Models of the Mind

Models of the Mind

A Framework for Biopsychosocial Psychiatry

Stephen L. Dilts, Jr., M.D.

WellSpan Health System
York, Pennsylvania

BRUNNER-ROUTLEDGE
Taylor & Francis Group

USA	Publishing Office:	BRUNNER-ROUTLEDGE *A member of the Taylor & Francis Group* 325 Chestnut Street Philadelphia, PA 19106 Tel: (215) 625-8900 Fax: (215) 625-2940
	Distribution Center:	BRUNNER-ROUTLEDGE *A member of the Taylor & Francis Group* 7625 Empire Drive Florence, KY 41042 Tel: 1-800-634-7064 Fax: 1-800-248-4724
UK		BRUNNER-ROUTLEDGE *A member of the Taylor & Francis Group* 27 Church Road Hove E. Sussex, BN3 2FA Tel: +44 (0) 1273 207411 Fax: +44 (0) 1273 205612

MODELS OF THE MIND: A Framework for Biopsychosocial Psychiatry

1 2 3 4 5 6 7 8 9 0

Printed by Edwards Brothers, Ann Arbor, MI, 2001
Cover photographs Copyright © 2001 Joseph Dieter Visual Communications and its licensors. All rights reserved.

A CIP catalog record for this book is available from the British Library.

♾ The paper in this publication meets the requirements of the ANSI Standard Z39.48-1984 (Permanence of Paper).

Library of Congress Cataloging-in-Publication Data

Dilts, Stephen L.
   Models of the mind : a framework for biopsychosocial psychiatry / by Stephen L. Dilts, Jr.
      p. cm.
   Includes bibliographical references and index.
   ISBN 1-58391-071-9 (alk. paper)
   1. Psychiatry. 2. Psychology, Pathological. I. Title.

RC454.D53 2000
616.89—dc21   CIP
                                                                   00-062987

ISBN: 1-58391-071-9 (paper)

To my wife, Jackie,
and to my parents

Contents

Foreword

Who are we, what do we do, and how do we understand our subject matter? These queries challenge and vex us as psychiatrists about our work and those we serve—our patients. We are all in need of models in solving problems. To paraphrase Einstein, our theories help us to identify the facts. In *Models of the Mind*, Dr. Steven Dilts, Jr., has diligently taken up this challenge to explain our work, our patients' needs, and the nature of their psychiatric dilemmas. He employs the "framework" of the biopsychosocial model introduced by George Engel and adopts it to explore the terrain of modern psychiatric practice and theory, and at the same time he enriches the model. Thus we are the beneficiaries of his elegant framework, the clarity of his writing, and the breadth and depth of his knowledge.

In an evenhanded and persistent way, Dr. Dilts strikes the theme that we cannot reduce our patients' problems to any one of the three domains—biological, psychological, or social—to explain or ameliorate their suffering and maladaptations. He uses the measure of "relevance" versus truth to guide practitioners in achieving understanding and efficacy with our patients. Best of all, he avoids the pitfalls of reductionism and polarized thinking in approaching understanding and in the treatment our patients. Although the scope of this book clearly reveals his sophisticated understanding of the biological bases of psychiatric illnesses, he also reflects a deep and abiding adherence to the humanistic underpinnings of sound psychiatric practice. He reveals his calling as a healer as much as a biological and social scientist. He guides us to do the same through case examples and an up-to-date review of the state of the art and science of our understanding of the psychiatric conditions we treat.

Dr. Dilts's book is a masterful guide to understanding the scope of our work as clinicians, using fresh, clear, and new language for modern times. It was only twenty years ago that George Engel introduced the term *biopsychosocial*. Dr. Dilts has seized the opportunity offered by this conceptualization to help modern practitioners in a manner that bygone master clinicians provided with their frameworks. Psychiatrists of each generation recall their favorite guides, whose that introduced them to psychiatric theory and practice. I believe this text by Dr. Dilts will be one such important guide for a new generation of students and clinicians embarking on—or already involved in—careers in psychiatry. It will do so in an enticing and stimulating way.

In this concise volume, Dr. Dilts covers it all—the models, the disorders, their treatments, and their theoretical underpinnings. However, it is not dry textbook reading. It is more like *lives in progress,* and how a modern-day practitioner guides the reader on matters of the mind and the brain in a lively and evocative style. He does this with grace, compelling case examples, and healthy tinctures of levity. This is instructive reading at its best, making new and complex material readily understandable, and making old hat stuff come alive (e.g., his review of Freudian theory and psychosexual development). Whether he's taking us through theory to help us understand the facts, or presenting one of his case examples in which we trust he will figure it out and help his patient, Dr. Steven Dilts, Jr., steadily and reliably guides us in this review of modern-day psychiatric practice and theory. With his scholarly, uncontentious, and very readable textbook on biopsychosocial psychiatry, he has provided a fresh and good start for us all.

—*Edward J. Khantzian, M.D.*
Harvard Medical School
The Cambridge Hospital and Tewksbury Hospital

Preface

> What a piece of work is a man, how noble in reason, how infinite in faculties, in form and moving, how express and admirable in action, how like an angel in apprehension, how like a god! the beauty of the world; the paragon of animals; and yet to me what is this quintessence of dust?
>
> *—Hamlet II.ii.303-07*

Hallucinations, delusions, depression, mania, substance dependence, anxiety, family problems, inner conflict—over one-third of the population will experience psychiatric problems such as these in their lifetimes. But despite their prevalence, psychiatric disorders seem mysterious. Are they the result of brain dysfunction? Unconscious anxiety? Group dynamics? No less mysterious are the people who try to solve such problems. The psychiatrist, making a new acquaintance and revealing his or her profession, is frequently met with one of several reactions. Predictable replies include:

"Uh, oh, you're probably analyzing me, aren't you?"

"Boy, could I use your help, ha, ha."

"I hear all you psychiatrists are crazy, too."

Psychiatric courses in medical school and residency training often do little to reduce this confusion. Psychiatry is a diverse field, comprising subjects from neuronal signal conduction to cultural effects on childhood development. Exhaustive literature is available on each topic, but students may not be shown how to integrate this information into a clinically useful whole. What is needed is a framework into which more detailed study on particular topics can be inserted.

Fortunately, such a framework is available, and it is used by all competent psychiatrists, whether they are researching cells or practicing psychotherapy. This framework is the *biopsychosocial model* of illness proposed by George Engel. In this model, the psychiatrist tries to understand the patient in biological, psychological, and social terms simultaneously, to arrive at a holistic picture with multiple strategies for treatment.

Recent successes in the basic sciences have given psychiatrists medical interventions previously unimagined. From Thorazine to Prozac to electroconvulsive therapy, these treatments have tempted psychiatrists to focus exclusively on the biological aspects of patient care. Generally, modern medicine has tended to turn all problems into problems of organ function. This tissue theory of illness—that all disease is ultimately cellular disease, as Rudolf Virchow said—has been a resounding success.

But this is not the only legitimate perspective on the problems of human beings. Virchow's tissue model has yet to explain and offer methods for coping with death, the conflicts of marital discord, bad habits, and economic difficulties, to name just a few. Nevertheless, human beings experience these sorts of problems, and they want to be helped with them. If medicine focuses solely on tissue problems, many other problems will be ignored. Worse still, potentially effective biological treatments may be undermined by such unresolved psychological or social problems.

Psychiatry in its modern incarnation is in a position to accommodate this diversity of problems. It can do this by shifting *models of the mind.* If a patient is hallucinating because he has a tumor infiltrating the temporal lobe of the brain, for example, psychiatry can turn to the biological model of tissue illness to explain the problem and offer solutions. If another is immersed in self-defeating behaviors, psychiatry can apply psychodynamic or behavioral psychology. If a child becomes depressed because of family interactions, a social model of family systems may help.

As we shall see, it is the practice of psychiatrists to assess patients in many dimensions simultaneously, with particular emphasis on the three domains described by Engel: the biological, the psychological, and the social. The focus of concern shifts constantly from one domain to another, and each domain interacts with and influences the others. But far from rendering psychiatric thinking confused and incoherent, the policy of shifting models depending on context is eminently practical. No single model serves in every setting. We should choose the ones we need for each particular problem.

That said, it is no simple matter to know which models to choose. It takes study, and it takes practice with patients. For that reason, I have used a number of clinical examples to illustrate the various models of the mind. They are real cases, although names and other identifying data have been changed to protect anonymity.

Models of the Mind is devoted to an examination of each of the three parts of the biopsychosocial model. Part 2, Biological Models, shows how symptoms are categorized and then examines the biological research behind each symptom cluster. Part 3, Psychological Models, discusses various psychological theories, and when each theory is applicable. Part 4, Social Models, covers the social theories of mental illness. The book ends with an outline of a psychiatric evaluation and a model diagnostic interview.

Each part of this book presents the modern psychiatric understanding of mental illness, not in an effort to show that it is absolutely right, but to illustrate why it is the best currently available. Most of the information here eventually will be supplanted by even better ideas. This is a compliment to the approach of psychiatry, and of the sciences in general. They are about being the best we have based on current information. The hope is always to improve, and history suggests that this will continue to happen through the constant critique of theories, as researchers look for error and improvement. Every model presented is the result of such critical inquiry.

The reader will note that in this text the *DSM-IV* syndromes of mental illness are detailed in Part 2. This strategy has been adopted for a reason: The biological understanding of each psychiatric syndrome is specific to that syndrome. The neurobiology of schizophrenia, for example, is different than the neurobiology of depression. Our understanding of the biology of each psychiatric syndrome has been derived from careful study of many patients with specific problems. It would be meaningless to discuss the neurobiology of mental illness in general without explaining the neurobiology underlying each specific syndrome. To tackle the question, "What is the biological basis of mental illness?" we must first answer the question, "Which mental illness?"

This is not the case for the psychological and social models of mental illness. The principles of these models of the mind are much more general and could be relevant for any and all of the psychiatric syndromes. It is generally uninformative to try to describe the specific psychology of depression versus that of anxiety disorders, for example. There may be a wide variability of psychological and social issues between individuals with the same psychiatric syndromes, and individuals with different diagnostic syndromes may have similar contributing psychological or social issues.

It is possible, for example, to find two depressed patients with widely divergent psychological issues, each requiring a different psychotherapeutic approach. Their neurobiology, however, is likely to be similar, and so the odds are decent that both will respond to the same antidepressant medication. An individual with schizophrenia will almost certainly have a different neurobiology than one with a substance use disorder, yet both patients may share many of the same social stressors within their families. Psychological and social factors tend to be less specific to individual syndromes.

The strategy of describing the individual syndromes within the discussion on biological models is therefore one of convenience; it is not meant to imply that the descriptive model is a purely biological model. It does reflect the greater specificity of biological models for particular psychiatric syndromes.

This book grew out of a series of lectures I gave to third-year medical students during their psychiatry rotation at the University of Colorado School of Medicine, and to primary care residents at the WellSpan System. It is written primarily for third- and fourth-year medical students, as well as psychiatric residents, as a framework for understanding the core concepts of psychiatry. Nursing students, psychology students, and others in the allied health fields will also find it useful. Although "psychiatry" is the subject, the biopsychosocial model is relevant to all of medicine. The method illustrated here is not the property of psychiatrists—it just happens that they frequently use it. Good ideas can and should be used by anybody.

Rather than survey the field comprehensively, my aim is to provide the basic information about psychiatry that students need, in a manner that corrects a bias toward the purely biological. *Psychiatry is holistic medicine.* I want to show how psychiatrists think holistically, and to provide some inkling of why they think as they do. Other texts and lectures can supply more detailed information on the topics introduced here. What I hope is that the reader will leave this book with a sense of where various subjects fit in an overall scheme of psychiatric thinking. No previous knowledge of psychiatry is presumed. Details are presented, but some oversimplification is needed at times. Psychiatry is an evolving field, and there is much controversy in each area surveyed here. What remains constant is the approach, which is biopsychosocial and scientific.

The scientific method is simply a way of looking at problems. Scientific investigation exposes any and all proposed solutions to criticism. Only those that withstand the scrutiny survive. The process of problem solving through critical inquiry does not eliminate all problems, however. Because science demands a constant search for improvements, there always are new problems, no matter how successful our solutions. In past ages, human beings debated whether the sun orbited the earth or the earth the sun; now we wonder whether there is life on other planets, whether our planet can sustain its population growth, and whether the mechanical production of carbon dioxide can cause the earth's temperature to rise. Human beings live in a world that is suitable, but not ideal, for our needs. This virtually guarantees an endless supply of problems.

Scientific "truths," therefore, are never absolute, but are tentative, contingent . . . and the best we have. The hope of science is that the best of now can be replaced by the even better. It is not a moment for sadness when a scientific "truth" is overthrown, but cause for rejoicing—we have improved our lot.

Psychiatry has not always lived up to its goal of being a scientific endeavor. Although Sigmund Freud—one of the founders of the psychiatric enterprise—was a decidedly free thinker, he had a clear tendency toward dogmatism. Freud's work was an attempt to explain all of human thought and behavior by using a single model. It was Freud's intent to develop a psychology that left no holes, one that could confidently explain anything human beings might do or feel. Given the complexity of human beings, this seems an overly ambitious project. Still, for much of the first half of the twentieth century, that hope drove the field of psychiatry, with the result that rival theories were shouted down as heretical.

But good ideas can't be kept down. Freudian psychology began to be modified and expanded as the decades of the twentieth century wore on. Innumerable schools of psychology developed, each with its particular insights. The invention of Thorazine in the 1950s heralded the explosion of biological models of psychiatry. New social theories looked at individuals as interrelated rather than as isolated specimens. In the 1980s, great strides in the field of neurobiology led to increasing understanding of the neurobiology of mental illness and to ever more potent biological therapies.

Although the successes of the biological models are to be lauded, there can be too much of a good thing. Despite biological advances, science is quite a long way from having a complete model that perfectly explains human beings in all their complexity. Although Freud and many others have thought so, there is no universal theory of human beings on the horizon. Such a model seems unlikely. People and the world are just too complicated to be summed up by a single perspective. I doubt that a single model will ever be devised to explain every facet of the immense complexity that is the human being. As scientists, psychiatrists must always be looking for defects and errors in current thinking, no matter how apparently seamless.

The scientific method applies not just to investigation in the basic sciences, but also to our day-to-day work with patients. The scientific method is not a group of subjects, such as chemistry or physics, but a way of looking at the world through critical inquiry. The practicing psychiatrist never knows for certain what will help the patient, and so the practice of psychiatry is one in which hypotheses are made and then tested, whether in trying a medication or in making a psychotherapeutic intervention.

This rational approach is all the more powerful when it is rendered through an ethic of humanism. The principles of beneficence, nonmaleficence, alleviation of suffering, and prevention of harm—which have been institutionalized in professional medicine since the time of Hippocrates—lessen the risk that a soulless science will coldly assess and manipulate human beings efficiently, perhaps, but without the care and compassion they require. I have truncated the introductory quotation from *Hamlet* to suit my purposes here. The ending, "Man delights me not—nor woman neither" I cannot endorse. Neither did Shakespeare and nor would Hamlet, I think, were he not depressed. We humans are one another's deepest fascination, and when we live the examined life,

we treat one another as we ought. This was Freud's founding principle—
that through self-examination we can free ourselves from thoughtless
action and live harmoniously.

Acknowledgments

I received invaluable help in the preparation of this book. My many teachers at the University of Colorado taught me biopsychosocial psychiatry from the beginning. The editors and staff at Taylor and Francis turned this idea into a finished product. John Dilts proofed the manuscript and has always been encouraging. My parents, Steve and Joann Dilts, spent innumerable hours editing and giving insights. They also instilled in me a love of learning that makes life a constant wonder. My wife, Jackie, is the joy of my life, my greatest friend, my best critic, and my inspiration. Thanks to everyone.

Models of the
Mind

What is mental illness? 1

The purpose of psychiatry is to diagnose and treat mental disorders. From the time of the ancients, physicians have attempted to describe and devise treatments for such problems as delirium, mania, and melancholia. Whether the theory was an excess of bodily humors, demonic infestation, unconscious conflict, or neurobiological dysfunction, the psychiatric enterprise has been moved by the practical desire to treat the suffering caused by mental disorders.

So just what are mental disorders? What do they look like, what are their essential elements, and what are their causes? Before defining what constitutes a mental disorder, we need to know how to define "the mental." Broadly, the basic elements of a mental state are *thoughts, feelings, perceptions, cognitions,* and *behaviors. Thoughts* are ideas, concepts, and the internal dialogue with one's self. *Feelings* are subjective emotional states, such as happiness or sadness. *Perceptions* are the functionings of the five sensory modalities—sight, hearing, touch, taste, and smell. *Cognitions* are the basic abilities of intelligence, such as memory, attention, calculation, and language. *Behaviors* are actions—the outward manifestations of internal mental states—that an individual undertakes in the world.

Together, these elements constitute a *mental state.* Just as normal physiological functioning can become disordered, so mental functioning can become disordered. A case example shows what this might look like.

> A *mental state* consists of one's thoughts, feelings, perceptions, cognitions, and behaviors.

Case example

G began to feel depressed and hopeless in her early 20s, after a particularly bad romantic involvement. She began to experience severe and recurrent abdominal pain. At first, doctors attributed this to adhesive scar tissue in G's abdomen as a result of surgery for ovarian cancer a few years before. Twice the adhesions were surgically removed, but the pain persisted. Finally, endometriosis was diagnosed and G's uterus was removed in an attempt to alleviate her pain. But still the pain continued.

G had always been what her friends called "compulsive." She had a driving, achievement-oriented style, graduating first in her high school class and attending a prestigious East Coast university. There she studied physics, supporting herself by working full time and compiling numerous academic honors. Then, in her junior year while she vacationed in Georgia, she met a young man who swept her off her feet. By the end of the school year G had decided to drop out of school and move to Georgia.

Then this relationship came to an end some months later, G was receiving death threats from the young man. She retreated to her home state, living with her parents again. Despite numerous attempts to correct her recurrent abdominal problems, G experienced worsening physical symptoms. The migraine headaches that had plagued her for much of her life became more frequent and severe. She found food less and less tolerable. Everything except fruit made her feel dizzy and confused. She felt a fullness in her abdomen, and she saw shadows out of the corner of her eye that disappeared when she turned toward them. Her perfectionistic style had turned into obsessional thinking and compulsive, repetitive behavior. She would clean her room, the bathroom, and the kitchen continuously, for hours every day, obsessed with a fear of germs that seemed irrational to her but that she could not ignore, despite her frustrated efforts. Mental rituals plagued her. She would find herself compelled to count items and mentally type words over and over.

G's food intolerance worsened, and she began to lose weight. Despite her petite, athletic figure, she viewed herself as ugly and grossly overweight. She thought it was inconceivable that anyone could be attracted to her if her weight was more than 120 pounds, although men complimented her looks and pursued her even when she weighed more. She denied wanting this attention, but she dressed seductively, wearing short dresses, low-cut tops, and elaborate hairstyles.

G's anxiety problems began to mount. In the grocery store one day she had a panic attack. She suddenly became exquisitely fearful; panting, sweating, her heart pounding, she felt dizzy and unreal. G curtailed her social activity dramatically after that, in part for fear of panic attacks, but more because of an inability to tolerate the feelings of dizziness and unreality that assailed her in noisy public gatherings. In such situations, she simply felt out of control.

Throughout all of this, G consulted physicians. She was convinced that some sort of medical illness was responsible for her woes. Doctors ran nnumerable tests, looking for anemia, lupus erythematosis, chronic fatigue syndrome, rheumatoid arthritis, anything that might explain her symptoms. Nothing was found. G invariably had normal lab tests and imaging studies. She was given trials of different antidepressant medications. All had intolerable side effects. G was able to take some antianxiety medications, which she began to administer to herself in high doses, but they provided little relief.

The psychiatrist who saw G at this time was impressed by the wide array of symptoms she presented. She also noticed that G's reported distress seemed markedly worse than her actual appearance. G was always carefully groomed, despite her claims to virtual incapacity, and she did not appear to be in any physical distress. Each session invariably began with the statement, "I'm doing so badly."

G's functioning was very poor. By this time, she was on disability and leading an isolated life. Her social contact was limited to her parents and a new boyfriend whom she found unsatisfactory. They no longer had sexual relations due to her chronic pelvic pain, and she was constantly irritated at the many ways he disappointed her. G was extraordinarily angry with everybody. She invariably portrayed her physicians as insensitive fools who would not give her the time and care she required. Her parents and the rest of her family could not understand her problems, and she found their encouragement to push through symptoms and go on living infuriating.

Perhaps surprisingly, the psychiatrist found G quite likeable in many ways. She was intelligent, witty, even hilarious at times, and she seemed genuinely committed to treatment, inspiring the psychiatrist to work diligently to find some end to G's suffering. Yet invariably, she found herself failing G. And though ostensibly working with the treatment plan, G missed appointments, saying she felt too bad to come in. She also started and stopped medications without involving her psychiatrist. G came to sessions informing the psychiatrist that she had felt suicidal over the weekend, but she had not called because every time she did, the psychiatrist was too problem-focused and not empathic enough. Yet when the psychiatrist simply listened to G's stories of suffering, G derided her as "silent" and "not having any ideas."

Using our definition of a mental state, we can discern which of G's problems might represent "mental disorders." G's symptoms can be organized as disturbances in the areas of thoughts, feelings, perceptions, behaviors, and cognitions. G was plagued with troublesome *thoughts*. For example, she held the irrational belief that any type of contamination was dangerous. She also was convinced that she was grossly physically defective. Her self-concept told her that she was a horribly deformed creature. G's *feelings* also proved disturbing. She suffered from depressed mood, anxiety, and overwhelming anger. Disruptive *perceptions*, such as a sense of abdominal fullness when she had not eaten and the sensation of shadows in her peripheral vision, also were present. G's *cognitive* capacities were altered as well. For example, she showed signs of confusion, particularly after eating, and poor concentration. Finally, G evidenced problematic and upsetting *behaviors*, such as repetitive cleaning and frequent fighting with her boyfriend.

G also had a number of physical, or *somatic*, symptoms, such as pelvic pain, food intolerance, headaches, and dizziness.

When psychiatrists see someone with disturbances in these areas, they are on the way to diagnosing a "mental disorder." A mental disorder is a disturbance in one or many of the basic elements of mental functioning: thoughts, feelings, perceptions, cognitions, or behaviors.

This list is a start, but it is not sufficient. After all, everyone has problematic mental states at one time or another. Is anger at a friend a mental disorder? What about test anxiety? How do we know when someone has a mental state that qualifies as a "mental disorder?"

> A *mental disorder* is a disturbance in thoughts, feelings, perceptions, cognitions, and behaviors.

The descriptive model

The Diagnostic and Statistical Manual of Mental Disorders

Serious human mental problems tend to have recurring features. Depressed mood, for example, often is seen in conjunction with appetite and sleep changes. Severe panic produces symptoms such as hyperventilation, heart palpitations, sweating, and tremor.

In the last 35 years, the serious mental problems people recurrently face have been classified. Research has found that certain symptoms reliably occur together, and these sets of symptoms can be organized as *syndromes*. These syndromes are thus *described* by the symptoms that compose them. The descriptive model of mental illness attempts to describe the appearance of the major mental disorders through their symptoms.

The current state of the art in descriptive psychiatry is *The Diagnostic and Statistical Manual of Mental Disorders*, which is now in its fourth edition (*DSM-IV*). In broad headings, the *DSM-IV* describes the most common causes of distress and dysfunction in human beings, as shown below. These are the major disruptions in thoughts, feelings, perceptions, cognitions, and behaviors which human beings often find distressing and functionally impairing.

- Psychosis
- Mania
- Depression

- Anxiety
  Obsessive-compulsive disorder
  Posttraumatic stress disorder
  Panic disorder
  Generalized anxiety disorder
  Social and specific phobias
- Psychiatric disorders secondary to general medical conditions
- Delirium
- Dementia
- Substance use disorders
- Personality disorders

The *DSM-IV* also contains listings for eating disorders, sleep disorders, disorders of childhood, somatoform and factitious disorders, dissociative disorders, sexual disorders, impulse-control disorders, and adjustment disorders.

For each disorder, the *DSM-IV* lists the symptoms that must be present to make a diagnosis. These disorders are defined and illustrated later in this book. Before proceeding to their descriptions, however, we must try to define what constitutes a mental disorder in general, compared to normal functioning.

Normal versus disordered

According to major epidemiological surveys, which have studied tens of thousands of people, over 30% of the population will experience a major mental disorder in their lifetimes. This is a large number, on par with the percentage who will die from cancer. This large number, however, raises a question. If almost one-third of the populace is going to have a serious mental disorder, are mental disorders so common that they might be said to represent the norm? If the list of mental disorders is expanded to include every conceivable human malaise, that list would be huge indeed.

Since the beginning of medical practice, the attempt to define health and normality has been an area of intense controversy. Is health simply the absence of disease? Or is it the absence of clinically significant disease, since most organisms have something about them that is not working right, if only a single cell out of trillions? Does adequate coping and functioning constitute health, even if abnormalities are present?

Psychiatry, too, has been embroiled in the question of what constitutes mental health, as well as mental illness. Sigmund Freud believed the concept of "the normal" was fictitious; in his model of mental illness, everyone has some degree of psychopathology (Sadock & Sadock, 2000). Freud did, however, suggest that a compromise was possible, and that adequate health could be said to exist when a person could "love and work" with relative freedom and facility. Others have attempted to define health and normality as *success*, whether in negotiating developmental stages, in adapting to the external world, or in mastering one's fears and anxiety. Still others define illness purely as tissue abnormality.

Defining normality statistically probably is not helpful. Coronary artery disease obviously is not a normal situation for human beings—clearly, it represents abnormal, detrimental functioning. But heart disease is very common, as is cancer. That these are statistically common situations does not make them normal, in the sense that people would not wish to intervene against them. Psychiatric disorders likewise may be statistically common, but they cause severe distress and impaired functioning and thus are states people usually want to eliminate. High intelligence is statistically uncommon, but it is usually desired and so is not a disease state, because it is adaptive rather than problematic. So statistical prevalence is not helpful in defining normal versus diseased.

More useful is the concept of *functional impairment*. Disease in this model is present when a disturbance reaches the level that it causes significant functional impairment. Occasional premature ventricular contractions represent abnormal functioning of the heart, but cardiologists do not usually consider them to be "disease" unless they interfere with functioning or lead to worsening arrhythmias. Most people have headaches from time to time, but they are considered abnormal only if they become functionally impairing or are a symptom of another illness, such as a brain tumor. Likewise, everyone experiences some degree of sadness in life, but depression is diagnosed only if it becomes functionally impairing.

From the foregoing, it should be obvious that there is no purely objective standard that can be applied to decide such questions. How we determine what constitutes health and normality is largely dependent on values in psychiatry and in medicine in general. However, most human beings wish to function well in their environment and be free of severe distress. Distress and dysfunction are usually considered possible indicators of a disease state. This definition is not perfect. Not all distress and dysfunction indicate disease (for example, a child's temper tantrum), while some diseases may be asymptomatic. But most disease states cause distress and dysfunction at some point in their course.

So how bad do distress and functional impairment have to be to warrant medical intervention? What problems are severe enough? The *DSM-IV* attempts to escape this dilemma in several ways. First, it lists specific criteria for each disorder. Simply having the blues, for example, does not warrant a diagnosis of depression. A number of other symptoms must be present, including changes in sleep, appetite, concentration, or energy; pervasive guilt; hopelessness; and suicidality. This type of depression, known as major depression, is a *syndrome*, a group of symptoms that are reliably found together.

One criterion for every *DSM-IV* disorder is that the symptoms must "cause clinically significant distress or impairment in social, occupational, or other important areas of functioning." This modifier is an attempt to ensure that a significant degree of distress and impairment is present for the diagnosis to apply. But it is far from perfectly effective in this task. The wording is so vague that, in theory, almost any amount of distress could be admitted as a diagnosis, since "significant" is poorly defined and obviously relative. What one person finds distressing and impairing, another might brush off as meaningless. Furthermore, the criterion may exclude states that are clearly pathological but nonimpairing, such as someone who hallucinates but is fully functional and not bothered by the experience. In practice, however, "significant distress and impairment" turns out to be relatively self-explanatory. Most of those seen in psychiatric practice are hurting badly and have areas of function that are blatantly impaired. This may be because, in the current medical–economic climate, psychiatrists usually see those whose disorders are severe enough that previous attempts at intervention—from family advice to consultation with a general physician—have proved inadequate.

The descriptive model has proved its usefulness in research and clinical practice. However, it does not capture everything that can be said about a particular disease state. All we need to know to make a diagnosis of depression is that someone has depressed mood and a few associated symptoms. We don't need to know at all what it is *like* to be depressed. A diagnosis of depression can be made solely on the basis of a report of depressed mood along with changes in sleep, appetite, concentration, and energy. These are often quantified with depression inventory rating scales, which ask subjects to rate their symptoms numerically. Depression thus begins to look very much the same in every case, differentiated only by a symptom or two and by the degree of severity.

This is extremely useful in some regards. Sameness leads to investigative power. If depression was a vastly different entity in each person who experienced it, if it had no recurring features, it would be extremely difficult to study or even to talk about. Language inevitably serves as a kind of condenser, organizing large amounts of information into concepts, which derive their utility from the very maneuverability of oversimplification.

Using the statistic that perhaps 15% of the population will develop major depression in their lifetimes, and multiplying that number by the current U.S. population of about 260 million, we obtain the result that 39 million people currently alive have had or will experience major depression. It would be absurd to believe that nine symptoms of depression would completely capture the depressive experience of 39 million people. Each individual has unique characteristics that may bear on the problem of depression. Reducing each individual to a few common features is useful in the sense that it may allow systematic development of powerful interventions, but those interventions will necessarily be generalized as a result. An antidepressant medication may be effective for many depressed people. But it will not work for everyone, and some people will find the side effects intolerable.

Systematic classification of illness runs the risk of missing real problems that do not fit neatly into the system. A woman might have a bad marriage that is wreaking havoc with her mood, but unless the problem extends into the domains of sleep, appetite, and energy, she won't "really" have *DSM-IV* major depression, if we are strict with our diagnostic criteria. Does this mean she does not have a problem worth solving?

If there is a consistent problem with the diagnostic categories, it is not that they are overly inclusive but, rather, that treatable illness often is missed, not just by individuals and their communities but by nonpsychiatric physicians. Estimates are that at least 50% of major depressions are not diagnosed and so go untreated. This is unfortunate, when one considers that major depression has a 15% mortality rate from suicide (Miles, 1977) and has been found to cause more distress and functional impairment than hypertension, diabetes, or chronic renal failure (Wells et al., 1989).

Ultimately, impairment embodies values—uncommon but valued states, such as high intelligence, are not diseases. Clear alterations in tissue structure that do not impair adaptation likewise are not usually diseases; for example, individuals may have the cellular changes associated with Alzheimer's disease, but they are not diagnosed with the syndrome of Alzheimer's disease unless they are functionally impaired. States that impair adaptation usually are considered diseases, since adaptation is highly valued. The desire to adapt to an environment appears to be universal in organisms. Without it, survival would be impossible over the long run.

The *DSM-IV* thus sets out to describe the major functionally impairing syndromes of mental disorder.

Validity and reliability

Validity is the degree to which a diagnosis represents what it is intended to.

The cornerstones of meaningful diagnosis are validity and reliability. *Validity* is the degree to which a diagnosis represents what it is intended to. A diagnosis is valid if it describes a syndrome in such a way that it remains stable even as new information is discovered about it. A valid diagnosis must also be useful, so that meaningful predictions can be made from it. Validity also can be conceptualized as the degree to which a particular diagnosis consistently represents the same underlying disease. Some diagnoses are easy to validate. For example, myocardial infarction or bone fractures can be seen in a post-mortem study. However, many general medical diagnoses have no gold standard by which they can be assessed. Examples of these include migraine headaches, lupus erythematosis, and seizure disorders. As yet there are no gold standard criteria for psychiatric diagnoses. However, succeeding chapters in this book show that many psychiatric diagnoses are valid, although some more so than others. Valid psychiatric diagnoses have remained stable and useful over long periods of time; in fact, some of them (such as depression, mania, and delirium) date from the time of Hippocrates.

Reliability is the degree to which diagnosticians agree that a particular diagnosis is present. The reliability for many *DSM-IV* diagnoses is quite high, at times surpassing the reliability of general medical diagnoses. For example, schizophrenia, major depression, and alcohol dependence each has a diagnostic reliability of about 95% (Guze, 1997). This means that 95% of the time, diagnosticians will agree on the presence or absence of these diagnoses in a particular individual. This degree of reliability surpasses that seen for many medical disorders, including pneumonia (about 72%), transient ischemic attacks (about 70%), and broken ankles (about 60%). As we will see, however, not all psychiatric diagnoses are as reliable as others. For example, the personality disorders have a diagnostic reliability of about 60%.

Reliability is the degree to which diagnosticians agree that a diagnosis is present.

The *DSM-IV* is neutral about cause

The *DSM-IV* is descriptive. It simply describes what the major mental disorders look like. It does not, however, attempt to explain what causes those disorders. It does not say whether a particular syndrome is caused by abnormal brain chemistry, Freudian psychology, or social circumstances.

This is because *all mental disorders have biological, psychological, and social causes.*

The biopsychosocial model

Psychiatry employs *models of the mind* to explain the causes of disorders in the areas of thought, feeling, perception, cognition, and behavior—the mental disorders. We can use these models to sort through G's problems, as presented earlier. How we look at her problems is going to depend very much on the models we use.

One way to look at G's problems is through biology. Modern investigative techniques have greatly increased our understanding of those alterations in the structure and function of the nervous system that result in mental disorders. For example, depression and anxiety are thought to be caused in part by dysfunction of the neuronal systems that use the neurotransmitter *serotonin*. Researchers have devised medicines to repair abnormal serotonergic neurotransmission, resulting in improved mood and decreased anxiety for thousands of people. This would be considered a biological model of mental illness. *The biological model of mental illness states that mental illness is caused by the dysfunction of tissues and cells.* Often, the tissues and cells in question involve the central nervous system, but this is not always the case.

There are other ways of seeing G's condition, however. Instead of looking at the nervous system, a clinician might turn her attention to how G's thinking influences itself. In other words, how do some thoughts G has cause others to emerge? If G interprets returning to her parents' house as a retrogression to her childhood years, then she might resent this return to dependency and react with anger, attempting to reassert her independence by pushing her parents away.

The *biological model* states that mental illness is caused by the dysfunction of tissues and cells.

This is a psychological model of mental illness. *The psychological model of mental illness states that mental disorders are the result of previous patterns of thinking, feeling, perceiving, cognating, and behaving.* In other words, mental states arise out of previous mental states.

Psychological treatment—or psychotherapy—might involve helping G see the causes of her anger, and so help her move to less damaging ways of expressing and coping with her emotions. The psychological model simply proposes that mental states of one kind influence later mental states. It makes no reference to the functioning of the nervous system by talking about the cells of the brain, nor is its treatment designed to affect cells specifically. Rather, it seeks to change how G thinks about things by using other thoughts, through talking and doing.

Alternatively, the clinician might look at the ways her interpersonal relationships have affected G. She began to become depressed after losing her boyfriend, for whom she gave up what had been a significant source of self-esteem, her achievements in education. The strain of the breakup forced G to return to her parents home, which (although a sanctuary) made her feel like a child again. G had worked hard, even compulsively, to establish her independence from her parents, moving across the country to attend college. Living again with her parents, G felt irritable and depressed about her perceived failure to emancipate, and the three people in the house began to engage in an escalating series of maladaptive interactions. G's growing hopelessness fueled a wish on the part of her parents to see G back on her feet and taking care of herself. Yet the more they suggested ways she might do this, the more G felt rejected and shamed by her failures. Using G's social situation as an explanation for illness serves as a social model. *The social model of mental illness proposes that mental disorders are caused by dysfunctional interpersonal interactions.* Intervention at the social level might occur through family therapy, which attempts to alter the structure of a family's relationships by seeing them as a group.

The *psychological model* states that mental disorders are the results of previous mental states.

How do we know which model is correct? The question itself reveals a bias. There is a tendency to believe that there is a single correct representation of the problem, one model that tells us the way things are. Is the psychological theory true? Or does G have an abnormality in her serotonin levels? Are these models mutually exclusive? What would it mean if researchers found, for example, that simply talking alters the cell biology of the brain? (As it turns out, this is exactly what happens in some types of psychotherapy.)

There is another way to approach the issue. Rather than asking which model is correct and true, it might be better to ask which model is relevant. All three models are internally consistent. They represent the facts of the case correctly within their given frameworks. In that sense they are all "true." But in G's case, relevance is more important than truth.

The reason for this is quite simple. There are innumerable representational models of G's condition that, while perhaps true, are irrelevant to her problems. It might be true, for example, that G is composed of subatomic particles all interacting in various ways. But current state-of-the-art particle physics cannot provide any information that can help G become less depressed and anxious, get along better with her family, and so on. Particle physics is a *true but irrelevant* model for G's problems.

What G needs are models of the mind that provide solutions for her problems. The three types of models we discussed earlier—biological, psychological, and social—all accomplish this task, but they do so using different theories about the problems, what causes them, and what to do about them. This creates difficulties if one insists there is a *single* right way to approach the patient.

For example, the biological model of mental illness currently has no way to explain psychological concepts such as conflict. It simply is not currently possible to describe psychological conflict using concepts like neurons and neurochemicals. Therefore, psychological conflict cannot be part of the current "truth" of the biological model. Conversely, psychological models cannot explain the fact that a large percentage of people with major depression have abnormalities in serotonergic neurotransmission. Wondering which one of these models is true needlessly excludes a lot of useful information.

If we are willing to accept any relevant model in order to come to some solutions, then our ability to cope with G's condition is greatly increased—we have three solutions instead of just one. The criterion of relevance rather than truth allows us to mix models. Using relevance as our signal for application of a model, we apply all three, saying that all are equally relevant perspectives on the case. This means that G has trouble with her brain chemistry *and* psychological conflict *and* social interaction. This is the *biopsychosocial model* of mental illness.

> The *social model* states that mental disorders are caused by dysfunctional interpersonal interactions.

Biopsychosocial medicine

In the early 1980s, George Engel introduced the concept of the biopsychosocial model of illness (Engel, 1980). According to this model, all illnesses have at once biological, psychological, and social causes.

Engel was aware that the biological model of illness—Virchow's "tissue" theory of illness, which says that all disease is ultimately cellular disease—had become the dominant model in medicine, to the extent that it virtually monopolized research and clinical practice. By focusing on the dysfunction of cells and tissue as the root of illness, medicine achieved tremendous successes, including penicillin, polio vaccinations, aspirin, and blood pressure control medications. Because of its successes, physicians had become so acculturated to the biomedical model that they were largely unaware of its influence. How else would one view disease, except as the dysfunction of cells and tissue? In the biomedical model, treatment is properly focused on intervention at those levels. Yet gradually, patients began to feel disenchanted with their physicians and with the medical care they provided. It seemed that the cells of the body could be adequately cared for and the person left unhealed.

The *biopsychosocial model* states that mental illness is caused by biological, psychological, and social causes.

As an antidote, Engel proposed that the biomedical model of illness be consciously replaced with what he called the *biopsychosocial model* of illness. Engel recognized a "continuum of natural systems" (Figure 1.1), from atoms and molecules to cells, tissues, and organs; to individuals; to pairs, groups, communities, and populations; and, finally to the biosphere at large.

For all its successes, the language of the biomedical model is inadequate to capture levels of organization beyond that of cells and tissues. It currently is impossible, for example, to describe international politics using the language of cell biology. Engel also recognized that, although one level of organization might be more relevant at a given moment, the levels are inextricably linked—that is, changes in one level precipitate changes in another. Thus, we must try to understand illness on multiple levels at once.

This does not mean that different models turn out to say the same thing. Physicians still have to talk about cells using the biological model, about people using psychological models, and about interpersonal relationships using social models. In a sense, using the biopsychosocial model the physician must always come up with three assessments, although once he has done so it may be possible to see where the models overlap.

The strength of the biopsychosocial model of mental illness is that it is a more thorough description of problems. Because it uses multiple vocabularies that can speak to the many different levels of organization, from the molecular to the community, it integrates data that a single perspective cannot. Furthermore, it gives practitioners humility before their patients. Whenever we assess a person, it is a given that our assessment is incomplete—indeed, there never can be a truly complete assessment. This does not mean we cannot develop a formulation that is sufficient for clinical purposes. A person in cardiac arrest requires only that one know how to work a defibrillator to restore the heart's rhythm at that moment. But seen across time, each person moves at each moment to a new area of concern. Recovering from her cardiac arrest, the patient may begin to worry about how her finances will be affected and about the loss of control she has experienced in her life. We speak to this perhaps with a "psychological" or a "social" model. But as worry impairs circulation to the heart, we may shift emphasis again to the cells of the

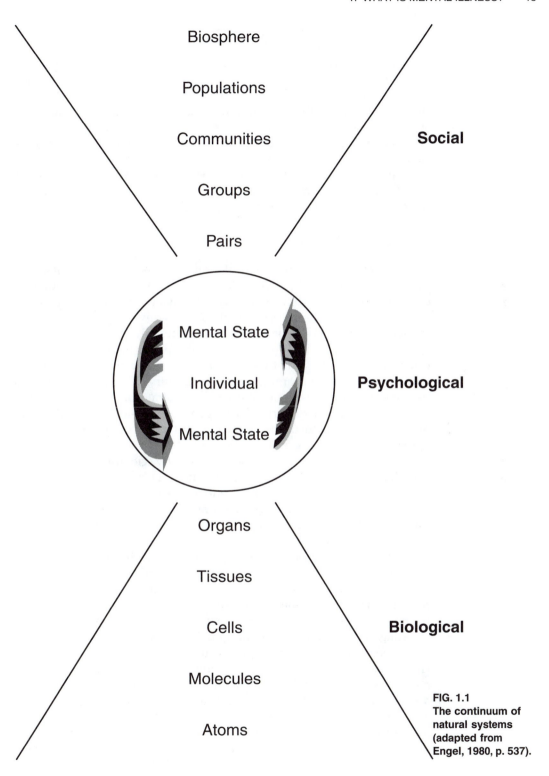

Biosphere

Populations

Communities

Social

Groups

Pairs

Mental State

Individual

Psychological

Mental State

Organs

Tissues

Cells

Biological

Molecules

Atoms

**FIG. 1.1
The continuum of
natural systems
(adapted from
Engel, 1980, p. 537).**

heart and the problem of maintaining blood flow so as to prevent another cardiac arrest.

The biopsychosocial model views the person not as a static entity,
but as one that constantly changes. These changes are not appraised
with complete objectivity, but in the context of our concerns. Because
the subject matter (the human patient) is in a state of constant flux—
shedding cells and replacing them, changing thoughts, processing food,
growing and withering, entering and leaving social contexts—and because the clinician's concerns shift as well, there is no ground on which
a "final" assessment might stand. It is better to recognize and accept this
than to attempt to suppress it with hopes that a single system will render all problems understandable in a single stroke.

Critical inquiry

We want our relevant models of the mind to be true in the sense that
they can be tested and withstand critical inquiry. This is the method of
science. A scientific model is not synonymous with a biological model.
Rather, a scientific model is one that has been developed in the spirit of
the scientific method, which involves critical inquiry.

Critical inquiry is a process in which theories are relentlessly criticized—and only those that withstand the process are retained. The scientific method is an example of critical inquiry. The scientific method
requires that a theory about the world generate predictions (hypotheses) that can be tested. If the predictions are not validated
by experiment, the theory is discarded, and a new theory must be generated.

Not every theory can be tested in a strictly scientific format. Events
are not always reproducible in the laboratory. This is particularly true of
clinical medicine—individual patients cannot be isolated in a laboratory so that the effectiveness of a treatment can be observed free of other
influences. But science is not about laboratories; it is about exposing
theories to criticism to see if they stand up.

In the practice of medicine it is important that the clinician approach the patient with a critical eye in the scientific spirit. Theories are
tentative, and if they are not working they must be discarded rather
than dogmatically retained. When several models are used at once, as in
the biopsychosocial approach, the chances of finding an accurate understanding and useful solutions are greatly increased.

The beauty of critical inquiry is not that it infallibly produces the
right answers, but that it is self-correcting. Science, after all, is predominantly a series of mistakes. Only a very small number of theories which
are thought at one time to be accurate are ultimately sustained over the
long run. However, since the scientific method actively searches for its
own errors rather than maintaining its theories in the face of conflicting
evidence, it has the potential for correcting itself. In this way, answers

and results are more likely to be obtained than if a cherished theory is held onto no matter the evidence to the contrary.

Less useful are models that purport to be true in an absolute sense. It used to be thought in psychiatry that Freudian psychology was the explanation for all mental life. The Freudian model, as we shall see later, was designed so as to make criticism of it impossible. Those who disagreed with the theory were thought to be suffering from the very elements of the theory with which they disagreed! The Freudian model thus attempted to turn any criticism into proof of its accuracy. The result of such dogmatism was that many useful models of mental life were ignored in the practice of psychiatry, since the truth was believed to lie entirely within Freudian psychology. No psychiatric model is beyond criticism. None fully explains all the facts of mental life.

Today, the various models of the mind used in psychiatric practice have been derived by a process of critical inquiry. Over time, a number of biological, psychological, and social models have proved their relevance by withstanding criticism. They are not accepted because of tradition or dogmatism, but because they have proved themselves in research and clinical practice. They have been deliberately tested and subjected to criticism. Since they can withstand criticism on their merits, they cannot be easily discarded.

Therefore, the various models need to be integrated and applied together—to discard a relevant model is to lose a piece of the clinical armamentarium.

The biopsychosocial model embraces the multifaceted and shifting nature of the human subject. It accepts that our vocabularies capture only *some* of the possible relevant perspectives on the subject at any given moment. Recognizing this, it tries to systematically think in several models at once. Thus, for any given patient, the psychiatrist applying the biopsychosocial model will come up with three different, although usually overlapping, assessments at once: biological, psychological, and social.

In the case of G, such an assessment might run as follows:

Descriptively, G appears to be suffering the clinical syndromes of major depression, panic disorder, an eating disorder, obsessive-compulsive disorder, and somatization disorder (we will see exactly what symptoms constitute these disorders later).

The *biological* bases of these various disorders have been partially understood, and all seem to implicate dysfunction of the neurotransmitter *serotonin*. Additionally, G has chronic pelvic problems (which have required surgical intervention), headaches, and an eating disorder, each of which may represent a medical disorder independent of any "mental disorder." In other words, she may have some "general medical" disorders that need to be addressed.

Psychologically, G has enormous anger, of which she keeps herself mostly unaware by using alternative thoughts and behaviors, such as bodily preoccupation (somatization and obsessions and compulsions). Her anger may be around issues of dependency, since it tends to be triggered by the sense that she is dependent on someone, such as her parents or therapist.

Socially, G is functioning below her predicted level based on her education and previous level of functioning. She has few interpersonal relationships, whereas before she had many, and those relationships are complicated by patterns of negative interaction. She does not work, despite a history of high achievement.

Combined, these three assessments give us a treatment plan. First, prescribe an antidepressant medication that works on the neurotransmitter serotonin, such as fluoxetine (Prozac), continue her treatment with a competent gynecologist, and search for medical causes for her weight loss, such as hyperthyroidism or brain tumors. Second, enroll Gina in psychotherapy, to focus on the issues delineated in the psychological formulation. Finally, through the first two treatment modalities, look toward improving her social functioning or, alternatively, encourage a group or family therapy.

Key points

- *Mental disorders* encompass problems in the areas of thoughts, feelings, perceptions, cognitions, and behaviors.

- There are recurring patterns of mental functioning that cause distress and impairment. The patterns can be classified by their recurring features as mental disorders. This is the descriptive model.

- The *descriptive model* does not attempt to delineate the causes of mental disorders, but simply describes their appearance.

- A *biological model* of mental illness explains mental disorders as the result of tissue and cell pathology.

- A *psychological model* of mental illness explains mental disorders as the result of preceding mental states.

- A *social model* of mental illness explains mental disorders as the result of dyfunctional interpersonal interactions.

- The *biopsychosocial model* states that mental disorders have at once biological, psychological, and social dimensions.

- The biological, psychological, and social dimensions of a mental disorder must be integrated through the biopsychosocial model into a unified assessment and treatment plan.

Biological Models ‖

Introduction to biological models 2

The biological model of mental illness posits that mental illness is the result of abnormal tissue function. Since the tissue that produces mental states is primarily the central nervous system, mental illness is thought to be the result of abnormal functioning of the central nervous system. The central nervous system can be disrupted either by primary psychiatric disorders or by general medical conditions to produce problematic symptoms.

Case example

S had been pistol-whipped. As a result, he had bled into the sub-dural space around his brain, a life-threatening injury. Once neurosurgeons had evacuated the blood clot that was compressing his brain, his condition stabilized and he began the process of recovery. On the rehabilitation unit he exhibited significant cognitive deficits, particularly in memory and judgment, but was able to participate in physical therapy, where he was pleasant and committed to recovery.

But the unit psychologist became concerned that S was having mood fluctuations. One day S would be happy and engaged. The next he would be oddly apathetic, conversing with the staff and visitors with a disconcerting vacancy of expression. He seemed to stare off into the distance even as he talked. Although he paid attention to the people around him, he could not or would not comply with any of the instructions the physical therapists gave him. He seemed unwilling even to leave his bed. Because S had a history of criminal behavior, including gang involvement, the psychologist wondered if he was reverting to oppositional behavior, or if he was becoming depressed. The rehabilitation staff was becoming irritated with him during such periods.

When the psychiatric consultant arrived, S was in just such a state. He was lying on his bed, staring off into the distance. Although awake and able to answer questions, he did not appear to be paying attention to his surroundings. His answers were fluent and grammatically normal, but dreamy and vague. He knew where

23

he was, but he could not name the date. He described his mood as fine.

Clearly, something more than a mood disorder was present. The psychiatrist performed a neurological exam, which revealed signs consistent with damage to the left cerebral hemisphere. Although these signs had been present since the injury, given S's changing mental state the possibility of rebleeding into the brain had to be considered. An emergent computed tomography (CT) scan of the brain was obtained, which showed no change from the scan taken after surgery. Were there other conditions that could be causing S's behavior? Seizure was a possibility, but the consulting neurologist thought S's symptoms were not consistent with seizure activity in the brain. More likely, he thought, it was one of the myriad changes in mental functioning which can accompany brain injury.

S's behavior was making it difficult to accomplish rehabilitation. Often he did not participate in his treatment. Staff members became frustrated. Finally, the psychiatrist ordered an electroencephalogram (EEG), more for the sake of completeness than out of any real hope of discovering a cause of the problem.

But there, in the left temporal lobe of the brain, he saw a spike of seizure activity. A small seizure focus in that location might have none of the dramatic manifestations that often accompany epilepsy, but it could easily render S unmotivated and unable to concentrate, despite remaining awake and aware. S was started on an anticonvulsant medication. The episodes disappeared.

Medical causes of mental illness

S's case raises several issues. First, it demonstrates that problems in the areas of thoughts, feelings, perceptions, cognitions, and behaviors—mental problems—can be the result of medical problems. In S's case, the problem was a brain injury, with a subsequent seizure disorder. The list of medical conditions that could result in a psychiatric problem of some kind is virtually as long as the list of medical problems itself. Poor thyroid function often leads to depressed mood. Drugs used to treat Parkinson's disease, such as L-dopa, can make people hallucinate. The suffocation caused by emphysema can trigger panic attacks.

Primary mental illnesses result from particular biologies.

But what do we mean, really, when we say that a medical problem can cause psychiatric problems? In what way are "medical" problems distinct from "psychiatric" problems? Sigmund Freud believed that his theories eventually would be found to have a neuroanatomical basis. Indeed, it was his hope that all psychiatric illness would one day have a neurological explanation. Freud was convinced that every mental state was the effect of specific causes, and that those causes were other brain states.

The "Decade of the Brain" that was the 1980s led many people to believe that Freud had not hoped in vain. The decade obtained its moniker precisely because advances in the neural science of psychiatric disorders were so impressive. Fluoxetine (Prozac), a type of antidepressant drug called a *selective serotonin reuptake inhibitor (SSRI)*, was released. The marvel of Prozac was not merely that it was a new and effective antidepressant, with generally fewer side effects than the older classes of antidepressants, but more importantly, it was rationally designed to target specific chemical receptors in the brain. The first antidepressant medications had been serendipitously discovered as effective against depression; only later was their chemistry understood. In the case of SSRIs, however, scientists attempted to design molecules that would engage only those proteins in the brain responsible for the activity of serotonin, knowing that serotonin was involved in the development of depression. They were successful, and the success of Prozac was paralleled in other areas of psychiatric research.

Secondary mental illnesses result from general medical conditions.

But if dysfunction of the central nervous system is the cause of psychiatric disorders, then how is it useful to think of "psychiatric" disorders at all? Why not call them "neurological disorders"? In fact, some have argued this very point, claiming that all psychiatry is essentially biological (Guze, 1989). While a large amount of evidence has accrued that psychiatric disorders have a biological basis, these disorders are still referred to as psychiatric, as distinct from general medical illnesses that may also result, as in S's case, in psychiatric symptoms. This is in part merely a convenience, since illnesses such as depression and schizophrenia have for so long been classified as psychiatric. It also serves, however, to distinguish the etiology of a particular group of symptoms.

Recall that the descriptive model is neutral toward etiology. Thus, for example, symptoms of depression as described in the *DSM-IV* (APA, 1994) are merely descriptive of the phenomena. Depressive symptoms could be the result of general medical conditions such as hypothyroidism or pancreatic cancer, or they could be the result of the illness known as *primary major depression*, which has a unique biology. As we will see, most of the psychiatric syndromes may be either *primary* (in which case they result from the particular biologies described herein), or *secondary* states—resulting from effects of general medical conditions, which are those conditions historically classified as the domain of general medicine, such as neurologic, cardiologic, oncologic, or endocrinologic ailments.

The tissue model of illness

Whether a particular psychiatric syndrome is primary or secondary, the argument for the biological model of psychiatry goes like this: All activities of thought, feeling, perception, cognition, and behavior—activities traditionally within the domain of psychiatry—are reducible to activities of the central nervous system. Indeed, centuries of investigation have so overwhelmingly localized the activities of thought, feeling, cognition, perception, and behavior in the nervous system that it now seems intuitively obvious. This follows the tissue theory of illness proposed by Rudolf Virchow and other anatomical pathologists of the nineteenth century, who believed that disease is the result of cellular dysfunction. This theory has had great success in general medicine, including neurology.

Attempts to explain disease processes in the nineteenth century began to focus on the abnormality of tissue structure and function as the cause of disease. Destruction of the heart muscle secondary to poor circulation produced the crushing chest pain of angina. Scarring of the liver produced jaundice and ascites. We have similar explanations for the problems that result from the disruption of neural structure and function. The death of brain cells from lack of blood flow produces the paralysis of stroke. The gradual death of brain cells from the accumulation of tangled cellular protein results in the failing memory of Alzheimer's disease. In the 1940s, neurosurgeon Wilder Penfield mapped out large sections of cortical function by electrically stimulating exposed brain tissue in awake patients during neurosurgical operations (Penfield & Jasper, 1954). Penfield found that when he stimulated certain nervous tissue, patients would report spontaneous experiences, such as a smell or a visual perception, the recollection of an old memory, or an intense emotion. This provided powerful evidence that the central nervous system is the seat, the substrate, of mental states.

But many activities of the "mind" have not been localized. Some would argue that we will never be able to reduce complex states of mind—such as being depressed, or angry, or in love—simply to the state of the nervous system. No matter how much we know about the neurotransmitter serotonin, for example, it is unlikely such knowledge will be able to describe these mental states completely. This is not necessarily a disagreement with the tissue model of mental activity. It simply claims that, although mind states may be rooted in neurological states, the complexity of the latter is too vast for us ever to be able to describe in sufficient detail.

The biological model of mental illness thus states that mind activities are the results of the functioning of the central nervous system—if we understand nervous system in the broadest sense to include the peripheral and autonomic nervous systems and their connections with the rest of the body, the endocrine system, and probably the immune system as well. Although it is crucial to understanding the neurobiology of mental illness, the central nervous system is intimately connected to the rest of the body. Neither can function without the other, and all organ systems exist to contribute to the whole. Although the focus of the biological model of mental illness is on neurobiology, we will see that neurobiology is intertwined with other biological domains, such as endocrinology.

The tissue model of function and dysfunction has withstood the critical inquiry of experimentation and produced real-world results in our ability to ameliorate malfunction and suffering. Investigation into the psychiatric disorders has led increasingly to an understanding of their basis in neurological dysfunction. Notable examples are schizophrenia, bipolar disorder, major depression, panic disorder, and obsessive-compulsive disorder. In fact, recent legislative debates have revolved around the question of parity in insurance coverage for these medical illnesses. Some states now require insurance companies that cover psychiatric illness to provide comparable benefits for the treatment of the above disorders as they do for high blood pressure, diabetes, back pain, and any other medical disorder. The biological model of mental illness, as well as for medical illness in general, is far from complete. Comprehensive understanding of the patient requires psychological and social models as well. But, as we will see in succeeding examples, the tissue theory has proved a powerful inspiration to the expansion of psychiatric knowledge and has resulted in efficacious treatments for many mental illnesses.

Key points

- The *biological model* of mental illness states that all mental activity is reducible to tissue activity, particularly that of the central nervous system.

- *Psychiatric disorders* may be conceptualized as being either *secondary* effects of other medical conditions or *primary* states with a unique neurobiology.

Neurobiology 3

The biological model of mental illness supposes that mental disorders are the result of physical processes. More specifically, the central nervous system (CNS) is thought to be the seat of mental activity, so mental disorders are seen as central nervous system disorders. Thus, a working familiarity of the anatomy and physiology of the CNS is necessary to understand the biological models of mental illness.

The neuron

In all, the CNS is composed of about one trillion cells. Neurons are the primary operating cells in CNS activity. Each neuron is supported by about ten structural cells, called glial cells. Each neuron consists of a *cell body* with numerous projecting *dendrites* that receive input from other neurons (Figure 3.1). From the cell body projects a single long extension called an *axon*, which terminates at a receiving cell—possibly another neuron or a muscle cell. The primary action of neurons is to conduct electrical impulses along the axonal length, by receiving input from and conducting impulses to other cells of the body, across a connection known as a *synapse*. A synapse is a tiny (60-micrometer) space between the terminal end of the axon and the receiving cell. Cells communicate across the *synaptic cleft*, as it is called, via chemical messengers called *neurotransmitters*. Neurotransmitters are secreted at the *presynaptic cell* from the axonal terminal, travel across the synaptic cleft, and reach the *postsynaptic cell*, where they interact with protein structures called *postsynaptic receptors*. Agents capable of stimulating a protein receptor are said to be *agonists* of that receptor. Agents that can block the action of an agonist at the receptor are called *antagonists*.

Stimulated by the presence of a neurotransmitter, these postsynaptic receptors trigger a series of chemical events in the postsynaptic cell; for example, they may cause the cell membrane to depolarize, thus creating electrical current, which is then transmitted along the length of the cell.

Neurons are the primary operating cells in central nervous system activity.

Dendrites are cell projections that receive input from other neurons.

29

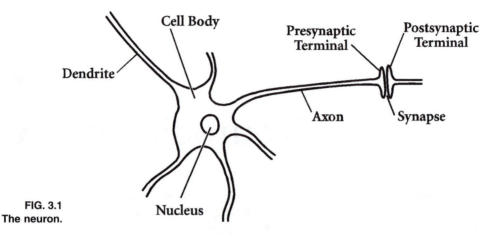

**FIG. 3.1
The neuron.**

Alternatively, neurotransmission may induce a series of chemical changes in the postsynaptic cell, called *second-messenger systems*. Some second-messenger systems include the cyclic AMP, cyclic GMP, and phosphotidyl-inositol systems—chemicals that communicate between the receptor and other parts of the cell.

Neurotransmitters may be classified as either *excitatory*, if they increase the firing rate of the postsynaptic neuron, or *inhibitory*, if they decrease the firing rate of the postsynaptic neuron.

There are hundreds of neurotransmitters. Some are long protein chains, some are derivatives of single amino acids, and some are simple molecules such as nitrous oxide. Six neurotransmitter systems appear commonly in the pathophysiology of the major mental disorders: the *biogenic amines* (dopamine, norepinephrine, serotonin, and acetylcholine), and the *amino acids* (g-aminobutyric acid or GABA and glutamate). The anatomy of these systems is detailed below.

Presynaptic neurons have receptors on their surfaces that are stimulated by their own neurotransmitters. These receptors are known as *autoreceptors*. The effect of stimulating these autoreceptors is to cause the cell to decrease its firing rate, and so release less neurotransmitter. This acts as a negative (or inhibitory) feedback loop. Once the cell has released a neurotransmitter, it must subsequently decrease its firing rate. The released neurotransmitter acts as a signal to the neuron that it has successfully accomplished its task and may reduce its firing rate until stimulated again. *Heteroreceptors* are presynaptic receptors that are agonized by neurotransmitters other than those released by the presynaptic neuron. Heteroreceptors in general have the same function as autoreceptors.

Any neurotransmitter that does not affect either the postsynaptic cell or autoreceptors of the presynaptic cell must be metabolized. This process occurs either in the synaptic cleft or in the presynaptic cell, after

Axons are extensions from a neuronal cell that conduct electrical pulses to a receiving cell.

Neuro-transmitters are chemical messengers between cells.

reuptake pumps channel remaining neurotransmitters back into the presynaptic cell. Once inside the presynaptic cell, enzymes degrade the neurotransmitter.

Receptors on the surface of cells receive messages from other cells.

Gross anatomy

The CNS may be conceptualized developmentally. The structures of the CNS arise from its embryological components (see Figure 3.1): the rhombencephalon, the mesencephalon, and the prosencephalon.

Rhombencephalon

The rhombencephalon develops into the medulla (myelencephalon) and the pons and cerebellum (metencephalon). The *medulla* controls basic physiologic functions such as respiration and blood pressure. The medulla is the seat of cranial nerves X through XII.

The *pons* gives rise to cranial nerves V through IX. Several major neurotransmitter systems, including norepinephrine and serotonin, also arise in the pons. The *cerebellum* coordinates movement and plays a role in higher cognitive functions such as memory.

Autoreceptors are receptors that are stimulated by neurotransmitters released by the presynaptic neuron.

Mesencephalon

The mesencephalon becomes the midbrain. The *midbrain* gives rise to the reticular activating system, as well as cranial nerves II through IV. Dopaminergic nuclei, containing the cell bodies of dopaminergic neurons, are found in the midbrain.

Prosencephalon

The prosencephalon becomes the thalamus and hypothalamus (diencephalon) and the amygdala, hippocampus, corpus striatum, and cerebral cortex (telencephalon). The *thalamus* relays neuronal conduction to and from the cerebral cortex. The *hypothalamus* controls the pituitary gland (the hypothalamic-pituitary-end organ systems) and regulates sleep, temperature, appetite, and thirst. The *amygdala* and *hippocampus* form part of the limbic system, which is intimately involved in emotion and memory. The *corpus striatum*, or basal ganglia—which includes the caudate, putamen, and globus pallidus—coordinates movement. The *cerebral cortex* (Figures 3.2a & 3.2b) is divided into two hemispheres, joined by and communicating across the *corpus callosum*. Each hemisphere has four lobes: the frontal lobe, the parietal lobe, the occipital lobe, and the temporal lobe.

Heteroreceptors are agonized by neurotransmitters other than those released by the presynaptic neuron.

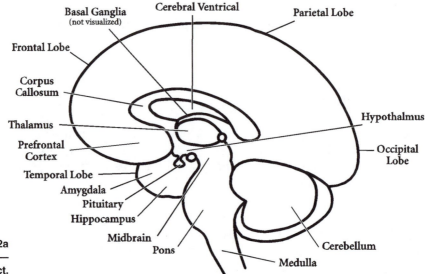

FIG. 3.2a
Right hemisphere—
medial aspect.

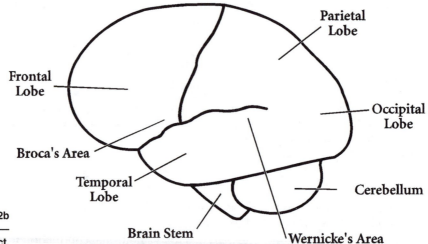

FIG. 3.2b
Left hemisphere—
lateral aspect.

The *frontal lobes* are the site of primary and association motor cortexes, as well as *Broca's area* (in the dominant hemisphere), which controls expressive language.

The *parietal lobes* contain primary and association sensory cortexes.

The *occipital lobes* contain visual cortex.

The *temporal* lobes are the site of auditory cortex, as well as *Wernicke's area* (in the dominant hemisphere), which controls language comprehension.

Injury to the cerebral cortex can result in several distinct syndromes that are psychiatrically important.

Aphasia

Aphasia is dysfunction in the production and/or comprehension of language. There are eight cortical aphasia syndromes, two of particular importance. Damage to Broca's area in the prefrontal cortex may result in an *expressive aphasia*, in which language comprehension is intact but linguistic expression is impaired. Damage to Wernicke's area in the temporal lobe may result in a *receptive aphasia*, in which linguistic expression remains fluent but comprehension of language is impaired.

Apraxia

Apraxia is the inability to plan and execute a motor task despite normal strength. *Ideational praxis* is a dominant hemisphere ability and is responsible for coordinating motor imitation and sequences. *Constructional praxis* coordinates visual-spatial motor tasks (such as drawing) and is a nondominant hemisphere function.

Agnosia

Agnosia is the inability to recognize objects. It is most commonly visual or tactile.

Neurotransmitter pathways

Several of the major neurotransmitters are found primarily in discrete groups of neurons with projections to specific areas of the brain. The following are particularly important to the neurobiology of mental illness.

Dopamine

Dopaminergic neurons (Figure 3.3) are found predominantly in the midbrain: from the *ventral tegmental area*, with projection to the limbic system and cerebral cortex (the mesolimbic and mesocortical tracts); and from the *substantia nigra*, with projection to the basal ganglia (the nigrostriatal tract).

Aphasia is dysfunction in the production and/or comprehension of language.

Apraxia is the inability to plan and execute a motor task, despite normal strength.

Agnosia is the inability to recognize objects.

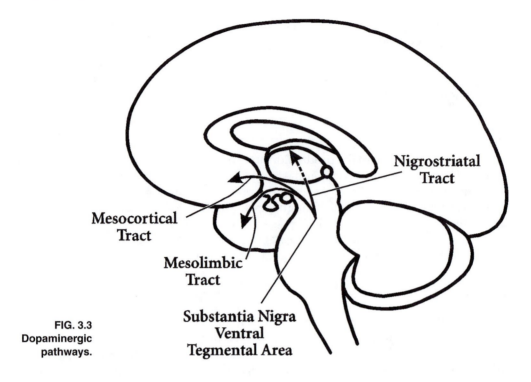

FIG. 3.3
Dopaminergic
pathways.

Norepinephrine

Noradrenergic neurons (Figure 3.4) arise largely from the *locus ceruleus* in the pons, with projections to the brain at large.

Serotonin

Serotonergic neurons (Figure 3.5) are found predominantly in the *dorsal raphe nucleus* of the pons, with projections to the cortex at large.

Acetylcholine

Cholinergic neurons are found diffusely throughout the brain, but are also concentrated in the *nucleus basalis of Meynert* (located ventral to the globus pallidus).

GABA

GABAergic neurons are found diffusely throughout the brain. GABA is the main inhibitory neurotransmitter of the central nervous system.

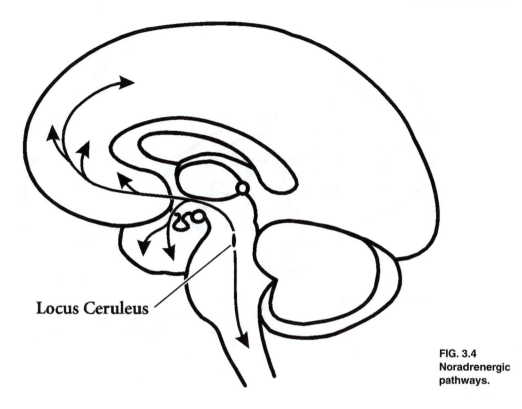

**FIG. 3.4
Noradrenergic
pathways.**

Locus Ceruleus

Glutamate

Glutamatergic neurons are found diffusely thoughout the brain. Glutamate is an excitatory neurotransmitter.

With this basic survey of neuroanatomy and neurophysiology, the neurobiology of the major mental disorders can be understood.

Key points

- Mental states arise primarily from activities of the *central nervous system*; however, the central nervous system is intimately connected with every organ system in the body.

- The principle acting cell in the central nervous system is the *neuron*, supported by neuroglial cells.

- The neuron consists of a cell body, which receives input from other cells via dendrites and transmits electrical signals down the axon.

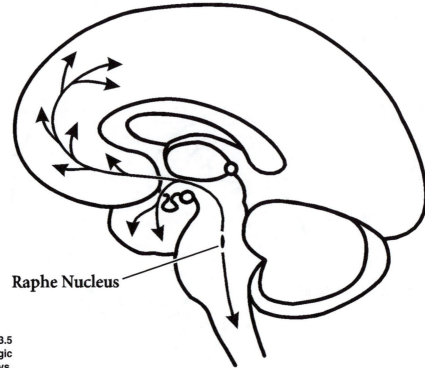

FIG. 3.5
Serotonergic
pathways.

Raphe Nucleus

- Electrical signals transmitted down the neuronal axon result in the secretion of chemical *neurotransmitters*, which cross the synapse to affect other cells.

- Of the hundreds of neurotransmitters, the *biogenic amines*—dopamine, serotonin, norephinephrine—are of particular importance in the pathogenesis of psychiatric disorders.

Psychotic disorders 4

Psychosis

Psychosis is one of the most debilitating of the psychiatric syndromes. When psychiatrists say a person is psychotic, they mean is that he or she is experiencing impaired *reality testing*. Impaired reality testing specifically refers to either *delusional thinking* or *hallucinatory perceptions*. Psychosis is the cardinal feature of schizophrenia, but it may result from many causes.

Psychosis is the experience of impaired reality testing.

Case example

Mr. B went to see a psychiatrist at the request of his primary care physician, but B was convinced the problem to be solved was his wife's. B and his wife lived in the mountains, in a fairly isolated cabin. B admitted he was feeling very depressed, hardly sleeping, losing weight, crying frequently, and wishing at times that he was dead. The reason for this, according to B, was that his wife was obsessed with other men. She flirted constantly, he claimed.

At first the details of this flirting seemed plausible. Then, as B talked, the rationality of his claims began to loosen. He said that when the two of them were sitting at night watching television, she would look at men outside their cabin. Recalling that B and his wife lived a mile from their nearest neighbor, the psychiatrist inquired if there were actually men outside the cabin. "Yes," B said, "And she looks at them, and winks at them in the dark when she thinks I'm not looking."

B's wife began crying as he told this to the psychiatrist. Nothing she could say could convince him that she was faithful. B was suffering from a paranoid delusion.

Impaired reality testing includes delusional thinking and hallucinatory perceptions.

Delusions

Delusional thinking is one variant of psychotic thinking. *Delusions are fixed beliefs that are untrue and not culturally accepted.* They are fixed in the sense that no amount of reasoning or contrary data can convince the believer otherwise. Such was the case with B. No matter what his wife or anyone else said, no matter how often it was demonstrated to him that no one was winking at his wife through the windows, B's belief that she was having an affair was entrenched.

Furthermore, the belief that she was having an affair was untrue. Although conceivable, it was simply not the case—the very idea stretched credulity—that B's wife was winking at men who were flirting with her in the dark of the woods surrounding their isolated cabin. Given that information and the tearful denials of his wife, most reasonable people would have doubted the story.

However, the story was conceivably true. And that means that the delusion was nonbizarre. *Nonbizarre delusions* are those that, although untrue in a given case, are at least plausible. They are conceivably true in the space-time world we understand ourselves to inhabit. Thus, in B's case, it would not have been impossible that someone was lurking outside his cabin. But no one was. Similarly, the CIA does follow people from time to time. However, for the average psychiatric patient who believes the CIA is watching, this is not the case.

On the other hand, if someone is convinced that all of his internal organs have been removed, or that everyone around her has been re-placed with an exact duplicate (a situation known as *Capgras syndrome*), such delusions are said to be *bizarre*, because they are not possible. There are no documented cases in which a person has remained fully func-tional with all of his or her internal organs removed. If a person experi-encing such a delusion is given a magnetic resonance imaging (MRI) scan of his or her body, and is showed the scan with all internal organs clearly visible, it does not make any difference at all. The nature of a delusion is that it is fixed.

Notice there is no claim that delusional thinking is objectively un-true. Rather, delusional thinking stands in the face of overwhelming conflicting evidence. Psychiatry is a scientific discipline, and so does not make claims to an objective truth to which all must adhere. The de-luded often believe they understand the world much better than others do. This might be so.

The psychiatrist is usually well advised to attempt to ascertain the truth or falsity of suspected delusions, if they are non-bizarre. Personnel of an inpatient unit once treated a woman who had been picked up by the police; she was wandering in and out of traffic, unkempt, and clearly gravely disabled. On the police report the arresting officers gave an ex-ample of what they thought was delusional thinking—the woman claimed to be an internationally famous writer, which seemed laugh-able given her dilapidated condition. But it was true. She had several other problems, including a severe case of alcohol withdrawal, and her behavior obviously held potential for imminent self-harm. But she was not delusional.

Delusions are fixed beliefs that are untrue and not culturally accepted.

The key difference between a deluded and a nondeluded person is the willingness to modify a belief based on evidence. Since the police and medical staff were quite willing to believe the woman was a writer once evidence to that effect had been produced, their incorrect belief that she was not a writer of international fame does not qualify as a delusion. Not all false beliefs are delusional. They are only so if the individual holds on to them despite overwhelming contrary evidence.

This does raise an intriguing question about how to regard some other fixed beliefs. Religious beliefs usually are not regarded as delusional because, although they are virtually never demonstrably true, they are also rarely demonstrably false either (although occasionally they are, such as when they make predictions that the world will end on a given date and it does not). Beliefs that are not clearly false cannot be classified as delusional. Furthermore, religious beliefs are held by large numbers of people. As such, they escape classification as delusional based on the *cultural congruency criterion*, which says that delusions are fixed, untrue beliefs that are not culturally accepted. Simply because everyone believes a particular statement is not necessarily a good reason for accepting that statement to be true, and hopefully belief systems revolve around some sort of criterion for proving and disproving beliefs. However, this is not always the case, and if psychiatrists were to classify as delusional all those who believed what others told them without independent evidence, virtually everyone would be delusional. In practice it is actually not difficult to locate truly delusional thinking when it occurs. Delusional beliefs are often testable, and deluded people are quite incorrigible in their adherence to their beliefs in the face of conflicting evidence. Virtually everybody else will perceive these features, not just the psychiatrist. B was referred to the psychiatrist by his primary care physician for delusional thinking, and B's wife certainly knew he was delusional.

Hallucinations are sensory perceptions that are internally generated.

Hallucinations

The other cardinal symptom of psychosis is the hallucination. *Hallucinations are perceptions, in any of the five sensory modalities (smell, taste, touch, sight, and hearing), that are internally generated.* They do not derive from outside stimuli. If an abnormal perception does result from outside stimuli, such as when someone taking LSD sees a painting melt down the wall, it is called an *illusion*. In that case, the painting is stimulating the visual system, which is then misperceiving the stimulus. Hallucinations arise without any outside stimulus. One common hallucination is to hear a voice speaking when there is no one there to speak. This might be as simple as hearing a voice call your name, or it might involve multiple voices talking about you or other topics. Sometimes auditory hallucinations tell people to do things. These hallucinations are called *command auditory hallucinations* and may be profoundly distressing. For example, people sometimes receive instructions to kill themselves or someone else, and resistance is difficult.

It should be noted that people normally speak to themselves in ongoing internal dialogues. Hallucinations are very different phenomena. As opposed to one's internal dialogue, hallucinations are distinctly perceived as arising from an external stimulus. But they do not.

The causes of psychosis

General medical conditions.   What causes psychosis? Since psychosis is a symptom and not a disease, the possible causes are numerous. Many medical conditions—such as tumors, head injuries, the effects of street drugs and prescription medications, and lupus erythematosis—can cause psychotic thinking (see Box 4.1). When psychotic symptoms arise from medical problems, the psychotic symptoms are said to be secondary to a general medical condition. General medical conditions are illnesses not classified as psychiatric illnesses, such as those listed above. Since many of the psychiatric illnesses have known neurological bases, the distinction between general medical conditions and psychiatric disorders is somewhat artificial, a holdover from the days when psychiatric disorders such as schizophrenia, depression, mania, and hysteria had no known biological causes. They were medically idiopathic. When, with the advent of the Wasserman antibody test, some of those who were thought to have schizophrenia were discovered to have syphilitic infection of the nervous system, those individuals were classified as having psychotic symptoms secondary to neurosyphilis, an infection and thus a general medical condition. Those with psychosis of undetermined cause who also displayed certain other symptoms continued to be classified as having schizophrenia.

When psychotic symptoms are clearly related to medical problems usually considered the province of general medicine, then the psychotic symptoms are said to be the result of—that is, secondary to—a general medical condition. When they are thought to be due to a substance use disorder, psychotic symptoms are described as being secondary to a substance use disorder. However, this leaves a large group of individuals who have psychotic syndromes that are primary—there is no known general medical condition causing the symptoms. Instead, the primary psychotic disorders have a unique neurobiology.

Primary psychotic disorders.   There are dozens of psychiatric syndromes classified in the *DSM-IV*. Mania, major depression, obsessive-compulsive disorder, panic disorder, and substance use disorders all are primary psychiatric disorders.

Many of these disorders are capable of causing psychotic symptoms. For example, it is common for manic individuals to have delusions of grandeur, in which their sense of self-worth becomes delusionally

BOX 4.1.   Medical Causes of Psychosis

Substance Use/Toxins
Alcohol intoxication/withdrawal
Stimulant intoxication
Hallucinogen intoxication
PCP/Ketamine intoxication
Cannibis intoxication
Heavy metal poisoning
Organic toxins

Autoimmune
Lupus erythematosis
Sjogren's syndrome
Sarcoidosis

Endocrine
Hypo/hyperthyroidism
Addison's/Cushing's diseases
Hypo/hyperparathyroidism

Metabolic
Wilson's disease
Hemochromatosis
Acute intermittent porphyria
Diabetic ketoacidosis
Hypoglycemia
Hypoxia
Liver failure/hepatic encephalopathy
Electrolyte/acid-base disturbances
Renal failure

Central Nervous System
Neoplasms
  Primary
  Metastatic
  Paraneoplastic syndromes
Hydrocephalus
  Obstructive
  Pseudotumor cerebri
  Normal pressure
Infections
  Meningitis
  Encephalitis
  Abscess
  HIV
  Progressive multifocal
    leukoencephalopathy
  Syphilis
Trauma
Subdermal/subarachnoid bleeding
Cerebral infarction

Vasculitis
Epilepsy/postictal states
Degenerative disorders
  Alzheimer's disease
  Lewy body dementia
  Vascular dementia
  Huntington's disease

Medications
Antiarrhythmics
Antibiotics
Anticholinergics
Antidepressants
Antihistaminics
Antineoplastics
Bromide compounds
Carbidopa/levodopa
Carbon disulfide
Cimetidine
Disulfiram
Dopamine agonists
Isoniazid
Reserpine
Steroids

Sleep Disorders
Central/obstructive sleep apnea

Hematologic
Hyperviscosity
Anemia
Malignancy
Sickle cell

Infection
Tuberculosis
Malaria
Typhoid
Subacute bacterial endocarditis

Developmental Disorders
Trisomy X

Nutritional Deficiencies
Thiamine
Nicotine acid
Folate
B_{12}
Protein
Essential fatty acids

inflated, so that they believe they can fly, are deities, or can stare at the sun for hours. Depression may result in hallucinations or delusions, as can substance intoxication and cognitive disorders. But although these disorders may result in psychosis, psychosis is not an elemental feature of them. Most people who become depressed, for example, do not become psychotic. Some do, but it is not a necessary feature of depression—it is a complication. The criteria for major depression are depressed mood, loss of interest, sleep and appetite disturbances, guilt or low self-esteem, hopelessness or suicidal thoughts, loss of energy, and decreased concentration.

Hallucinations and delusions are not listed as elemental criteria for major depression, since, if they occur in the course of an episode of major depression, that depression is understood as major depression with psychotic features.

There is, however, a group of primary psychiatric disorders known as the *primary psychotic disorders*. These are distinguished by requiring the presence of psychotic thinking to diagnose the disease process. The classic example of a primary psychotic disorder is schizophrenia. Schizophrenia, as we will see later, is thought to be a neurodevelopmental disorder that results in the cardinal symptoms of psychosis, as well as other associated symptoms.

The pathophysiology of psychosis

The dopamine hypothesis. In the early 1950s, it was discovered serendipitously that a drug called chlorpromazine, which was used as an anesthesia adjunct, also relieved psychotic symptoms. Investigation of the drug's activity revealed that it has the capability of blocking postsynaptic dopamine receptors in the brain. There are three major dopamine pathways in the brain. The best known arises from the *nucleus substantia nigra* (literally, black substance, named for its dark tincture). Cell bodies in this brainstem nucleus send axons to an area in the middle of the brain known as the *basal ganglia*, which helps regulate movement. Degeneration of this neuronal tract, known as the *nigrostriatal tract* (because it runs from the substantia nigra to the basal ganglia, otherwise known as the striatum), causes Parkinson's disease, an illness characterized by slowed movements (*bradykinesia*), muscle rigidity, and tremors.

Two other dopaminergic pathways arise from a second area of the brainstem called the *ventral tegmental* area of the midbrain. Axons from the ventral tegmental area project into a portion of the brain called the *limbic system* (which includes structures such as the hippocampus, amygdala, cingulate gyrus, and mammillary bodies) and the frontal lobes of the cerebrum. These pathways are known respectively as the *mesolimbic* and *mesocortical tracts*.

The antipsychotic effect of chlorpromazine, and of antipsychotic medications in general, appears to arise from its ability to block postsynaptic dopamine receptors at the end of the mesolimbic and mesocortical tracts. Blockade of the postsynaptic dopamine receptors reduces the ability of dopamine secreted by the mesolimbic and mesocortical tracts to act on the receptors (Janicek, Davis, Preskorn, & Ayd, 1997).

Chlorpromazine is 60% to 70% effective (versus 20% for placebo) in treating the symptoms of schizophrenia (Janicek et al., 1997). It has become famous under its trade name—Thorazine. When chlorpromazine was discovered to be effective in the treatment of psychosis, intense investigation as to possible mechanisms of action ensued. The drug's ability to block postsynaptic dopamine receptors was hypothesized to be the reason for its antipsychotic activity; this suggested that some abnormality in dopamine function might be responsible for psychotic symptoms. This became known as the *dopamine hypothesis* of schizophrenia. It has now become apparent that dopamine receptor blockade is a common feature of all antipsychotic medications (Creese, Burt, & Snyder, 1984; Nordstrom et al., 1993).

Further support for the dopamine hypothesis of schizophrenia comes from drug-induced psychoses. Amphetamines and cocaine are notorious for precipitating psychosis during the state of intoxication after repetitive use (Byne, Kemether, Jones, Haroutunian, & Davis, 1999). The primary mechanism of these drugs is to enhance the release of dopamine from dopaminergic neurons of the mesolimbic, mesocortical, and nigrostriatal tracts into the synaptic cleft, thus increasing the stimulation of postsynaptic dopamine receptors (Carboni, Imperato, Perezzani, & Di Chiara, 1989). This is the opposite effect of antipsychotic medications, which not surprisingly can be used to treat amphetamine- and cocaine-induced psychoses. Other dopaminergic agents such as L-dopa and bromocriptine also may cause psychosis (Byne et al., 1999).

Glutamate

Other neurotransmitter systems also are implicated in the pathogenesis of psychosis. The drug phencyclidine (PCP) is an antagonist of the neurotransmitter glutamate, at NMDA (N-methyl-D-aspartate) receptors. Like cocaine and amphetamines, PCP can cause symptoms of psychosis (Byne et al., 1999). This finding has been replicated in animals with both PCP and the anesthetic ketamine, which, like PCP, is an NMDA antagonist. This has led researchers to look for glutamate agonists as possible antipsychotic agents. Unfortunately, glutamate agonists to date have proved toxic to humans.

Serotonin

Lysergic acid diethylamide (LSD) is well-known for ability to induce hallucinations. The primary effect of LSD appears to be stimulation of postsynaptic serotonin receptors—most importantly, the 5-HT$_{2A}$ receptor (Aghajianian, 1994). As we will see shortly, many of the newer antipsychotic agents have the ability to block postsynaptic 5-HT$_{2A}$ receptors, further supporting the hypothesis that dysregulation of these neurons is part of the pathophysiology of psychosis (Sadock & Sadock, 2000).

Schizophrenia

Schizophrenia has been investigated intensely for more than one hundred years, yet, although the biology of schizophrenia is better understood now more than ever, much of the disease remains mysterious.

Schizophrenia presents most commonly in the second to fourth decades of life. It is characterized by psychotic symptoms: most often delusions and/or hallucinations, but also disorganized thinking; negative symptoms such as poverty of speech and facial expression, inability to experience pleasure, or lack of interest and initiative; and catatonia, a state of withdrawal, immobility, and imitative actions. Persons with schizophrenia inevitably experience deterioration in their functioning, sometimes to the point of severe inability to take care of even basic hygiene and feeding.

Case example

S had gone to college, where he was a promising literature student who planned to attend graduate school. However, in his senior year friends and teachers began to notice changes in S. First, he became withdrawn and no longer participated in his habitual activities. Those who called on him were surprised at the deteriorating condition of his apartment. S's personal hygiene also became noticeably inadequate. He went days without bathing. His behavior became odd. When he became hot in church one Sunday he took off his shirt and sat comfortably in the pew, despite the stares of the congregation. He seemed surprised and a little annoyed when he was asked to put his shirt back on.

S's conversations also had taken a strange turn. Although he remained affable, his features were curiously free of expression— he seldom blinked, let alone smiled or frowned—and he began to say his mother had malign plans to destroy him. S had always been close to his mother, and the family became extremely worried when he refused to speak with any of them except his father. S was not specific about how his mother planned to destroy him, except to say that she wanted "world dominion." S also was observed giggling to himself when sitting alone. When asked about this, he admitted he heard voices that often told jokes. But the voices could also be harshly critical. In these times, the voices would sound like his mother's.

S failed his last semester of college. He began wandering the streets. Late one night, he was drinking heavily and finally attempted to kill himself by lying on a highway, waiting for a car to run over him. He was struck in the foot, which was seriously fractured. At that point, S was hospitalized.

S's case was severe. Between 0.5% and 1% of the population has schizophrenia (American Psychiatric Association, 1994). Some people with schizophrenia have only minor hallucinations and mild delusions, which they keep to themselves. Their functioning may be only slightly impaired, and they may have a completely unremarkable lifestyle.

DSM-IV diagnostic criteria for schizophrenia

A. **Characteristic Symptoms:** Two (or more) of the following, each present for a significant portion of time during a 1-month period (or less if successfully treated).

(1) delusions

(2) hallucinations

(3) disorganized speech (e.g., frequent derailment or incoherence)

(4) grossly disorganized or catatonic behavior

(5) negative symptoms (i.e., affective flattening, alogia, avolition)

Note: Only one Criterion A symptom is required if delusions are bizarre or hallucinations consist of a voice keeping up a running commentary on the person's behavior or thoughts, or two or more voices conversing with each other.

B. **Social/Occupational Dysfunction:** For a significant portion of the time since the onset of the disturbance, one or more major areas of functioning such as work, interpersonal relations, or self-care are markedly below the level achieved prior to the onset (or when the onset is in childhood or adolescence, the failure to achieve expected levels of interpersonal, academic, or occupational achievement).

C. **Duration:** Continuous signs of the disturbance persist for at least 6 months. This 6-month period must include at least 1 month of symptoms (or less if successfully treated) that meet Criterion A (i.e., active-phase symptoms) and may include periods of prodromal or residual symptoms. During these prodromal or residual periods, the signs of the disturbance may be manifested by only negative symptoms or two or more symptoms listed in Criterion A present in an attenuated form (e.g., odd beliefs, unusual perceptual experiences).

D. **Schizoaffective and Mood Disorder Exclusion:** Schizoaffective Disorder and Mood Disorder With Psychotic Features have been ruled out because either (1) no Major Depressive, Manic, or Mixed Episodes have occurred concurrently with the active-phase symptoms; or (2) if mood episodes have occurred during active-phase symptoms, their total duration has been brief relative to the duration of the active and residual periods.

E. **Substance/General Medical Condition Exclusion:** The disturbance is not due to the direct physiological effects of a substance (e.g., a drug of abuse or a medication) or a general medical condition.

F. **Relationship to a Pervasive Developmental Disorder:** If there is a history of Autistic Disorder or another Pervasive Developmental Disorder, the additional diagnosis of Schizophrenia is made only if prominent delusions or hallucinations are also present for at least a month (or less if successfully treated).

Reprinted with permission from the ***Diagnostic and Statistical Manual of Mental Disorders,*** Fourth Edition. Copyright 1994, American Psychiatric Association.

Positive and negative symptoms

The symptoms of schizophrenia have been divided usefully into positive and negative symptoms. Positive symptoms are additions onto a usual state of mental functioning and so include hallucinations and delusions, thought disorganization, and catatonia (discussed later). Negative symptoms represent deficits in normal functioning and include lack of facial expression (flat affect), amotivation, and illogical thinking. There appears to be distinct pathophysiology for the positive and negative symptoms of schizophrenia, and they have differential responses to antipsychotic medication.

Catatonia.   Catatonia is a syndrome that may occur in schizophrenia but is not specific to the psychotic disorders. It also may be present in mood disorders and can be caused by the use of dopamine receptor antagonists.

Catatonia is characterized by negativism (failure to care for the self and resistance to help), mutism, echolalia (parroting of words or phrases), echopraxia (imitation of movements), and catalepsy (postural immobility).

Catatonia is not a primary symptom of psychosis, but can be present in a variety of disorders including the primary psychotic disorders. Since catatonia may be caused by antipsychotic medication, it should come as no surprise that the treatment of catatonia does not rely on antipsychotic medications. Instead, the treatment of choice is the benzodiazepine agent *lorazepam* (see Chapter 6). *Benzodiazepines* increase the activity of the inhibitory neurotransmitter GABA, but how this finding relates to the pathophysiology of catatonia is not well understood.

The pathophysiology of schizophrenia

Genetics.   A century of investigation has yielded much information about the pathology of schizophrenia. There is a significant genetic contribution to the disorder. If an individual has one parent with schizophrenia, the chances of him or her developing the disorder rises to 12%; two parents, and the chances increase to 40%. If someone has an identical twin with schizophrenia, there is a 47% chance he or she will eventually have it too. Monozygotic twins, who share the same genetic makeup, show a concordance rate of between 33% and 78%, while dizygotic twins show rates between 8% and 28% (Sadock & Sadock, 2000). Despite this increased genetic risk, single genes clearly related to the pathogenesis of schizophrenia have not been discovered. Genetic linkage studies have implicated chromosomes 6, 8, and 22 as possible candidates for genetic loci.

Neuroanatomy.   The brains of persons with schizophrenia show consistent anatomical differences from normal controls. The brains of those with schizophrenia often show enlargement of the cerebral ventricles (Berman & Weinberger, 1999). The cellular architecture of the hippocampus and prefrontal cortex often is abnormal, and the temporal lobes often show an abnormal asymmetry (Akbarian, Vinuela, Kim, Potkin, Bunney, & Jones, 1993; Arnold, Hyman, van Hoesen, & Damasio, 1991; Bogerts, Ashtari, Degreef, Alvir, Bilder, & Lieberman, 1990; Jeste & Lohr, 1989; Kovelman & Scheibel, 1980).

This abnormal cellular architecture is not thought to be related to neurodegeneration, as is seen in degenerative disorders such as Alzheimer's disease (see Chapter 7), since evidence of neurodegeneration (*cellular gliosis*) is not found in schizophrenic brains (Sadock & Sadock, 2000). Instead, the defect is thought to be developmental. Prime candidates are (a) abnormal cellular migration during embryonic development and (b) abnormal cellular "pruning" during adolescence. The result is ventricular enlargement and abnormal cellular architecture, particularly in the frontal and temporal lobes.

Functional dysregulation.   Functional as well as structural differences also are evident. Persons with schizophrenia show abnormalities in their ability to track moving objects visually (Braff, 1999). They also evidence abnormal electrical function in the brain following a sensory stimulus such as a loud noise. Consistently, people with schizophrenia show prolonged responses on reaction-time tests and, unlike comparison subjects, do not benefit from a warning stimulus. On continuous performance tests measuring sustained attention, people with schizophrenia do less well than control subjects as the information processing load increases. Verbal, nonverbal, and visual recall are decreased. People with schizophrenia also show reduced frontal lobe activity in studies of regional cerebral blood flow (Berman & Weinberger, 1999). Abnormal nonspecific findings on the neurological exam are more common than in controls.

One finding, which perhaps explains some of the thought disorganization of schizophrenia, is that the brains of those with schizophrenia do not decrease their reaction to repeated sensory stimuli. If an EEG is placed on a normal control, exposure to a sound will generate a spike on the EEG tracing, known as a P50 (Braff, 1999). If the first stimulus is followed closely by a second, the P50 in response to the second stimulus will be of lesser amplitude than the first. The brain has adjusted to the stimulus and does not respond as dramatically to a second presentation. Individuals with schizophrenia fail to attenuate their P50 response. This ability to adjust probably is what allows repetitive and unimportant stimuli to be screened from conscious perception. For example, as you read this you are probably unaware of small sounds such as traffic outside, birds chirping, the light buzzing, and so on, although you can become aware of these stimuli if you choose to direct your attention toward them. As can easily be imagined, losing this ability would be extremely detrimental.

Neural networks

From the foregoing it might be clear that there is no single, discrete neuroanatomical lesion responsible for the symptoms of schizophrenia. Rather, it appears to be the result of complex interactions between abnormally functioning neurotransmitter systems, specifically involving dopamine, glutamate, serotonin, and probably others, in conjunction with diffuse disturbances in the cellular architecture of the brain. Schizophrenia is a *systems illness*. Although there are some brain functions (such as language) that are controlled by relatively discrete centers in the brain, much brain function—particularly as it relates to the domains of thinking, feeling, perceiving, cognating, and behaving—is controlled diffusely by a "neural net." Neural nets may be conceptualized as feedback loops between neurons in the brain.

Recall that when a neuron secretes a neurotransmitter, that neurotransmitter may have three fates. It can stimulate the postsynaptic neuron, be transported into the presynaptic neuron for degradation, or stimulate presynaptic autoreceptors. Stimulation of autoreceptors reduces the firing rate of the presynaptic cell. This is an example of a simple feedback loop involving a single cell. More complex feedback loops involving many neurons also are present in the brain.

Two examples of this are the cortico-striatal-thalamic (CST) and the cortico-cerebellar-thalamic-cortical (CCTC) loops (see Figure 4.1). While the specific defect remains to be fully elucidated, it seems likely that a disorder in interneuronal regulation and feedback, such as in the CST loop and/or the CCTC loop, is responsible for the symptoms of schizophrenia, perhaps through impairment in information processing (Andreasen, 1999; Sadock & Sadock, 2000). Much as tracts from the frontal lobe to the cerebellum coordinate movement (such as eye movement, which is often aberrant in schizophrenia), so some CST and CCTC tracts may help modulate cognitive functions. Dysfunction in these tracts is perhaps induced by neurotransmitter defects at multiple sites.

Fortunately, as we will see, some relief from the symptoms of schizophrenia is available through antipsychotic medication. Interestingly, it

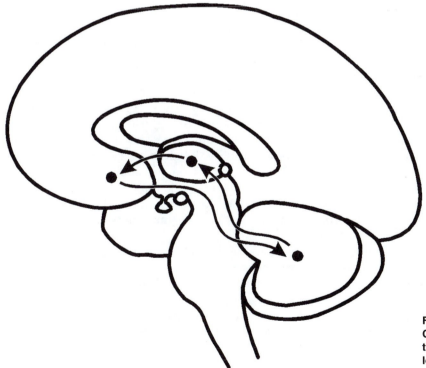

**FIG. 4.1
Cortico-cerebellar-
thalamic-cortical
loop.**

turns out that effective symptom control also can be achieved through the use of a particular type of psychotherapy. As we will see, better treatment for psychiatric problems comes through an integrated approach that includes the biological, psychological, and social models.

Other primary psychotic disorders

In addition to schizophrenia, there are several other primary psychotic disorders. *Schizoaffective disorder* is characterized by baseline psychosis with a superimposed mood disorder (bipolar disorder or unipolar major depression). *Schizophreniform disorder* presents with symptoms of schizophrenia, but a decline in functioning of less than 6 months. *Brief psychotic disorder* consists of psychotic symptoms of less than 1 month duration. *Delusional disorder*, in which the only symptom is a nonbizarre delusion, comes in jealous, grandiose, erotomanic, and persecutory subtypes. When two people share a delusional system, *shared psychotic disorder*, also known as *folie à deux*, is diagnosed.

Antipsychotic medications

Dopamine receptor antagonists

The antipsychotic medications (see Table 4.1) are, without exception, dopamine receptor antagonists. Dopamine receptor antagonism is responsible not only for the putative antipsychotic effect of these medications but also for much of their side effect profile.

When dopamine receptor antagonism occurs in the mesolimbic and mesocortical tracts, this action is thought to decrease psychosis. Dopamine receptor antagonism at other sites, however, may result in side effects. Recall the other primary dopaminergic tract in the brain— the nigrostriatal tract. This tract runs from the substantia nigra to the basal ganglia and is integral to the regulation of movement. Degeneration of this tract results in Parkinson's disease. Usually, 80% of nigrostriatal neurons must be lost before symptoms of Parkinson's disease become evident.

Pharmacologic blockade of dopamine receptors results in a syndrome identical to Parkinson's disease. When 78% of nigrostriatal dopamine receptors are antagonized (Kapur, Zipursky, Jones, Remington, & Houle, 2000), the result is a classic syndrome: masked facies (lack of expression); slowed movements (bradykinesia); cogwheel rigidity (movement of the limbs is stiff and "ratchets"); decreased postural reflexes; resting tremor (regular, at three to seven cycles per second); stooped, shuffling gait (festinating gait); and micrographia (minute handwriting).

TABLE 4.1. Antipsychotic Medications

Potency	Dose Equivalents (mg.)
High Potency	
* Risperidone (Risperdal)	0.1
Haloperidol (Haldol)	1
Droperidol (Inapsine)	1
Fluphenazine (Prolixin)	1
Pimozide (Orap)	1
Trifluoperazine (Stelazine)	2
Medium Potency	
Thiothixene (Navane)	4
Perphenazine (Trilafon)	4–8
* Olanzapine (Zyprexa)	10
Molindone (Moban)	15
Prochlorperazine (Compazine)	15
Loxapine (Loxitane)	20
Low Potency	
Chlorpromazine (Thorazine)	100
Thioridazine (Mellaril)	100
Mesoridazine (Serentil)	100
* Clozapine (Clozaril)	100
* Quetiapine (Seroquel)	100

* Atypical antipsychotics.

In addition, other symptoms of dopamine antagonism may be seen, including dystonia (rigidity), akathisia (motor restlessness), neuroleptic malignant syndrome (severe rigidity associated with high fever), and tardive dyskinesia (a writhing, or "choreoathetotic," movement of the mouth, trunk, or limbs).

Dopamine receptor antagonists may be described as lying on a spectrum of affinity for the type-2 dopamine receptor (D2), a property known as "potency." High-potency dopamine receptor antagonists like haloperidol bind with greater affinity to the D2 receptor than do low potency agents such as chlorpromazine. Thus, only 1 milligram of haloperidol achieves the same dopamine receptor antagonism as 100 milligrams of chlorpromazine (Janicek et al., 1997). Both medications are equally effective in terms of alleviating psychosis (60% to 70% versus 20% to 30% for placebo). However, potency determines the side effect profile of the medications. Since haloperidol has greater affinity for the D2 receptor than chlorpromazine, it is more prone to produce parkinsonism and other symptoms of dopamine blockade than is chlorpromazine. On the other hand, chlorpromazine is more likely to bind to assorted other receptors.

Nondopamine receptor antagonism.   The dopamine receptor antagonists all bind to other chemical receptors in the body. Blocking these receptors produces additional side effects. The most important nondopamine receptors antagonized by these agents are these:

- *Muscarinic cholinergic receptors.* Blockade of these receptors produces "anticholinergic" symptoms including dry mouth, constipation, blurred vision, and urinary retention.

- *Histaminic receptors.* The "antihistiminic" effect results in sedation and weight gain.

- *Alpha–1–adrenergic receptors.* Blockade of these receptors reduces the effect of norepinephrine on blood vessels, resulting in hypotension.

- *Fast sodium channels.* Blockade here results in antiarrythmic effects similar to quinidine.

High-potency dopamine receptor antagonists are more likely to cause symptoms of parkinsonism, and are less anticholinergic, antihistaminic, and hypotensive than low-potency agents such as chlorpromazine. Conversely, low-potency agents produce more anticholinergic, antihistaminic, and hypotensive effects, and produce less parkinsonism than do high-potency agents.

Atypical antipsychotics.   Atypical, or novel, antipsychotics also are dopamine receptor antagonists, but they have the unique property of blocking postsynaptic 5-HT_{2A} receptors as well (Janicek et al., 1997). As discussed earlier, this receptor is implicated in the pathogenesis of psychosis. The result is that atypical antipsychotics are somewhat more effective than typical agents in treating psychosis. This is particularly true for the negative symptoms of psychosis (Kane, Honigfeld, Singer, & Meltzer, 1988; Wahlbeck, Cheine, Essali, & Adams, 1999). Additionally, the atypical agents produce less parkinsonism than do typical agents, also as a result of 5-HT_{2A} antagonism.

Key points

- *Psychosis* is a symptom complex of delusions, or hallucinations, or both.

- *Hallucinations* are internally generated sensory perceptions.

- *Delusions* are false, culturally incongruent beliefs not amenable to correction by conflicting data.

- The causes of psychosis include general medical conditions, substance use, mood disorders, posttraumatic stress disorder, and the primary psychotic disorders.

- *Primary psychotic disorders* are those in which psychosis *must* be present to make the diagnosis.

- Primary psychotic disorders include schizophrenia, schizoaffective disorder, schizophreniform disorder, brief psychotic disorder, delusional disorder, and shared psychotic disorder.

- The primary biological treatment for psychosis is the use of dopamine receptor antagonists.

Mood disorders 5

Mood is the subjective experience of emotion that is pervasive and colors other mental functioning, including self-image and expectations about the environment. Mood is usefully conceptualized on a spectrum, from pessimistic withdrawal and self-abnegation (depression), to a general sense of well-being (euthymia), to euphoria with excessive optimism and engagement (mania). The ends of the spectrum, depression and mania, are classified as mood disorders.

Mood is the subjective experience of emotion.

Depression

Depression is characterized by a marked decline in interest and energy; sadness, pessimism, or even nihilistic hopelessness; and alterations in sleep, appetite, energy, and concentration. Recognized since the time of Hippocrates, depression represents more than simple sadness or discouragement; it is a disabling and potentially lethal mental disorder.

Depression is a mood disorder characterized by sadness; hopelessness; low self-esteem; declines in interest and energy; and changes in sleep, appetite, and concentration.

Case example

Ms. C had broken up with a boyfriend. Then her sister, with whom C was very close, moved out of the house, leaving C and her parents. As a result, C found herself fighting with her sister and her parents. C had spent two years away at college but had been forced to move back home because of financial difficulties. She began to cry "all the time." Without warning, alone or with others, she would begin to weep. Although she was very tired and seemed to have no enthusiasm, she had difficulty sleeping. It took hours of tossing and turning before she finally nodded off, and then she would awaken at 5 A.M. unable to return to sleep. She craved sweets and began gaining weight. She admitted, with tears in her eyes, that there were times when life seemed so hopeless she wished she would die, although she was opposed to suicide on religious grounds. In her times of hopelessness, C's main concern was that if her parents died she would be left alone, since she was fighting

55

with her sister and no longer spoke to her boyfriend, who had formerly been her "best friend." C had been depressed on several occasions before, and had been treated with fluoxetine (Prozac). Her mood had improved soon after starting the medication, which she continued taking for about 4 months. Her mood began to deteriorate not long after she stopped taking the fluoxetine.

C was treated with the antidepressant medication venlafaxine (Effexor). Within two weeks her symptoms were predominantly resolved, and in a month they were gone completely. While she continued to struggle with her relationship with her family and with fear of loneliness and abandonment, she did so without overwhelming hopelessness, suicidal thoughts, or disturbing physical symptoms.

Major depression is one of the most common of the major mental disorders, occurring in approximately 10% to 25% of women and 5% to 12% of men (Sadock & Sadock, 2000). The prevalence of major depression is roughly similar cross-culturally, as is the discrepancy in prevalence between men and women.

DSM-IV criteria for major depressive disorder

A. Five (or more) of the following symptoms have been present during the same 2-week period and represent a change from previous functioning; at least one of the symptoms is either (1) depressed mood or (2) loss of interest or pleasure. Note: Do not include symptoms that are clearly due to a general medical condition, or mood-incongruent delusions or hallucinations.

   (1) Depressed mood most of the day, nearly every day, as indicated by either subjective report (e.g., feels sad or empty) or observation made by others (e.g., appears tearful). Note: In children and adolescents, can be irritable mood.

   (2) Markedly diminished interest or pleasure in all, or almost all, activities for most of the day, nearly every day (as indicated by either subjective account or observation made by others).

   (3) Significant weight loss when not dieting or weight gain (e.g., a change of more than 5% of body weight in a month), or decrease or increase in appetite nearly every day. Note: In children, consider failure to make expected weight gains.

   (4) Insomnia or hypersomnia nearly every day.

   (5) Psychomotor agitation or retardation nearly every day (ob-

servable by others, not merely subjective feelings of restlessness or being slowed down).

(6) Fatigue or loss of energy nearly every day.

(7) Feelings of worthlessness or excessive or inappropriate guilt (which may be delusional) nearly every day (not merely self-reproach or guilt about being sick).

(8) Diminished ability to think or concentrate, or indecisiveness, nearly every day (either by subjective account or as observed by others).

(9) Recurrent thoughts of death (not just fear of dying), recurrent suicidal ideation without a specific plan, or a suicide attempt or a specific plan for committing suicide.

B.   The symptoms do not meet criteria for a Mixed Episode.

C.   The symptoms cause clinically significant distress or impairment in social, occupational, or other important areas of functioning.

D.   The symptoms are not due to the direct physiological effects of a substance (e.g., a drug of abuse, a medication) or a general medical condition (e.g., hypothyroidism).

E.   The symptoms are not better accounted for by Bereavement; i.e., after the loss of a loved one, the symptoms persist for longer than 2 months or are characterized by marked functional impairment, morbid preoccupation with worthlessness, suicidal ideation, psychotic symptoms, or psychomotor retardation.

Reprinted with permission from the ***Diagnostic and Statistical Manual of Mental Disorders,*** Fourth Edition. Copyright 1994, American Psychiatric Association.

The pathophysiology of depression

The monoamine theory of depression.   It became apparent in the 1950s that a group of neurotransmitters called the biogenic amines—norepinephrine, serotonin, and dopamine—are dysregulated in depressive states. *Reserpine*, an antihypertensive drug that works by depleting the brain of monoamine neurotransmitters, was found to cause depression in individuals with a history of depression (Janicek et al., 1997). A class of drugs called the *monoamine oxidase inhibitors* (*MAOIs*), which increase the amount of biogenic amines in the brain by inhibiting their metabolism, was found to relieve depression in 60% to 80% of patients, versus 20% to 40% for placebo (Janicek et al., 1997).

Biogenic amines are neurotransmitters that become dysregulated in depressive states.

Intense interest in biogenic amines led to development of a group of medications called the *tricyclic antidepressants* (*TCAs*), named for their three-ringed chemical structure. Like the MAOIs, the TCAs proved to inhibit the metabolism of the biogenic amines, but by a different mechanism. Whereas MAOIs work by blocking the mitochondrial enzyme that degrades the biogenic amines, TCAs block the major transport route to this enzyme. By inhibiting the membrane pumps that transport biogenic amines from the synapse into the presynaptic cell for subsequent degradation, the amount of biogenic amine available in the synaptic cleft is increased. This process is called *reuptake inhibition* (Janicek et al., 1997).

Reuptake inhibition is the process of inhibiting the presynaptic membrane pumps that transport biogenic amines.

In later decades, research focused on finding chemicals that would inhibit the reuptake of serotonin selectively, where the TCAs blocked the reuptake of all three biogenic amines (norepinephrine more so than serotonin, with minimal dopamine reuptake inhibition). The result was fluoxetine, commonly known by its trade name, Prozac.

The success of the various antidepressant agents, and their common ability to increase the amount of biogenic amine available in the synaptic cleft, provided powerful evidence that aminergic neurotransmission is dysregulated in depressed states. However, the theory is complicated by the consistent finding that antidepressants take weeks to months to achieve maximum efficacy (Janicek et al., 1997). This suggests that simply increasing the amount of biogenic amine in the synaptic cleft, an effect that can be seen within hours after the administration of an antidepressant medication, is not the complete mechanism of action for antidepressants. It is currently believed that postsynaptic receptor changes resulting from abnormal presynaptic neurotransmission may be the critical link in the neurobiology of depression.

Endocrine abnormalities. It is clear that a structure in the diencephalon called the *hypothalamus* is implicated in the pathophysiology of depression. Depressed individuals almost invariably have abnormalities in hypothalamic function. Sleep and appetite are regulated by the hypothalamus and are often dysregulated in depression. About 60% of depressed individuals evidence abnormal secretion of the hormone cortisol, which is hypothalamically controlled via a hormonal circuit known as the *hypothalamic-pituitary-adrenal (HPA) axis* (see Figure 5.1) (Young, Haskett, Murphy-Weinberg, Watson, & Akil, 1991). The secretion of cortisol by the adrenal glands is controlled by the hormone ACTH (adrenocorticotropic hormone), which is secreted from the pituitary gland. The secretion of pituitary ACTH is, in turn, controlled by the hormone CRF (corticotropin releasing factor), which is secreted by the hypothalamus to stimulate the pituitary. CRF has been shown to be increased in the cerebrospinal fluid of depressed individuals (Nemeroff et al., 1984). The cortisol analog dexamethasone may be administered as a dexamethasone suppression test, after which blood levels of ACTH are obtained. The presence of circulating dexamethasone suppresses ACTH secretion

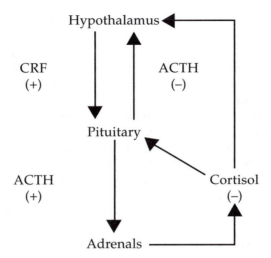

FIG. 5.1
The HPA axis.

by the pituitary, thus reducing the amount of cortisol secreted by the adrenals. Administration of dexamethasone should therefore lead to a reduction in circulating cortisol levels. In contrast with controls, up to 50% of individuals with major depression fail to fully suppress cortisol secretion in response to dexamethasone (Gastpar, Gilsdorf, Abou-Saleh, & Ngo-Khac, 1992).

Thyroid function also may be abnormal in depression. One common and effective strategy for augmenting the effect of antidepressants is to add synthetic thyroid hormone (Janicek et al., 1997). Like cortisol secretion, thyroid function is controlled by hormones originating in the hypothalamus. Hypothalamic thyrotropin releasing hormone (TRH) stimulates the pituitary to secrete thyroid stimulating hormone (TSH), which in turn promotes the secretion of thyroid hormone by the thyroid gland. TRH has been shown to be increased in depressed patients relative to controls, while TRH levels are normal in anxiety states (Shelton, Winn, Ekhatore, & Loosen, 1993). TRH may be administered to subjects in a TRH stimulation test. Approximately 25% to 30% of depressed individuals show reduced secretion of TSH in response to a TRH stimulation challenge (Loosen & Prange, 1982). A like percentage show abnormalities in serum concentrations of thyroid hormones (Janicek et al., 1997).

Neuroanatomical abnormalities.   Unlike schizophrenia, unipolar major depression seems to have few consistent associated structural brain abnormalities. One important finding is that of reduced hippocampal volume. It has been shown that this reduction can be induced by stress, which causes increased secretion of cortisol, as well as by administration of glucocorticoid hormones. This effect is thought to be mediated both by the direct atrophic effects of cortisol on hippocampal cells and by the decreased production of the protein BDNF (brain-derived neu-rotrophic factor) during stress (Charney, Nestler, & Bunney, 1999). Treat-ment with antidepressant medications has been shown to increase the expression of BDNF in neurons, and this in turn has been shown to pro-mote growth, arborization (number of dendritic projections), and syn-aptic signal strength in hippocampal neurons.

Depression has been consistently shown to be associated with al-tered regional cerebral blood flow and glucose metabolism. Depression leads to decreases in prefrontal cortical blood flow and a reciprocal in-crease in blood flow in the limbic system specifically to the amygdala (Coffey, Wilkinson, Weiner, Parashos, Djang, & Webb, 1993). Recovery from depression reverses these findings. The precise contribution of re-gional blood flow alterations to depressed mood, however, remains to be elucidated.

Furthermore, depression is a recurrent illness. The more episodes of depression an individual has, the more likely another episode be-comes. After a single episode of depression, there is a 50% chance of experiencing a recurrence of depression. After three episodes of depres-sion, the likelihood of a fourth episode rises to over 90%. Probably the best interpretation of depression's tendency to recur with greater fre-quency and severity is the "kindling" hypothesis of Robert Post, who suggested that repeated stimulation of neurons sensitizes them, so that subsequently it takes much less stimulation to induce firing (Post, 1990; Post, Rubinow, & Ballenger, 1986). The tendency toward depression ap-pears to become "hard-wired" into the synapses of the brain, so that relatively little is required in later years to precipitate another episode.

Infant and primate studies.   Further evidence that depression is not a normal human response to a challenging world comes from infant and animal research. In the 1950s, René Spitz made a series of famous obser-vations of infants in orphanages. Despite adequate food, warmth, and diapering, these infants became seriously depressed and often died from what Spitz called *anaclitic depression*. It became apparent that those in-fants spared this condition were receiving extra interpersonal attention from the nursing caregivers (Sadock & Sadock, 2000). Spitz presumed that anaclitic depression resulted from interpersonal deprivation.

Anaclitic depression is a condition that results from interpersonal deprivation.

In addition to revealing the necessity of social interaction for in-fant survival, these results show that depression can occur in organisms that lack the cognitive capacity to experience philoso-phical distress at a disappointing world. Because infants lack a language system and a dis-crete sense of self-representation through which to experience meaning, they likely do not experience meaninglessness in the way adults do. Social deprivation, however, apparently induces a biological condition of withdrawal that may ultimately prove fatal.

Primate research has provided a parallel model for human depres-sion. Social isolation of infant rhesus monkeys leads to a state that looks like major depression—sadness of expression, anhedonia (loss of interest and pleasure), withdrawal, physical slowing, and decreased initiative. More impressive, these monkeys show many of the same physiological changes seen in human depression, such as elevations in serum cortisol. These states respond to the same biological treatments that are effective in humans, specifically TCAs and electroconvulsive therapy (discussed later).

Sleep abnormalities.   Sleep abnormalities are common in major depression (Kupfer, Frank, Perel, Cornes, Mallinger, & Thase, 1992). Increased time to sleep onset (sleep latency), decreased total amount of sleep time, and changes in REM sleep (occurring earlier in sleep and in greater quantities than usual) have been observed consistently (Janicek et al., 1997).

Melancholic depression is a condition characterized by pervasive anhedonia.

Subtypes of depression

Major depression occurs in three subtypes, which has implications for treatment. These three subtypes are classic melancholic, atypical, and psychotic.

Melancholic major depression is characterized primarily by the presence of pervasive anhedonia. Those with melancholic depression have little respite from their suffering, in contrast to atypical depression, which often shows marked mood reactivity to positive and negative events. Melancholic depression usually is associated with decreased sleep, decreased appetite, and diurnal mood variation. Melancholic major depression responds preferentially to TCAs.

Atypical major depression is characterized by mood reactivity to positive and negative events. Individuals with an atypical major depression may brighten considerably, even to the point of transient euthymia, when positive events occur. However, it takes little impetus for the depressed mood to return. In contrast to melancholic major depression, individuals with atypical major depression usually have increased sleep requirements, increased appetite (often with carbohydrate craving), and a "leaden" feeling of fatigue. Atypical major depression responds preferentially to SSRIs and MAOIs, and somewhat less well to TCAs (Janicek et al., 1997).

Atypical major depression is a condition characterized by mood reactivity to positive and negative events.

Psychotic major depression is more common than is often appreciated and may occur in over 50% of major depressions. Often, symptoms of psychosis are limited to mild hallucinatory events (such as occasionally hearing a voice say one's name, or seeing shadows out the corner of the eye) or ideas of reference with relatively intact reality testing (feeling like everyone is staring at one, while knowing this is probably not true). More severe psychosis can occur, however, including florid hallucinations and frank delusions, usually having to do with personal worthlessness. Psychotic depression responds much less well to antidepressants than nonpsychotic depression, with a response rate of 20% to 40%, as compared to 60% to 80% for nonpsychotic depression (Chan, Janicek, Davis, Altman, Andriukaitis, & Hedeker, 1987; Janicek et al., 1997). Psychotic depression often requires the addition of an antipsychotic medication for successful resolution of symptoms (Anton & Burch, 1990).

Psychotic major depression is a condition characterized by symptoms of psychosis.

Regardless of subtype, major depression also may be characterized as seasonal or postpartum. When the onset of episodes of major depression consistently coincides with changes in season, *seasonal affective disorder* may be diagnosed. Seasonal affective disorder afflicts perhaps 5% of the population (roughly accounting for one-third of depressive disorders). Women are four times more likely than men to experience the disorder. It is more common at higher latitudes, and usually occurs in the fall. A springtime variant has been described and appears to be more severe (Janicek et al., 1997). Seasonal depressive episodes often are of the atypical subtype. Some evidence has accrued for the use of phototherapy in the treatment of seasonal affective disorder (Eastman, Young, Fogg, Liu, & Meaden, 1998). Phototherapy involves exposure to high-intensity, full-spectrum light in the morning and is thought to help regulate circadian cycles.

While *postpartum blues* is extremely common and may occur in up to 85% of women during the several weeks postpartum, major *postpartum depression* afflicts between 10% and 20% of women after delivery (Bright, 1994). The specific pathophysiology of postpartum depression is unclear, but it may be related to abrupt changes in hormone levels.

Dysthymia.   Dysthymia is characterized by the same symptoms seen in major depression, but of lesser severity and with a duration of at least 2 years. The presence of psychotic symptoms rules out a diagnosis of dysthymia and instead represents major depression with psychotic features. Dysthymia responds to the same treatments as major depression.

Dual depression is diagnosed when an episode of major depression is superimposed on dysthymia.

Costs

Major depression is a different entity than a simple case of the blues, the vicissitudes of mood that trouble the daily life of every human being. It is normal to feel sad, it is normal to grieve, it is normal to worry and cry. But the syndrome of major depression is not normal in the sense that, although all too common, it is a state of devastating pain and dysfunction. About 15% percent of those suffering from major depression will ultimately die from suicide (Guze & Robins, 1970; Henriksson, Aro, Marttunen, Heikkinen, Isometsa, & Kuoppasalmi, 1993; Miles, 1977). Depression is present in over 50% of completed suicides (Asgard, 1990). Major depression causes diminished immune response, as evidenced by the decreased activity of lymphocytes (Schliefe, Keller, Bond, Cohen,

Stein, & 1989; Schliefe, Keller, Camerino, Thornton, Stein, & 1983). Depressed people have a much higher mortality in the period immediately after a heart attack than the nondepressed (Frasure-Smith, Lesperance, & Talajic, 1993). Major depression causes more morbidity than hypertension, kidney failure, and diabetes mellitus, and costs the U.S. economy nearly $50 billion a year in health care and lost productivity (Greenberg, Stiglin, Finkelstein, & Berndt, 1993; Wells et al., 1989).

Half of major depressive episodes go unidentified, and many that are identified are inadequately treated. This is a serious problem; not only do those with major depression suffer both physically and mentally, they go on to have more episodes of depression, often with increasing frequency and of greater severity. A person who has had a single episode of major depression has about a 50% chance of having a second. After three episodes of depression, the chances of having a fourth increase to 90% (Maj, Veltro, Pirozzi, Lobrace, & Magliano, 1992). And, contrary to older teaching, major depressive episodes often are not self-limited. Major depression tends to recur and it tends to persist. This is particularly true of psychotic depression.

Dysthemia is a condition characterized by the same symptoms seen in major depression, but of lesser severity and shorter duration.

Antidepressant medications

Monoamine oxidase inhibitors.   The monoamine oxidase inhibitors (phenelzine or Nardil, and tranylcypromine or Parnate) irreversibly inhibit the enzyme monoamine oxidase. Because they inhibit the enzyme irreversibly, patients must follow medication and dietary restrictions while taking an MAOI. Diets rich in the amino acid tyramine must be avoided, since large levels of dietary tyramine cannot be metabolized by inhibited monoamine oxidase. The result can be a hypertensive crisis. Foods to be avoided include cheeses, beer and wine, aged or smoked meats, pickled foods, fava beans, caffeine, and chocolate.

Serotonergic medications, including SSRIs and TCAs, must be avoided due to the risk of developing a potentially lethal central serotonin syndrome, symptoms of which include delirium, mania, tremor, incoordination, tachycardia, hypertension, diaphoresis, elevated temperature, and diarrhea.

Other side effects of the MAOIs include weight gain, insomnia, and sexual dysfunction. MAOIs are particularly effective in the treatment of atypical and refractory depressions.

Tricyclic antidepressants.   The TCAs may be categorized as either tertiary or secondary, depending on their chemical structure. The tertiary tricyclics include amitriptyline (Elavil), imipramine (Tofranil), doxepin (Sinequan), and clomipramine (Anafranil). Secondary tricyclics include desipramine (Norpramin) and nortriptyline (Pamelor).

All the TCAs inhibit the reuptake of norepinephrine, and to a lesser extent serotonin, with only slight degrees of dopamine reuptake inhibition. Tertiary TCAs, especially clomipramine, are in general more sero-tonergic than are secondary TCAs.

The side effects of TCAs are due to the binding of additional receptors beyond reuptake pumps. Like antipsychotic medications, TCAs inhibit histamine receptors, leading to weight gain and sedation; acetylcholine receptors, leading to dry mouth, blurred vision, constipation, and urinary retention; adrenergic receptors, leading to hypotension; and sodium channels, predisposing to cardiac arrhythmias (Janicek et al., 1997).

Secondary TCAs have somewhat lower affinity for these receptors than tertiary TCAs. TCAs are more effective for melancholic than atypical depression, and may also have uses in anxiety disorders.

Selective serotonin reuptake inhibitors.   The SSRIs include fluoxetine (Prozac), sertraline (Zoloft), paroxetine (Paxil), fluvoxamine (Luvox), and citalopram (Celexa). All of these inhibit the reuptake of serotonin into presynaptic neurons to a substantially greater degree than either norepinephrine or dopamine. SSRIs are more effective than TCAs for atypical depression.

The side effects of the SSRIs can be understood from the effects of increased levels of serotonin on postsynaptic serotonin receptors (Dubovsky, 1994):

- 5-HT_{1A}—serotonin syndrome
- 5-HT_{1D}—headache
- 5-HT_{2A}—anxiety, tremor, insomnia, sexual dysfunction, decreased appetite, sweating
- 5-HT_{3}—nausea

Other antidepressants.   Bupropion (Wellbutrin) is an energizing antidepressant that is, in part, a dopamine reuptake inhibitor. It has little propensity to cause weight gain or sexual dysfunction, but seizures can result at high doses. It also is effective in treating smoking.

Venlafaxine (Effexor) is a serotonin-norepinephrine reuptake inhibitor (SNRI), like the TCAs. However, it has little affinity for histamine, acetylcholine, or adrenergic receptors, or for fast sodium channels, so it lacks many of the side effects associated with TCAs.

Nefazodone (Serzone) is an SSRI that also blocks postsynaptic 5-HT_{2A} receptors, and so has fewer side effects associated with the stimulation of that receptor.

Mirtazapine (Remeron) increases norepinephrine by acting as an antagonist at presynaptic a-2 adrenergic receptors (thus blocking the effect of norepinephrine on the autoreceptor in order to reduce firing).

Indirectly, this stimulates increased serotonergic neurotransmission. Mirtazapine also blocks 5-HT$_{2A}$ and 5-HT$_3$ receptors, and is a potent antihistamine.

Electroconvulsive therapy. Electroconvulsive therapy (ECT) is perhaps the most maligned therapy in all of medicine. With its Frankensteinian character and little-understood mechanism of action, ECT, the passage of a small amount of current through the brain to induce a seizure, is much feared. Yet ECT is enormously effective, ameliorating depression in up to 70% of medication nonresponders (Sadock & Sadock, 2000). In its older incarnation, ECT could indeed be cruel therapy, particularly when administered on an involuntary basis, as it was all too often. The scene from the movie ***One Flew Over the Cuckoo's Nest*** in which Jack Nicholson is given ECT involuntarily and while fully awake is unfortunately an accurate representation of ECT treatment prior to the 1970s and has caused many who might benefit from the treatment to fear it. ECT is now done under general anesthesia, using the short-acting barbiturate methohexital and the paralytic agent succinylcholine. The brain is induced to seizure, but muscular contractures, incontinence, and other effects of generalized seizures are prevented by the anesthesia. ECT is remarkably safe and effective, particularly in contrast to the potentially devastating effects of treatment-resistant major depression (Janicek et al., 1997).

ECT is effective for both bipolar and unipolar major depression. It also has been shown to be of benefit in treating mania, delirium, catatonia, neuroleptic malignant syndrome, schizophrenia, and obsessive-compulsive disorder (Janicek et al., 1997).

Some critics have claimed that ECT causes "brain damage." Research has failed to demonstrate any evidence of damage to the central nervous system from ECT in brain imaging studies, measurement of central nervous system breakdown products, and neuropsychiatric testing (Coffey, Weiner, Djang, Figiel, Soday, & Patterson, 1991). ECT does cause amnesia for the events immediately preceding treatments, because the electrical current and seizure disrupt the formation of new memories for that interval. Individuals who receive ECT often show some impairment in the formation of new memories (anterograde amnesia) for perhaps 6 to 8 weeks after treatment. However, by 6 months neuropsychiatric testing does not show consistent evidence of impaired cognition (Janicek et al., 1997). On the other hand, there is growing evidence that ongoing untreated mood disorders result in damage to the central nervous system. As we have seen, depression can lead to atrophy in certain areas of the brain, and depression is clearly a recurrent illness, such that the risk of relapse rises with each successive episode. When the costs of depression, in terms of both mortality from suicide and lost productivity, are factored in, it becomes clear that ECT is preferable to untreated depression (Kupfer et al., 1992).

Bipolar disorder

When an individual experiences manic episodes, with or without a history of depression, bipolar disorder is said to be present. *Mania* represents the opposite of depression. The manic individual is euphoric (though possibly irritable), full of energy, enthusiasm, and creativity. Unfortunately, like depression, mania is profoundly disabling and may even be fatal.

Mania

Case example

Mania is a condition characterized by euphoria, energy, grandiosity, and impulsivity

Ms. M was 19 and talking a blue streak. She had been picked up by the police as she was running down a heavily trafficked avenue, apparently heedless of her surroundings, alternately singing and screaming. When she was interviewed, M spoke very rapidly and could not be kept focused on a topic. She appeared effusive and, when asked how she was feeling, said, "Great, I'm trying to get a rock concert organized at Giant's Stadium. It's going to be like Woodstock, only it's sponsored by a group I've formed to feed the world by collecting pennies. I could snap my fingers and have 10,000 bikers here to protect me." At this point she looked over at a potted plant nearby. "And I know everything there is to know about botany."

Abruptly, she became fierce and hostile. "Why do you need to know this, anyway?" M had not slept in several days. Her family reported that in the preceding months she had been quite depressed, but then seemed to recover. They were unable to cite any precipitant to M's mood changes.

M was manic. She was experiencing euphoric mood but, like many manic people, she could become irritable in an instant. M was also evidencing the associated symptoms required for a formal diagnosis of mania. She had required little or no sleep for several days in a row. Her sense of self-esteem was dramatically inflated to grandiose proportions. Indeed, M was delusionally grandiose, believing she had special powers and abilities and was the center of important activity. Her speech was "pressured," rapid-fire and difficult to interrupt. Her thinking was tangential, wandering from topic to topic, and at times she experienced "flight of ideas," in which her thinking was so florid she made illogical leaps from one idea to another. Finally, she was extremely impulsive, as evidenced by her wandering in a busy street without concern for her safety.

Like all psychiatric syndromes, mania can have many causes. In M's case, for example, it was important to rule out mania as a result of an intoxicating substance, such as amphetamines or cocaine, by obtaining a toxicology screening. Other lab tests were ordered to look for medical conditions such as anemia and electrolyte abnormalities. When these tests came back negative, M was diagnosed with primary mania.

Primary mania is one phase of bipolar disorder, known popularly as manic-depression. In the psychiatric literature, manic-depression is called bipolar disorder, since individuals usually cycle between two polar extremes—the hopelessness of depression and the euphoria of mania (cases of isolated mania without depression occur uncommonly). Typically, cycling occurs over periods of months to years. However, a subset of between 10%and 15% of individuals with bipolar disorder may cycle four or more times a year, a state known as "rapid cycling." If cycling occurs within a matter of days, it is known as "ultrarapid cycling," and cycling mood within a single day is termed "ultradian."

DSM-IV criteria for manic episode

A. A distinct period of abnormally and persistently elevated, expansive, or irritable mood, lasting at least 1 week (or any duration if hospitalization is necessary).

B. During the period of mood disturbance, three (or more) of the following symptoms have persisted (four if the mood is only irritable) and have been present to a significant degree:

(1) inflated self-esteem or grandiosity

(2) decreased need for sleep (e.g., feels rested after only 3 hours of sleep)

(3) more talkative than usual or pressure to keep talking

(4) flight of ideas or subjective experience that thoughts are racing

(5) distractibility (i.e., attention too easily drawn to unimportant or irrelevant external stimuli)

(6) increase in goal-directed activity (either socially, at work or school, or sexually) or psychomotor agitation

(7) excessive involvement in pleasurable activities that have a high potential for painful consequences (e.g., engaging in unrestrained buying sprees, sexual indiscretions, or foolish investments)

C. The symptoms do not meet criteria for a Mixed Episode.

D. The mood disturbance is sufficiently severe to cause marked impairment in occupational functioning or in usual social activities or relationships with others, or to necessitate hospitalization to prevent harm to self or others, or there are psychotic features.

E. The symptoms are not due to the direct physiologic effects of a substance (e.g., a drug of abuse, a medication, or other treatment) or a general medical condition (e.g., hyperthyroidism). Note: Manic-like episodes that are clearly caused by somatic antidepressant treatment (e.g., medication, electroconvulsive therapy, light therapy) should not count toward a diagnosis of Bipolar I disorder.

Reprinted with permission from the ***Diagnostic and Statistical Manual of Mental Disorders***, Fourth Edition. Copyright 1994, American Psychiatric Association.

Pathophysiology of bipolar disorder

Bipolar disorder is about as common as schizophrenia, affecting between 1% and 2% of the population. Men and women are equally affected. Like schizophrenia, there is a strong genetic component to bipolar disorder. Monozygotic twins, who share the same genetic makeup, have a concordance rate of between 33% and 90% for bipolar disorder (Sadock & Sadock, 2000). That is, if one twin has bipolar disorder, there is a 33% to 90% chance the identical twin will have bipolar disorder. Dizygotic twins, who gestate at the same time but have a different genetic makeup, show a concordance rate of 5% to 20%, implying that there is a powerful hereditary component to bipolar disorder. Recently, linkage studies have suggested that chromosome 18 may be involved in part of the genetic predisposition to bipolar disorder, and the X chromosome also may be a contributor.

Like unipolar depression, bipolar depression is associated with decreased metabolism in the left frontal cortex, which reverses upon resolution of the episode of depression, and with increased metabolism in the amygdala. Mania may be associated with decreases in cerebral blood flow to the right frontal cortex (Sadock & Sadock, 2000). Abnormalities in second messenger systems, including protein kinase C and G proteins, as well as abnormalities in intracellular sodium and calcium, are seen in bipolar depression. Lithium and divalproex sodium (see below) may affect these second messenger systems and electrolyte disturbances.

Antimanic medications

Lithium.   In the late 1960s, it was discovered that lithium salt was effective in reducing manic episodes. Indeed, lithium will ameliorate a manic episode about 60% of the time, compared with 25% for placebo (Janicek et al., 1997). Lithium also is useful in long-term prophylaxis against recurrent manic or depressive episodes (Goodwin & Jamison, 1990).

Lithium is handled by the body like sodium, and so is excreted entirely by the kidneys. Decreased lithium excretion can easily lead to lithium toxicity, characterized by severe tremor, slurred speech, uncoordinated movement (ataxia), confusion, and even death. Therapeutic levels of lithium range from 0.6 to 1.5 mEq/L, depending on the laboratory used. Lithium levels of 2.0 to 3.0 mEq/L are classified as severely toxic, and levels above 3.0 mEq/L often require dialysis.

Even in the therapeutic range, lithium has a number of side effects. These include hypothyroidism (10% of patients), A-V conduction abnormalities, tremor, gastrointestinal upset, sedation, and confusion. Rarely, long-term use is associated with renal failure. Lithium can increase the chance of fetal malformation.

Anticonvulsants.   Antiseizure medications such as divalproex sodium (Depakote) and carbamazepine (Tegretol) have proven effective in the treatment of mania (Freeman, Clotheir, Pazzaguia, Leser, & Swann, 1992; Keck, McElroy, Tugrul, & Bennett, 1993). The reason for this is not clear. It may be that, as with seizures, the manic brain is in a hyperexcitable state, which can be "cooled" with antiseizure medications. Divalproex enhances GABA neurotransmission, which is inhibitory. It also inhibits the enzyme protein kinase C, which has been implicated in the pathogenesis of mania. Both medications may cause sedation, weight gain, hepatitis, and hematopoeitic failure.

Antipsychotics.   Antipsychotic agents are useful in the treatment of mania if psychotic symptoms are present. However, they may have pure mood stabilizing properties as well, even if symptoms of psychosis are absent. This may be particularly true of chlorpromazine, and the atypical antipsychotics. Controlled trials of atypical antipsychotics such as olanzapine (Zyprexa) have shown them to have promising antimanic properties as monotherapy (Tohen, Sanger, McElroy, Tollefson, Roy, & Daniel, 1999).

Benzodiazepines.   The benzodiazepines increase the rate of GABA inhibitory neurotransmission (see Chapter 6). Several, including lorazepam and clonazepam, have been shown to have acute antimanic effects (Janicek et al, 1997). Long-term antimanic efficacy has not been established, however, and extended use may be associated with habituation.

Hypomania

Mania also can appear in a milder form, known as hypomania. The symptoms of hypomania resemble mania, but they are much less severe. Hypomania cannot cause psychotic symptoms. Whereas a manic person might become delusionally grandiose, hypomanic grandiosity is limited to excessive enthusiasm for plans that a person might not normally undertake and might even consider unrealistic, such as writing a novel or starting a new business. Hypomanic grandiosity typically consists of ideas that are not abnormal per se, but might be unusual for a given individual. The need for sleep may lessen, perhaps to only 4 hours a night, but not be eliminated.

Case example

Mr. K presented with severe depression, which was successfully treated with antidepressant medication. However, although his subsequent mood usually was normal, he could not regain his former level of functioning. He remained unemployed, and his relationship with his girlfriend was strained. K seemed to get bursts of enthusiasm, during which he would form plans for employment, such as buying an ice cream truck. Typically, he would do several job interviews during these periods. He felt full of energy and enthusiasm. Then suddenly, he would crash. So tired he could barely move, he would lie in bed for 3 to 4 days, and all of his previous plans would disintegrate in a fog of hopelessness. For several weeks after, his mood and energy would be normal. Then the cycle would repeat.

K was started on divalproex sodium. Almost immediately he felt better, and he never again experienced either mood swing, but felt normally energetic and confident. He began working regularly, and his relationship with his girlfriend (who had thought he was simply being lazy and manipulative) improved greatly.

Hypomania is characterized by the same symptoms as mania, but in milder form.

One of the difficulties in treating hypomania is that it usually is a pleasant state. Not only do hypomanic people often feel an expansive sense of self-esteem and good mood, this good mood—along with increased energy and creative ideas—is highly valued in Western societies. The hypomanic individual is energetic and enthusiastic, highly productive to the point of seeing sleep as an interference, and sparkling with creative projects. Indeed, an unusually large percentage of creative artists—poets, writers, and musicians—have bipolar disorder. Some famous historical examples include Lord Byron, Percy Bysshe Shelley, William Blake, and Georg Frederick Handel. Not surprisingly, hypomanic people doubt that what they are experiencing is really an illness. If people with bipolar disorder were only ever hypomanic, they might have a point. But sooner or later, with rare exceptions, they become manic or depressed. The drug treatments for bipolar disorder are effective, but only if they are taken. One of the real therapeutic tasks in treating bipolar disorder is convincing euthymic, and particularly hypomanic, individuals that they need to stay on the medication, or they will become depressed or manic again.

Key points

- *Major depression* probably results from dysregulation of biogenic amines and of the hypothalamic-pituitary-end organ axes.

- Major depression occurs in 10% to 20% of individuals over the lifespan.

- Major depression causes great morbidity and, left untreated, has a 15% mortality rate from suicide.

- Treatment efficacy approaches 90%.

- *Antidepressant medications* increase the amount of available biogenic amines.

- *Monoamine oxidase inhibitors* inhibit the enzyme monoamine oxidase.

- *Tricyclic antidepressants* block the reuptake of norepinephrine and serotonin.

- *Selective serotonin reuptake inhibitors* block the reuptake of serotonin.

- *Electroconvulsive therapy* is safe and effective in up to 90% of depressive episodes.

- *Bipolar disorder* consists of cycles of mania, usually with intervening episodes of depression.

- Bipolar disorder is treatable primarily with lithium and anticonvulsants, but may also respond to adjunctive treatment with antipsychotics and benzodiazepines.

Anxiety disorders 6

Fear is a basic response to danger. As such, fear is adaptive. If danger did not rapidly induce an unpleasant mental state and avoidance behavior, animals might quickly be overwhelmed by a hostile environment. Although human beings still face dangers, the modern environment is relatively safe. Yet the neurobiology that induces fear responses persists. If a fear response occurs in a setting where it is maladaptive, an anxiety disorder is present. The anxiety disorders include panic disorder and agoraphobia, specific and social phobias, generalized anxiety disorder, posttraumatic stress disorder, and obsessive-compulsive disorder.

Anxiety disorders are characterized by fear responses in settings where they are maladaptive.

Panic disorder and agoraphobia

A panic attack is a sudden rush of intense fear in a nondangerous situation, typically accompanied by symptoms of sympathetic nervous system activity. The fear of recurring panic attacks is called panic disorder, and the avoidance of places where escape might be difficult is called agoraphobia.

Panic attacks are sudden rushes of intense fear in nondangerous situations.

Case example

Ms. S was moving, with the help of her older brother. She was driving behind her brother's truck to her new house when, while crossing a bridge, her brother had to swerve to avoid a pedestrian and rolled his truck on its side. Fortunately, he was unhurt. But the experience was unnerving to S. Seeing his truck swerve, she thought for a moment that he would topple over the side of the bridge, and she was convinced for an instant that he was going to die.

Months later, S was still fearful. Not long after the accident, she was driving on a highway overpass when she was suddenly overwhelmed with the sensation that she was going to lose control of the car and kill someone in the resulting accident. As this thought flooded her mind, she began to hyperventilate. She felt she could barely catch her breath, and this heightened fear that she would lose control of the truck. S was afraid she would pass out. Her heart pounded, she broke into a sweat, she felt dizzy, and she had a bizarre sensation of being outside her body. In a panic, she pulled her car to the side of the road, got out, staggered to a pay phone, and called her mother to pick her up.

Panic disorder is the fear of recurring panic attacks.

After this experience, S was terrified to drive over bridges. She refused to drive herself over highway overpasses and could only ride as a passenger by closing her eyes and counting out loud until it was over. Even this tactic was not always successful. Often, the panic would occur anyway, and she would make the driver turn around. This became a significant problem, because her workplace was on the other side of the highway from her house, and she was needed to cross a bridge in order to work. Gradually, she became so terrified of having an anxiety attack that she began to avoid public places altogether, and stayed largely at home.

S had recurrent panic attacks. Panic attacks are the sudden onset of intense anxiety, of the intensity that would be expected if one were in a life-threatening situation. The anxiety is accompanied by symptoms of autonomic arousal, the fight or flight response—hyperventilation, palpitations, sweating, and dizziness are prominent. When S began to fear the occurrence of more panic attacks and took steps to avoid them, such as refusing to drive over bridges, she had developed a panic disorder. Her life was significantly disrupted by her anxiety, and she was in great distress. This constriction of her lifestyle, with marked avoidance of locations where she feared panic and loss of control would occur and from which escape might be difficult, is called agoraphobia.

Agoraphobia is Greek for "fear of the marketplace." Loosely translated, it means fear of places where help might not be available or from which escape might be difficult.

DSM-IV criteria for panic attack

A. A discrete period of intense fear or discomfort, in which four (or more) of the following symptoms develop abruptly and reach a peak within 10 minutes:

(1) palpitations, pounding heart, or accelerated heart rate

(2) sweating

(3) trembling or shaking

(4) sensation of shortness of breath or smothering

(5) feeling of choking

(6) chest pain or discomfort

(7) nausea or abdominal distress

(8) feeling dizzy, unsteady, lightheaded, faint

(9) derealization (feeling of unreality) or depersonalization (being detached from oneself)

(10) fear of losing control or going crazy

(11) fear of dying

(12) paresthesias

(13) chills or hot flushes

Reprinted with permission from the *Diagnostic and Statistical Manual of Mental Disorders*, Fourth Edition. Copyright 1994, American Psychiatric Association.

DSM-IV criteria for agoraphobia

A. Anxiety about being in places or situations from which escape might be difficult (or embarrassing) or in which help may not be available in the event of having an unexpected or situationally predisposed Panic Attack or panic-like symptoms. Agoraphobic fears typically involve characteristic clusters of situations that include being outside the home alone; being in a crowd or standing in a line; being on a bridge; and traveling in a bus, train, or automobile. Note: Consider the diagnosis of Specific Phobia if the avoidance is limited to one or only a few specific situations, or Social Phobia if the avoidance is limited to social situations.

B. The situations are avoided (e.g., travel is restricted) or else are endured with marked distress or with anxiety about having a Panic Attack or panic-like symptoms, or require the presence of a companion.

C. The anxiety or phobic avoidance is not better accounted for by another mental disorder, such as Social Phobia (e.g., avoidance limited to social situations because of fear of embarrassment), Specific Phobia (e.g., avoidance limited to a single situation like elevators), Obsessive-Compulsive Disorder (e.g., avoidance of dirt in someone with an obsession about contamination), Posttraumatic Stress Disorder (e.g., avoidance of stimuli associated with a severe stressor), or Separation Anxiety Disorder (e.g., avoidance of leaving home or relatives).

Reprinted with permission from the ***Diagnostic and Statistical Manual of Mental Disorders,*** Fourth Edition. Copyright 1994, American Psychiatric Association.

DSM-IV criteria for panic disorder with/without agoraphobia

A. Both (1) and (2):

(1) Recurrent unexpected Panic Attacks.

(2) At least one of the attacks has been followed by 1 month (or more) of one (or more) or the following:

(a) persistent about having additional panic attacks

(b) worry about the implications of the attacks or its consequences (e.g., losing control, having a heart attack, "going crazy")

(c) a significant change in behavior related to the attacks

B. Absence/presence of Agoraphobia.

C. The Panic Attacks are not due to the direct physiological effects of a substance (e.g., a drug of abuse or a medication) or a general medical condition (e.g., hyperthyroidism).

D. The Panic Attacks are not better accounted for by another mental disorder, such as Social Phobia (e.g., occurring on exposure to feared social situation), Specific Phobia (e.g., on exposure to a specific phobic situation), Obsessive-Compulsive Disorder (e.g., on exposure to dirt in someone with an obsession about contamination), Posttraumatic Stress Disorder (e.g., in response to stimuli associated with a severe stressor), or Separation Anxiety Disorder (e.g., in response to being away from home or close relatives).

Reprinted with permission from the ***Diagnostic and Statistical Manual of Mental Disorders,*** Fourth Edition. Copyright 1994, American Psychiatric Association.

The symptoms of her panic make sense if one considers that S was actually experiencing a very normal physiological event: the fight-or-flight response. When panic sets in, it often is accompanied by an overwhelming urge to flee the situation. This would be normal and adaptive if a tiger had just jumped out of the woods and attacked. But if one is driving a car on a busy street, this physiologically normal response becomes significantly maladaptive, not to mention extremely distressing.

Pathophysiology of panic disorder

Panic disorder occurs in between 1.5% and 3.5% of the population, with females accounting for more than twice as many cases as males (American Psychiatric Association, 1994). There seems to be a genetic contribution to the pathogenesis of panic disorder. Familial risk for panic, which measures the rates of panic in individuals who have a first-degree relative with panic, suggests that the rate of panic disorder rises to between 13.2% and 17.3%. Monozygotic twins have 47% concordance rate for panic compared to 17% of dizygotic twins, again suggesting a genetic contribution (Crowe, Noyes, Pauls, & Slyman, 1983; Skre, Onstad, Torgerson, & Kringlen, 1993).

There is considerable evidence that panic and other anxiety disorders involve the abnormal regulation of the neurotransmitter norepinephrine (Gorman, Kent, Sullivan, & Coplan, 2000). With epinephrine, norepinephrine is responsible for regulating the fight-or-flight response. It is well-documented that anxiety-provoking situations, such as public speaking or flying in airplanes, produces an elevation in noradrenergic function, as revealed by elevated levels of urinary norepinephrine metabolites (homovanillic acid, or HVA). The physical symptoms of anxiety are produced by noradrenergic arousal—sweating, hand tremor, palpitations, rapid breathing, and pupillary dilation are all effects of a discharging sympathetic nervous system. The administration of drugs that increase noradrenergic neurotransmission, such as yohimbine (Yocon, a presynaptic a-2 receptor antagonist that leads to increased neuronal release of norepinephrine) may cause panic in individuals predisposed to panic attacks (Charney, Heninger & Breier, 1984).

Panic appears to be associated with abnormal sensitivity to sensations of smothering. The drive to breathe is regulated by blood levels of carbon dioxide (CO_2), which is produced by the consumption of energy sources in the body. Rising CO_2 levels produce an urge to breathe faster. If severe, this urge can become profoundly anxiety-provoking. It turns out that many individuals who experience panic attacks are extremely sensitive to CO_2 levels in the blood. When they are given inhaled CO_2, a panic attack ensues, whereas normal controls are less anxious (Gorman et al., 1994). Panic disordered individuals are similarly sensitive to an infusion of lactate, another byproduct of energy metabolism (Liebowitz et al., 1985). Again, controls do not share this sensitivity.

Anxiety apparently also involves abnormalities in the neurotransmitter g-aminobutyric acid, or GABA. GABA is the main inhibitory neurotransmitter of the brain, acting to reduce the firing rate of neurons. Anxiety often is successfully treated using benzodiazepines, which increase the activity of GABA. Benzodiazepines bind to the GABA receptor, which is located on chloride channels, and enhance the conduction of chloride ions. This action hyperpolarizes the neuron, making it more difficult for the cell to fire. Benzodiazepines have been shown to be effective in the treatment of panic disorder (Janicek et al., 1997; Lydiard et al., 1992).

A similar mechanism of action explains the anxiolytic and sedative effects of the barbiturates. However, barbiturates bind to a different subunit on the GABA receptor and are much more potent. Because they are more sedating, barbiturates currently are seldom used for treatment of anxiety.

Additionally, as in depression, the neurotransmitter serotonin is implicated in pathogenesis of anxiety. Antidepressants, including the SSRIs, TCAs, and MAOIs, are demonstrably effective in treating panic and other anxiety disorders (Janicek et al., 1997; Pohl, Wolkow, & Clary, 1988). As already discussed, these drugs enhance serotonergic neurotransmission by making more serotonin available in the synapse. It is not understood precisely why this results in anxiolysis but, as with depression, anxiolysis is thought to be due to down-regulation of postsynaptic serotonin receptors. Conversely, fenfluramine (Pondimin), which increases the release of serotonin from serotonergic neurons, can precipitate panic (Targum & Marshall, 1989) as can the serotonin receptor agonist m-CPP (Klein, Zohar, Geraci, Murphy, & Uhde, 1991).

Treatment

The pharmacologic treatment of panic may be divided into two groups: the sedative-hypnotics and the antidepressants.

As noted, medications that increase the activity of GABA, an inhibitory neurotransmitter, are effective in decreasing panic. These medications include the benzodiazepines, the barbiturates, chloral hydrate, meprobamate, and paraldehyde, the sedative-hypnotics. The sedative effect of a medication refers to its ability to decrease anxiety, while the hypnotic effect refers to its ability to promote sleep. Because they are safer, the benzodiazepines are the only sedative-hypnotic agents frequently used in the treatment of panic.

The benzodiazepines may be usefully divided along two dimensions (see Figure 6.1). On one dimension is the potency of the drug, which refers to its affinity for the GABA receptor. Fewer milligrams of a high-potency drug such as alprazolam (Xanax) or clonazepam (Klonopin) are required to produce the same GABA receptor binding compared to a low-potency benzodiazepine such as chlordiazepoxide (Librium). Duration of action depends on the half-life of the drug—that is, how long it takes the drug to be metabolized and excreted. Half-life, the time it takes

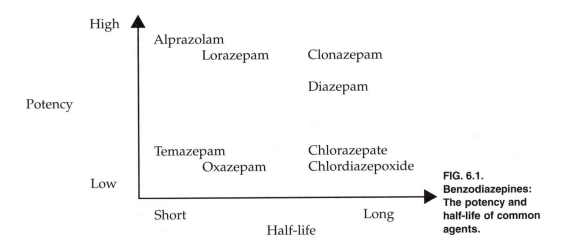

FIG. 6.1. Benzodiazepines: The potency and half-life of common agents.

to metabolize and excrete 50% of a concentration of drug, ranges among the benzodiazepines from a few hours to nearly a week.

In general, high-potency drugs have a more abrupt onset of action. This may be desirable, but it also may promote misuse of the medication, since it can produce a "high." Longer acting drugs tend to produce fewer problems with withdrawal (characterized by anxiety, tremor, sweating, tachycardia, nausea, and rarely seizures and delirium; see sedative-hypnotic withdrawal, Chapter 8), but they also may inadvertently build to toxic levels.

Antidepressants from several drug classes have been shown to be effective in reducing symptoms of panic (Janicek et al., 1997). The MAOIs and the TCAs, particularly the tertiary TCAs, are highly effective, but have some problems with tolerability. The SSRIs also are effective against panic. Nefazadone (Serzone), venlafaxine (Effexor), and mirtazapine (Remeron) have shown promise as anxiolytic agents.

Social and specific phobias

As noted in the *DSM-IV*, agoraphobia must be distinguished from two other disorders of anxious avoidance. *Social phobia* is characterized by a specific fear of social situations. Socially phobic individuals fear embarrassment and the attention of others. This usually includes situations of public performance, but socially phobic individuals also may fear small gatherings or even eating in front of loved ones. Panic attacks may occur in social settings. Social phobia affects perhaps 10% of the population (Sadock & Sadock, 2000). Like panic disorder, it responds to SSRIs, and MAOIs, but it does not respond as well to TCAs (Janicek et al., 1997). Benzodiazepines also may be effective.

Social phobia is characterized by a specific fear of social situations.

Specific phobias are fears of specific situations or objects, such as spiders, heights, and flying. Specific phobias probably affect about 10% of the population. Unlike the other anxiety disorders, they respond poorly to medications, and are usually treated with psychotherapy (Janicek et al., 1997).

Generalized anxiety disorder

Specific phobias are fears of individual situations or objects.

When anxiety is chronic rather than punctuated, as in the case of panic attacks, generalized anxiety disorder (GAD) is present. The primary feature of generalized anxiety disorder is chronic, disproportionate, and uncontrollable worry, accompanied by symptoms of edginess, insomnia, irritability, muscle tension, fatigue, and poor concentration.

GAD occurs in 3% to 5% of the population (American Psychiatric Association, 1994). Its pathophysiology is poorly understood, but like other anxiety disorders it appears to involve abnormalities in GABA and serotonergic neurotransmission. Benzodiazepines are effective, as are the antidepressants venlafaxine and imipramine. Buspirone (Buspar), an agonist at serotonin 1a receptors, also is effective (Janicek et al., 1997).

Posttraumatic stress disorder

When an individual is exposed to a life-threatening event, the resultant extreme fear response may persist, leaving symptoms of arousal, reexperience of the trauma, and withdrawal. This is the syndrome of posttraumatic stress disorder.

Case example

Generalized anxiety disorder is characterized chronic and uncontrollable worry.

S began to realize she lived with the experience of the accident in ways besides panic and avoidance. She seldom slept well, and when she did she was plagued with nightmares of automobile accidents. She worried constantly about the safety of her family, and she felt continually on guard, looking out for danger. She preferred not to leave the house by herself, and she was terrified when she did not know where and what her parents and brother were doing.

In addition to panic, S also had posttraumatic stress disorder (PTSD). She had witnessed a major trauma, defined as an event in which someone's physical integrity is threatened. S intrusively reexperienced the trauma through nightmares and flashbacks (a state in which she felt that the trauma was recurring). She was hyperaroused—that is, she was in a perpetual state of fight-or-flight that caused her difficulty in sleeping and ease of startling—and she had withdrawn from social interaction as a protection from overstimulation.

DSM-IV criteria for posttraumatic stress disorder

A. The person has been exposed to a traumatic event in which both of the following were present:

(1) The person experienced, witnessed, or was confronted with an event or events that involved actual or threatened death or serious injury, or a threat to the physical integrity of self or others.

(2) The person's response involved intense fear, helplessness, or horror. Note: In children, this may be expressed instead by disorganized or agitated behavior.

Posttraumatic stress disorder is a persistent extreme fear response resulting from a life-threatening event.

B. The traumatic event is persistently reexperienced in one (or more) of the following ways:

(1) Recurrent and intrusive distressing recollections of the event, including images, thoughts, or perceptions. Note: In young children, repetitive play may occur in which themes or aspects of the trauma are expressed.

(2) Recurrent distressing dreams of the event. Note: In children, there may be frightening dreams without recognizable content.

(3) Acting or feeling as if the traumatic event were recurring (includes a sense of reliving the experience, illusions, hallucinations, and dissociative flashback episodes, including those that occur on awakening or when intoxicated). Note: In young children, trauma-specific reenactment may occur.

(4) Intense psychological distress at exposure to internal or external cues that symbolize or resemble an aspect of the traumatic event.

(5) Physiological reactivity on exposure to internal or external cues that symbolize or resemble an aspect of the traumatic event.

C. Persistent avoidance of stimuli associated with the trauma and numbing of general responsiveness (not present before the trauma), as indicated by three (or more) or the following:

(1) efforts to avoid thoughts, feelings, or conversations associated with the trauma

(2) efforts to avoid activities, places, or people that arouse recollections of the trauma

(3) inability to recall an important aspect of the trauma

(4) markedly diminished interest or participation in significant activities

(5) feeling of detachment or estrangement from others

(6) restricted range of affect (e.g., unable to have loving feelings)

(7) sense of a foreshortened future (e.g., does not expect to have a career, marriage, children, or a normal life span)

D. Persistent symptoms of increased arousal (not present before the trauma), as indicated by two or more of the following:

(1) difficulty falling or staying asleep

(2) irritability or outbursts of anger

(3) difficulty concentrating

(4) hypervigilence

(5) exaggerated startle response

E. Duration of the disturbance (symptoms in Criteria B, C, and D) is more than 1 month.

F. The disturbance causes clinically significant distress or impairment in social, occupational, or other important areas of functioning.

Reprinted with permission from the ***Diagnostic and Statistical Manual of Mental Disorders***, Fourth Edition. Copyright 1994, American Psychiatric Association.

Pathophysiology of PTSD

Like panic disorder, PTSD is thought to be due in part to the dysregulation of aminergic neurotransmission, specifically of norepinephrine and serotonin, as well as GABA. Individuals with PTSD show pronounced increases in their secretion of the stress hormone cortisol (Baker, West, Nicholson, Ekhatore, Kasckon, & Hill, 1999). Unfortunately, as we saw in the discussion on depression, chronically high levels of cortisol are neurotoxic, and individuals with PTSD show loss of hippocampal nerve cells corresponding to their production of cortisol. The pathogenesis of this neurotoxicity may be similar to that seen in depression, but PTSD seems to result in greater hippocampal cell loss (Charney et al., 1999).

Treatment

The treatment of PTSD has not been studied as extensively as other anxiety disorders. Like panic, PTSD responds to benzodiazepines and antidepressants, specifically the SSRIs, TCAs, and MAOIs (Janicek et al., 1997).

Obsessive-compulsive disorder

Individuals with obsessive-compulsive disorder are assailed by fears that seem senseless and yet are relentless and often compel compensatory behavior. Typical obsessions and compulsions revolve around themes of cleanliness, orderliness, doubt, hoarding, and religiousity.

Obsessive-compulsive disorder is characterized by senseless fears that compel compensatory behavior.

Case example

In his teens, Mr. L had begun to experience the sensation that his clothes were always dirty. At first he assuaged this fear by washing his clothes frequently. As time went on, however, he obtained less and less relief with washing. He began to dread contamination from any number of sources. Sitting in public became impossible, since it risked contamination. L also developed a need for symmetry. He would spend hours straightening a picture and experienced intolerable anxiety if he could not achieve the symmetry he craved. Since most of his time was engaged in compulsive rituals, and he could not leave the house for fear of contamination, L became severely disabled.

L had developed obsessive-compulsive disorder, or OCD. OCD occurs in about 2.5% of the population (American Psychiatric Association, 1994). OCD is the presence of obsessive ideas that produce anxiety or compulsive behavior, or both.

DSM-IV criteria for obsessive-compulsive disorder

A. Either obsessions or compulsions.

Obsessions as defined by (1), (2), (3), and (4):

(1) Recurrent and persistent thoughts, impulses, or images that are experienced, at some time during the disturbance, as

intrusive and inappropriate and that cause marked anxiety or distress.

(2) The thoughts, impulses, or images are not simply excessive worries about real-life problems.

(3) The person attempts to ignore or suppress such thoughts, impulses, or images, or to neutralize them with some other thought or action.

(4) The person recognizes that the obsessional thoughts, impulses, or images are a product of his or her own mind (not imposed from without as in thought insertion).

Compulsions as defined by (1) and (2):

(1) Repetitive behaviors (e.g., hand washing, ordering, checking) or mental acts (e.g., praying, counting, repeating words silently) that the person feels driven to perform in response to an obsession, or according to rules that must be applied rigidly.

(2) The behaviors or mental acts aimed at preventing or reducing distress or preventing some dreaded event or situation; however, these behaviors or mental acts either are not connected in a realistic way with what they are designed to neutralize or prevent or are clearly excessive.

B. At some point during the course of the disorder, the person has recognized that the obsessions or compulsions are excessive or unreasonable. Note: This does not apply to children.

Ego-systonic fears are those the sufferer recognizes as senseless.

C. The obsessions or compulsions cause marked distress, are time-consuming (take more than 1 hour a day), or significantly interfere with the person's normal routine, occupational or aca- demic functioning, or usual social activities or relationships.

D. If another Axis I disorder is present, the content of the obsessions or compulsions is not restricted to it (e.g., preoccupation with food in the presence of an Eating Disorder; hair pulling in the presence of Trichotillomania; concern with appearance in the presence of Body Dysmorphic Disorder; preoccupation with drugs in the presence of a Substance use Disorder; preoccupation with having a serious illness in the presence of Hypochondriasis; preoccupation with sexual urges or fantasies in the presence of a Paraphilia; or guilty ruminations in the presence of Major Depressive Disorder).

E. The disturbance is not due to the direct physiological effects of a substance (e.g., a drug of abuse, a medication) or a general medical condition.

Reprinted with permission from the *Diagnostic and Statistical Manual of Mental Disorder,* Fourth Edition. Copyright 1994, American Psychiatric Association

Typically, obsessive fears lead to compulsive behavior. In the case of L, his fear of contamination led him to attempt to assuage this fear by compulsively washing his person and clothes. Eventually, however, compulsive behaviors take on a life of their own and are no longer as effective in reducing anxiety. Failure to engage in the behavior, however, still causes anxiousness. In most cases, the obsessions of OCD are seen as absurd and mystifying. Rationally, individuals with OCD know that there is no reason to fear what they do. In that sense, the fears are said to be *ego-dystonic.* In those cases where the individual with OCD has lost insight into the senselessness of the fears, the obsessions are said to be *ego-syntonic.* Ego-dystonic obsessions may occasionally be of delusional proportions. Major depression often is comorbid with OCD.

Ego-dystonic fears are those the sufferer recognizes as senseless.

Pathophysiology of OCD

OCD occurs in 1% to 3% of the population (American Psychiatric Association, 1994). The male-to-female ratio for OCD is 1:1. First-degree relatives of those with OCD are 4.6 times more likely to have OCD than the general population, suggesting a genetic contribution. Monozygotic twins appear to have greater concordance for OCD than dizygotic twins. However, a specific genetic locus has yet to be elucidated.

OCD seems to be caused in part by alterations in serotonergic neurotransmission in the cingulate gyrus, prefrontal cortex, and basal ganglia, which show increased metabolic activity on positron emission tomography (PET) (Baxter, 1999). OCD is known to be associated with blood flow abnormalities in these same sites (Cohen, Hollander, & Stein, 1997). Brain imaging studies have shown consistently that individuals with OCD have decreased caudate nucleus volume compared to control subjects (Robinson et al., 1995). Animal models of OCD, including repetitive canine forepaw licking and feather picking in parrots, respond to the same medications that are used to treat OCD in humans (Dodman, Moon-Fanelli, Mertens Pfluger, & Stein, 1997). The pharmacologic treatment of OCD provides further evidence for the role of serotonin in the pathogenesis of OCD. The medications that improve compulsive behaviors in both human and animal subjects are serotonergic (and are limited to the SSRIs and the TCA clomipramine).

One intriguing model proposed by Lewis Baxter (1999) attempts to combine these findings. Social behavior often is not consciously controlled, but is instead learned implicitly. Like riding a bicycle or playing a guitar, many social behaviors are learned through performance and repetition rather than didactically, and activation of these behaviors often occurs without conscious effort. In many social settings, we simply know without conscious reflection the "right" thing to say or do. Baxter proposes that these implicitly learned behavioral patterns are driven by a circuit running from the prefrontal cortex to the striatum (particularly the caudate nucleus) and then to the thalamus. Balance in this system activates or inhibits various social behavioral patterns that are organized around basic themes such as cleanliness, aggression, and territoriality. In OCD, this balance may be shifted by deficient serotonergic neurotransmission such that particularly defensive as opposed to aggressive behavioral patterns become preferentially activated. This may explain why the prefrontal cortex and caudate nucleus show increased activity in OCD. Increases in serotonergic neurotransmission decrease overactivity of these areas of the brain, restoring balanced behavior.

Treatment

OCD appears to respond only to high doses of serotonergic antidepressants, such as the SSRIs or the TCA clomipramine (Anafranil). These medications have been shown to be between 60% and 80% effective in reducing symptoms of OCD. Placebo response in OCD is between 5% and 15%, dramatically lower than the 20% to 30% seen in many medical and psychiatric disorders (Greist et al., 1995). In some cases, relief has been obtained through anterior cingulotomy, a neurosurgical procedure in which the connections between the frontal lobe and the basal ganglia are severed. As we will see, OCD also responds to behavioral psychotherapy, which has been shown to induce the same changes in the caudate nucleus as the SSRIs.

Key points

- *Panic disorder* and *posttraumatic stress disorder* are thought to be caused by dysregulation of biogenic amines and GABA.

- Panic disorder and PTSD are treatable with benzodiazepines, which potentiate GABA, as well as MAOIs, TCAs, and SSRIs.

- *Obsessive-compulsive disorder* is caused by serotonergic dysfunction in the caudate, prefrontal cortex, and cingulate gyrus.

- Biologically, OCD responds only to serotonergic antidepressants in high doses and to cingulotomy.

Cognitive disorders 7

The cognitive disorders are dysfunctions in the basic elements of intelligence, such as memory, attention, language, calculation, praxis, abstract ability, sequencing, and planning. They also include delirium and dementia. Unlike other psychiatric presentations, the cognitive disorders have no primary state, but are thought always to be secondary to general medical conditions.

Delirium

Delirium is the onset, usually abruptly, of alterations in level of consciousness, attention, and other cognitive deficits. Delirium represents a disruption of arousal caused by general medical conditions.

Case example

Mr. J was 60 and had been living with schizophrenia for more than 30 years. Then, over a few days, he went into a curious decline. Although chronically disorganized as a result of psychotic symptoms, he began to have difficulty walking and caring for himself, admittedly a complicated task given J's numerous health problems, which included emphysema and a colostomy. The nursing home where he resided reported that J fell frequently, despite using a walker. He was often sleepy and difficult to arouse, although when awake he could still converse coherently. During those times he complained of losing control of his bladder. J's primary physician ran some blood tests, which came back normal. Finally, he referred J to the emergency room for an evaluation of his symptoms. The emergency room physician looked J over and pronounced him "medically clear," a common euphemism for describing a situation believed to be a primary psychiatric and not medical problem. The doctor requested a psychiatry consult to address J's symptoms of "psychosis."

Delirium is the onset of alterations in level of consciousness, attention, and other cognitive deficits.

89

When the psychiatrist went to see J, he was immediately struck by J's emaciated appearance. Although J was generally awake and conversant, he tended to drift off momentarily. This was fairly subtle; but the remainder of J's neurological exam revealed other abnormalities. Not only could J not recall any objects presented to him for memory testing, he could not even initially repeat the objects for later recall. He tended to perseverate, or repeat a single item over and over. When asked to spell "world," for example, he said, "W-o-r-l-r-l-l-l." He also had an apraxia, an inability to organize and carry out a task despite having normal strength in his extremities. J evidenced "primitive" reflexes, or reflexes that are present in infants but which disappear as the child ages. The reappearance of such reflexes is an indication of damage to the frontal lobes of the brain. When asked what he thought was happening, J said, "I think I'm going crazy, Doc. I keep pissing myself."

The psychiatrist diagnosed delirium. Delirium, sometimes known as an "acute confusional state," is marked by an altered level of consciousness and an inability to sustain attention to the environment, with associated cognitive deficits such as memory impairment, and hallucinations.

DSM-IV criteria for delirium

A. Disturbance of consciousness (i.e., reduced clarity of awareness of the environment) with reduced ability to focus, sustain, or shift attention.

B. A change in cognition (such as memory deficit, disorientation, language disturbance) or the development of a perceptual disturbance that is not better accounted for by a preexisting, established, or evolving dementia.

C. The disturbance develops over a short period of time (usually hours to days) and tends to fluctuate during the course of the day.

D. There is evidence from the history, physical examination, or laboratory findings that the disturbance is caused by the direct physiological consequences of a general medical condition.

Reprinted with permission from *Diagnostic and Statistical Manual of Mental Disorders*, Fourth Edition. Copyright 1994, American Psychiatric Association.

Level of consciousness refers to the ability of an organism to maintain a level of arousal that is "awake and alert." Psychiatrists routinely describe six levels of consciousness, in descending order: hyperaroused, awake and alert, somnolent (sleepy but arousable), obtunded (barely arousable), stuporous (not arousable, but still responsive to painful stimuli), and comatose. The ability to maintain a waking and attentive state is controlled by brain structures in the *ascending reticular activating system*, which arises primarily in the midbrain (Nolte, 1988). This system uses norepinephrine, serotonin, dopamine, and acetylcholine to regulate the level of consciousness and attention.

As one might expect, the ability to sustain arousal and attention to the environment is imperative for survival. The capacity to do so thus appears in the brainstem, where critical functions such as respiration and heart rate are controlled. Impairment in arousal and attention are always abnormal. Other higher cognitive capacities, such as memory and praxis, depend on intact attention and so may be impaired in delirium. Delirium also may be a cause of psychotic symptoms. However, impairment in memory and praxis or the appearance of psychotic symptoms are not specific to delirium. These symptoms may be present in other disorders and may not be present in delirium. Impairment in arousal and attention, on the other hand, are unique to delirium. Such dysfunction often is mistaken for schizophrenia, depression, mental retardation, or other psychiatric disorders. But inability to sustain arousal is not a symptom of any mental disorder except delirium.

Delirium and dementia are not primary conditions, but are always the result of general medical conditions. Although the symptoms of depression may represent "primary major depression" and not the result of a general medical illness, delirium and dementia are, by definition, always due to general medical causes. In the majority of cases of delirium (95%), a definite causative medical condition is found. This far exceeds the percentage of cases caused by general medical conditions for any of the psychiatric syndromes except dementia, which also is considered to be only the result of a general medical condition. Delirium most commonly arises from the following conditions, in descending order of frequency (Guze, 1997):

- Multifactorial
- Drug or alcohol intoxication and withdrawal
- Metabolic disturbances
- Intracranial processes (e.g., subdural hematoma or tumors)
- Infection
- Electrolyte disturbances
- Postsurgical

The 6-month mortality of delirium is about 25%, and the mortality rate during hospitalization for the elderly delirious ranges from 22% to 76%, depending on the population studied (Francis, Martin, & Kapoor, 1990; Lipowski, 1987; Sirous, 1988; Weddington, 1982). This high mortality rate is not the effect of delirium per se, but reflects the fact that delirium is so often a symptom of devastating medical illness. Thus, even when a definite medical cause for a delirium cannot be located, it is thought to be due to an undiscovered medical problem; treatment consists primarily of an exhaustive search for such problems, which can then be corrected. The laboratory evaluation of delirium might include a complete blood count, electrolytes/glucose/blood urea nitrogen/creatinine/calcium, liver function tests, urinalysis, chest x-ray, electrocardiogram, thyroid studies, vitamin B12/folate, HIV/RPR (for neurosyphilis), brain imaging (CT or MRI), lumbar puncture, and electroencephalogram.

Dementia is a disturbance in memory, with accompanying cognitive deficits.

J's neurological examination, combined with his history of falling and incontinence, indicated a problem in the central nervous system. Because delirium is so often associated with serious medical problems such as meningitis, sepsis, metabolic disturbances, tumors, and strokes, it constitutes a medical emergency. The psychiatrist recommended an emergency CT scan of J's head, which revealed numerous space-occupying lesions, or "mass lesions" compressing J's brain, directly disrupting function and also inhibiting the flow of cerebrospinal fluid, the fluid that surrounds the central nervous system. The resulting expansion of fluid spaces disrupted the function of nearby neuronal circuits responsible for the control of continence and gait. The other symptom they produced was the alteration in attention and level of consciousness distinctive to delirium. In J's case, the mass lesions were metastatic lung cancer.

Dementia

Dementia is a disturbance in memory, with other accompanying cognitive deficits. The most common dementia is Alzheimer's dementia, but many other dementing illnesses exist. Like delirium, true dementia syndrome is always the result of a general medical condition.

Case example

Mr. E, 87 years old, was found wandering aimlessly about the city. When questioned about his purposes, E could not explain where he was or what he was doing. Concerned, the police took him to the hospital for evaluation. Emergency room physicians obtained a psychiatric consultation to address the question of competency—

that is, whether or not E was capable of making decisions for himself.

The first thing the psychiatrist noticed was that E had infections in both eyes, which were bloodshot and oozing pus. Nevertheless, he was able to look at the examiner and was awake and alert throughout the interview. The emergency room physician corroborated that he had been so since admission. The psychiatrist introduced himself, and began with a standard inquiry: "Tell me what's happening."

E did not know. His response to the question was exceedingly slow. When asked if he knew where he was, he did not appear at first to understand the question. He was given options: Was he in a restaurant? A bank? Someone's home? E said he thought he was in a home. When told he was in a hospital and asked if he knew where he lived, he was unable to reply. Surprisingly, he was perfectly oriented to the date. When E's memory was tested, he was unable to repeat a list of words for later recall. When asked to identify a pen, he took 30 seconds of close inspection before correctly naming the object.

E was exhibiting the syndrome of dementia, defined as a memory impairment with associated cognitive deficits such as apraxia (as in J's case, an inability to plan and execute a task despite normal strength, an ability regulated by the parietal and frontal lobes), agnosia (an inability to recognize objects, caused by impairments in parietal and occipital lobe function), aphasia (language deficits, a dominant hemisphere function), or impaired executive function (diminished speed of cognition and poor planning, sequencing, and organization). Because E was able to maintain a consistent level of arousal and sustain attention to the environment, a diagnosis of delirium was not made.

The causes of dementia break down roughly as follow (Sadock & Sadock, 2000):

Alzheimer's disease	50%–60%
Vascular (numerous strokes, deep white matter atherosclerosis)	10%–20%
Alcohol-related	10%
Hydrocephalus	4%–8%
Tumors	1%–2%
Other causes such as hypothyroidism, vitamin B12 deficiency, HIV, neurosyphilis, Parkinson's, or Huntington's disease	5%–10%

About 10% of dementia syndromes are not actually due to the degenerative effects of general medical conditions, but instead represent impaired cognitive function due to other psychiatric disorders. It is common, for example, for depressed people to have poor concentration and low energy, which may significantly impair their ability to perform on cognitive testing. Adequate treatment of the depression, however, will eliminate the cognitive problems. The prevalence of pseudodementia has been called into question. The cognitive impairments of schizophrenia may be permanent and related to neurological abnormalities, as previously discussed, and depression may result in persistent cognitive deficits.

Pseudo-dementia is characterized by dementia symptoms that are caused by other psychiatric disorders.

Although dementia often is distinguished from delirium by the usually abrupt onset and fluctuating character of the latter, the only completely reliable distinction between the two is the altered level of consciousness and impaired attention specific to delirium. It also must be remembered that delirium can be superimposed onto any mental state, including dementia.

Alzheimer's disease

Alzheimer's disease is the most common dementing illness, affecting over 10% of the population and accounting for the majority of dementia cases. Alzheimer's disease becomes more common as age advances, such that the incidence doubles at approximately 5-year intervals between the ages of 65 and 85 (Evans et al., 1989). Alzheimer's disease is a progressively degenerative disease with a widely variable course, ranging from 2 to 20 years after diagnosis.

Pathophysiology.   Alzheimer's disease is caused by neuronal cell death due to an accumulation of abnormal cellular products, known as b-amyloid *plaques* and cytoskeleton protein *tangles*. The disease usually affects the parietal cortex first, and then inexorably progresses to involve the temporal and finally the frontal lobes.

Genetically, Alzheimer's disease is thought to involve chromosome 21. This chromosome is the location for the b-amyloid precursor protein gene. Individuals with Down's syndrome, who have an extra chromosome 21, always show histopathological evidence of Alzheimer's disease once they reach the age of 40, although they may not always show evidence of dementia (Wisniewski et al., 1985). Since these individuals have an extra copy of the b-amyloid precursor protein gene, it is thought that extra production of this protein leads to the invariable presence of Alzheimer's histopathology (Games et al., 1995). A form of autosomal-dominant early-onset Alzheimer's disease shows a genetic abnormality localized to chromosome 14. This abnormality is a mutation in the presenilin gene, which also has been implicated in the pathogenesis of Alzheimer's disease (Cruts, Hendricks, & Van Broeckhoven, 1996).

Another genetic finding is the higher prevalence of the apoE4 gene in individuals with Alzheimer's disease. Apolipoprotein, which is involved in the metabolism of cholesterol and triglycerides, is coded for by the genes apoE2, apoE3, and apoE4. Individuals homozygous for apoE4 (i.e., with one apoE4 gene derived from each parent) show increased risk for developing Alzheimer's disease (Corder et al., 1993). Conversely, apoE2 may decrease the risk of developing Alzheimer's disease. The reason for this association is not yet known.

Individuals with Alzheimer's disease show progressive loss of cholinergic neurons arising from the nucleus basalis of Meynert. This has led investigators to attempt replenishment of the cholinergic deficit by giving cholinergic medications. Alzheimer's dementia is partially responsive to a class of drugs called *cholinesterase inhibitors* (tacrine or Cognex, donepezil or Aricept, and rivastigmine or Exelon). Cholinesterase inhibitors increase the amount of the neurotransmitter acetylcholine by inhibiting the enzyme acetylcholinesterase, which is responsible for acetylcholine degradation. These drugs have been shown to delay the progression of the illness (Rogers et al., 1998). Some benefit also has been seen from antioxidants such as vitamin E, which may protect from damage caused by b-amyloid proteins (Sano et al., 1997).

Key points

- *Delirium* is an altered level of consciousness with associated cognitive deficits.

- Delirium may be superimposed on any other psychiatric condition.

- Delirium is always the result of a general medical condition.

- *Dementia* is a syndrome of impaired memory with associated aphasia, apraxia, agnosia, or decreased executive function.

- The most common dementing illness is Alzheimer's-type dementia.

- *Pseudodementia* is the mimicking of dementia by other psychiatric disorders, such as depression or schizophrenia.

Substance use disorders 8

The central nervous system operates to reinforce biologically desirable behaviors, such as eating and reproduction. These reward systems, however, are susceptible to manipulation by some substances that are not biologically desirable but, in fact deleterious. Once taken, they can induce addictive consumption.

Substance abuse and dependence

There are numerous substances of abuse, including alcohol, stimulants, opiates, marijuana, sedative-hypnotics, nicotine, caffeine, PCP, hallucinogens, and inhalants. About 16% to 26% of the general population will use a substance (excluding nicotine and caffeine) to a degree sufficient to adversely impact their lives (Sadock & Sadock, 2000). The majority of adverse substance uses are nicotine and alcohol consumption.

Psychiatrists speak of two broad ways in which substance use can adversely impact a person's life: abuse and dependence.

Substance abuse is the use of a substance in ways that cause repeated detrimental consequences.

Abuse

Substance abuse is the use of a substance in such a way that adverse consequences have repeatedly occurred in important areas of functioning, such as work, social interactions (including legal problems related to substance use), and health. Examples might include people who use a substance such that their work is impaired or they incur a driving under the influence (DUI) charge. About 10% of women and 20% of men will meet the criteria for alcohol abuse in their lifetimes (Sadock & Sadock, 2000).

DSM-IV criteria for substance abuse

    A. A maladaptive pattern of substance use leading to clinically significant impairment or distress, as manifested by one (or more) of the following, occurring within a 12-month period:

(1) recurrent substance use resulting in a failure to fulfill major role obligations at work, school, or home (e.g., repeated absences or poor work performance related to substance use; substance-related absences, suspensions, or expulsions from school; neglect of children or household)

(2) recurrent substance use in situations in which it is physically hazardous (e.g., driving an automobile or operating a machine when impaired by substance use)

(3) recurrent substance-related legal problems (e.g., arrests for substance-related disorderly conduct)

(4) continued substance use despite having persistent or recurrent social or interpersonal problems caused or exacerbated by the effects of the substance (e.g., arguments with spouse about consequences of intoxication, physical)

B. The symptoms have never met the criteria for Substance Dependence for this class of substance.

Reprinted with permission from **_Diagnostic and Statistical Manual of Mental Disorders,_** Fourth Edition. Copyright 1994, American Psychiatric Association.

Dependence

Substance dependence is defined as loss of control over the use of a substance. Substance abuse does not imply that individuals have lost control of the use of the substance, but only that they have had serious problems when they do use the substance. The loss of control seen in substance dependence can include physical dependence, as evidenced by the phenomena of *tolerance* (development of the capacity to consume at least 50% more of a substance than previously possible with the same effect) and *withdrawal* (the appearance of a physiological syndrome upon removal of the substance). Physical dependence may, however, occur without a formal diagnosis of substance dependence if the psychological experience of loss of control is lacking. For example, the antihypertensive medication clonidine can be tolerated in increasing doses over time and can produce a severe rebound hypertension if abruptly withdrawn. Because users of clonidine do not experience the psychological sensation of loss of control, however, it is not classified as a drug of dependence. Psychological symptoms of dependence include using the substance more often or in greater quantities than was intended, repeated or unsuccessful attempts to reduce use of the substance, continuing to use the substance despite serious adverse physical consequences, and using the substance to the exclusion of other activities. Although com-

Substance dependance is loss of control over use of a substance.

mon, physical dependence is not required to diagnose substance dependence. It is possible to lose control over the use of a substance without developing tolerance or withdrawal.

DSM-IV criteria for substance dependence

A maladaptive pattern of substance use, leading to clinically significant impairment or distress, as manifested by three (or more) of the following, occurring at any time in the same 12-month period.

(1) Tolerance, as defined by either of the following:

    (a) a need for markedly increased amounts of the substance to achieve intoxication or desired effect,

    (b) markedly diminished effect with continued use of the same amount of the substance.

(2) Withdrawal, as manifested by either of the following:

    (a) the characteristic withdrawal syndrome for the substance,

    (b) the same (or a closely related) substance is taken to relieve or avoid withdrawal symptoms.

(3) The substance is often taken in larger amounts or over a longer period than was intended.

(4) There is a persistent desire or unsuccessful efforts to cut down or control substance use.

(5) A great deal of time is spent in activities necessary to obtain the substance (e.g., visiting multiple doctors or driving long distances), use the substance (e.g., chain-smoking), or recover from its effects.

(6) Important social, occupational, or recreational activities are given up or reduced because of substance use.

(7) The substance use is continued despite knowledge of having a persistent or recurrent physical or psychological problem that is likely to have been caused or exacerbated by the substance (e.g., current cocaine use despite recognition of cocaine-induced depression, or continued drinking despite recognition that an ulcer was made worse by alcohol consumption).

Reprinted with permission from ***Diagnostic and Statistical Manual of Mental Disorders***, Fourth Edition. Copyright 1994, American Psychiatric Association.

Tolerance is the capacity to consume at least 50% more of a substance than previously possible with the same effect.

Withdrawal is the appearance of a physiological syndrome upon removal of the substance.

The pathophysiology of addiction

Addictive behaviors include reward response, conditioning, and compulsive self-administration. Early in this century, it was widely believed that addictive behavior was specific to human beings. However, investigation has revealed that reward-based reinforcing behavior occurs in many animals, and that animals may develop addictive behavior to the same substances as do human beings. The dominant neurotransmitter system controlling these behaviors is the dopaminergic mesolimbic system. With the exception of alcohol, all addictive substances enhance the activity of the mesolimbic dopaminergic system. Cocaine and amphetamines increase the release of dopamine from mesolimbic neurons by inhibiting the reuptake of dopamine and increasing dopamine secretion respectively (Goeders & Smith, 1983, 1993). Nicotine has been shown to increase dopamine activity in the nucleus accumbens and basal ganglia (Pontieri, Tanda, Orzi, & DiChiara, 1996; Salokangas et al., 2000). Opiates appear to stimulate the cell bodies of dopaminergic neurons (Johnson & North, 1992).

With the exception of LSD, virtually all substances that induce dependency states in humans also induce self-administration in animals (London, Grant, Morgan, & Zukin, 1996). That is, given free access, animals will self-administer the substance. Chemical lesioning of the mesolimbic system interrupts the self-administration of drugs of abuse in experimental animals, as does lesioning of the nucleus accumbens (Vaccarino, Bloom, & Koob, 1985), a structure in the limbic system that is a primary projection of the mesolimbic dopamine system. Drugs that stimulate dopamine receptors reduce cocaine self-administration in animals, while drugs that block dopamine receptors increase self-administration (Yokel & Wise, 1975). It also has been discovered in both animals and humans that electrical stimulation of areas such as the septal area, which receives dopaminergic projections, produces a feeling of euphoria and precipitates self-stimulation of this area (Olds & Milner, 1954).

But is addictive behavior purely a function of dopaminergic neurotransmission? Despite strong evidence for this view, it is clear that other factors are involved. Genetics play a role in the development of addiction, as has been shown in twin/adoption studies (in which the rate of addiction in identical twins raised together is compared to that in twins raised apart, with the hope of separating environmental from genetic influence). How genetic predisposition translates into behavior, however, is not understood. Social context also plays a role, as do adverse consequences for using addictive substances. Even the most addicted individuals will inhibit their use in the presence of a police officer (although, of note, animals will endure pain to self-administer substances such as cocaine; in fact, given free access to cocaine, rats will self-administer the drug to the exclusion of all other rewards, including food). The dopamine reward system may play a crucial role in addictions but, like most psychiatric disorders, there probably is not a single mechanism exclusively responsible for the problem.

Free will.   What about free will? The biological mechanisms described seem to imply that individuals in the throes of addiction do not have free will to behave otherwise. Animals often are assumed not to have free will, and human biology is closely analogous to other animals. Yet, clearly, people can and do make conscious decisions regarding their intake of substances. Rather than viewing free will as an all-or-nothing phenomenon, it may be more useful, in terms of explaining the biological evidence, to consider individuals as possessing free will within certain constraints. For individuals not addicted to a substance, it requires no exercise of will at all not to consume an addictive substance such as alcohol. Indeed, they may be disinclined to use it. Addicted individuals may ultimately be in control of whether they take a substance, but they exercise this control within certain constraints. They must fight severe, biologically driven impulses to consume the substance.

Since the brain depends on dopaminergic tracts to impel biologically desirably behavior, such as the drives for food and sex, substances that stimulate the dopamine system ultimately become biological imperatives to the addicted organism. For a rat addicted to cocaine, it is more conceivable to go without food and water than cocaine. Likewise in humans, addicting substances take on a life or death imperative that can be resisted only with great effort. In these individuals, the free will must labor against a brain giving signals that to do without the addicting substance is to run great risk. Such resistance takes tremendous effort that the nonaddicted individual need not exert. In essence, addictive substances hijack a biological system designed to reward biologically necessary behavior, and instead compel addictive behavior as a biological imperative. This is not to imply that addicted individuals do not bear responsibility for the decisions they make. Rather, it is to make clear that they labor under a biological duress that makes it challenging for them to make the decisions that are most adaptive.

Specific substance abuse disorders

Alcohol and sedative-hypnotics

Alcohol and the sedative-hypnotic drugs (benzodiazepines, barbiturates, chloral hydrate, meprobamate, paraldehyde) are identical in their intoxication and withdrawal syndromes. As a result they are *cross-tolerant*: Tolerance to alcohol results in tolerance to the sedative-hypnotic drugs, and vice versa. This can be used to advantage in detoxification from sedative-hypnotic addiction. Alcohol and sedative-hypnotic withdrawal is the result of the adaptation of the brain to the chronic administration of sedative substances. The nervous system accomodates to such exposure by increasing the activity of catecholamines such as norepinephrine. If the use of alcohol or sedative-hypnotics is abruptly interrupted, the nervous system remains in a hypercatecholaminergic state for a period of time. This results in the hyperautonomic symptoms of alcohol/sedative-hypnotic withdrawal. Using the principle of cross-tolerance, this withdrawal syndrome can be treated with gradually decreasing doses of benzodiazepines, which are the safest of the sedative-hypnotics. This can be life-saving, since, untreated, the alcohol/sedative-hypnotic withdrawal delirium has a mortality rate of 15% to 20% (Griffin, Gross, & Teitel-baum, 1993).

Cross-tolerance is a tolerance for one substance that results from a tolerance for another.

Symptoms of alcohol/sedative-hypnotic intoxication include decreased memory or attention, slurred speech, nystagmus (the inability to maintain a fixed, lateral gaze), gait and coordination impairment, and sedation. Alcohol/sedative-hypnotic withdrawal is characterized by: hyperautomicity (increased heart rate, increased blood pressure, and sweating), fine tremor, insomnia, nausea/vomiting, anxiety and agitation, hallucinations, and seizures.

The pharmacologic treatment of alcohol dependence rests on the use of disulfiram (Antabuse) and naltrexone (ReVia). Disulfiram inhibits the metabolism of alcohol by decreasing the activity of the enzyme aldehyde dehydrogenase, resulting in the buildup of ethyl aldehyde upon alcohol consumption. The presence of large quantities of ethyl aldehyde causes the "Antabuse reaction": flushing, sweating, vomiting, choking and palpitations. Administered chronically, the threat of the Antabuse reaction provides an incentive to avoid alcohol consumption. Naltrexone is a long-acting opiate antagonist that decreases the euphoria associated with alcohol intoxication and has been shown to decrease alcohol consumption (Volpicelli, Alterman, Hayashida, & O'Brian, 1992).

Case example

By age 38, Mr. P had been drinking for more than 25 years, and when he was admitted to the hospital with severe pancreatitis, he was drinking up to a half-gallon of vodka a day. In the emergency department, he was still intoxicated from his latest drinking bout: His speech was slurred, his gait was wide-based and staggering, and he was somnolent and largely apathetic, but could be aroused to a state of lethargic irritability. Once admitted to the hospital, he rapidly cleared his alcohol intoxication. However, his irritability persisted. Twenty-four hours later, he developed a worsening fine tremor in his hands and became sweaty. His heart rate and blood pressure climbed. In another 12 hours, he was confused and disoriented, talking nonsensically, and seeing animals in his room. P was diagnosed with alcohol withdrawal delirium (the DTs).

Opiates

The opiates are all either natural or synthetic analogs of morphine and, as such, they interact with opiate receptors. Examples include heroin (diacetylmorphine), morphine, codeine, oxycodone, propoxyphene, and dilaudid.

Opiate intoxication is characterized by euphoria, usually followed by apathy/sedation, pupillary constriction (miosis), and decreased attention/memory.

Opiate withdrawal is characterized by pupillary dilatation (mydriasis), nausea/vomiting, lacrimation/rhinorrhea, fever, muscle and joint aching, insomnia, yawning, diarrhea and abdominal cramping, and dysphoria.

Tolerance to the effects of opiates develops through a hyperadrenergic state. Unlike alcohol/sedative-hypnotic withdrawal, however, opiate withdrawal is physiologically nonlife-threatening (except in the case of pregnancy, where it may result in spontaneous abortion). Opiate withdrawal may precipitate dangerous attempts to alleviate the withdrawal symptoms, however, such as prostitution or burglary to obtain opiates or the use of contaminated needles. Increased firing of noradrenergic neurons can be decreased by the use of clonidine, a presynaptic a-2 receptor agonist.

The long-term treatment of choice for opiate addiction is methadone maintenance. Methadone (or Dolophin) is a long-acting opiate that has a slow onset of action. Because of this slow onset, it does not produce the high associated with other opiates. Methadone's long half-life prevents the withdrawal associated with discontinuation of opiate use and also inhibits the ability of other opiates, such as heroin, to produce a high. Thus, patients in methadone maintenance treatment do not become high on the methadone, do not generally experience opiate withdrawal (which often leads to drug use to alleviate the symptoms), and cannot get high if they use another narcotic. If it is prescribed properly, methadone maintenance decreases crime and disease transmission, and increases employment rates in opiate users (Cooper, 1989; Sees et al., 2000). It does substitute addiction to methadone for heroin or other opiates. However, the relapse rate to opiate use without methadone is well over 95%. Thus, for the majority of opiate addicts, methadone represents a better alternative than repeated relapse.

Case example

Ms. Y was found unconscious in a lavatory, a needle and syringe still protruding from a vein in her arm. At that point she was observed to have pinpoint pupils and labored respiration. Vomitus was observed on the floor around her. [When given a dose of naloxone (Narcan), a short-acting opiate receptor antagonist, she revived briefly, only to slip again into a stupor when the drug's effect waned.]

Eight hours later, Y was wide awake and extremely uncomfortable. Her eyes and nose ran, she yawned repeatedly, and she was wracked by shaking chills and abdominal cramping. Her skin developed gooseflesh (piloerection), and her joints ached. At this point, she insisted upon leaving the hospital, but she was convinced to stay when her opiate withdrawal was treated with clonidine.

Stimulants

The stimulants—cocaine, amphetamine, dextroamphetamine (Dexedrine), methylphenidate (Ritalin), and pemoline (Cylert)—directly increase the activity of dopamine, either by inhibiting dopamine reuptake or by increasing the rate of its release. As a result, overstimulation and psychosis are frequent complications of stimulant use. Dopamine antagonists, conversely, can relieve this state. Since stimulants directly affect the dopamine reward system, their use results in particularly severe addictions. As yet, there are no definitive pharmacologic treatments for stimulant addiction.

Stimulant intoxication is characterized by tachycardia (rarely bradycardia), pupillary dilatation (mydriasis), elevated blood pressure (rarely decreased), sweating, nausea/vomiting, arrhythmia, confusion, seizures, dyskinesias (writhing movements), decreased cardiac perfusion, and weight loss in chronic use. Stimulant withdrawal is characterized by hypersomia (or insomnia), psychomotor slowing (or agitation), and increased appetite.

Case example

Mr. Z had overdosed on dextroamphetamine in a suicide attempt. Initially, he presented agitated and twitching, with pronounced visual hallucinations of people and animals. He also believed that everyone around him was trying to hurt him. His heart rate and blood pressure were elevated. These symptoms decreased with the administration of the dopamine antagonist risperidone (Risperdal). Once he had cleared the dextroamphetamine from his system, he became lethargic and depressed.

Phencyclidine

Phencyclidine (PCP) antagonizes glutamate receptors (NMDA receptors). It also increases the activity of prefrontal dopaminergic neurons. PCP intoxication results in severe agitation, psychosis, and seizures. It may lead to rhabdomyolysis (muscle damage) and renal failure. PCP usually is ingested accidentally, often with another substance (or it may be used to "spike" cannabis or cocaine).

PCP withdrawal and dependence syndromes are rare. The PCP intoxication state can be treated with benzodiazepines and the dopamine antagonist haloperidol, as well as acidification of the urine to enhance excretion.

Case example

Mr. W was picked up by the police screaming and combative. When he was brought to the emergency department, it took half a dozen people to restrain him. He was paranoid and his thinking was disorganized. His heart rate and blood pressure were elevated. A urine drug screen showed the presence of phencyclidine.

Cannabis (marijuana)

The active ingredient in marijuana is tetrahydrocannabol (THC), which may be inhaled or ingested. THC binds to a specific cannabinoid receptor (London et al., 1996). Cannabis intoxication is characterized by bloodshot conjunctiva, increased appetite, mood changes (euphoria or dysphoria, anxiety, and paranoia), dry mouth, and increased heart rate. Rarely, cannabis intoxication can result in severe psychosis or delirium.

Cannabis has no withdrawal syndrome but, contrary to popular belief, dependence can develop with chronic use. Chronic use also may result in impaired memory and "amotivation syndrome," characterized by apathy.

Case example

When Ms. V used marijuana she typically became extremely giggly and euphoric. At times, however, she became paranoid, believing that everyone knew everything about her. Observers noticed bloodshot eyes and increase appetite. When V tried at times to discontinue her daily use of marijuana, she experienced craving. Even when not using, she lacked motivation and some difficulties with her memory.

Hallucinogens

The hallucinogens include lysergic acid diethylamide (LSD), psilocybin (mushrooms), and mescaline (peyote cactus). Their mechanism of action is not well-understood, but it is clear that LSD is serotonergic, acting as an agonist of 5-HT$_{2A}$ receptors. Hallucinogen intoxication is characterized by perceptual disturbances (hallucinations, illusions, and synesthesia—the experiencing of one sensory modality in another, such as seeing musical sounds), pupillary dilatation, hyper-autonomicity (increased heart rate and sweating), and tremor or lack of coordination. Persistent use is infrequent, and there are no tolerance or withdrawal syndromes. "Flashback" experiences of hallucinogen-induced hallucinations are not unusual, however. A persistent psychotic disorder is unusual, but has been described. It is thought to occur in individuals already predisposed to psychotic disorders.

Case example

Mr. D had taken LSD, which he had licked from a stamp. Several hours later, he experienced euphoria, time distortion, vivid visual hallucinations of swirling colors, and a delusion that he was being followed across the rooftops of buildings by a beaver. This lasted for a number of hours.

Nicotine

Nicotine is an agonist at nicotinic acetylcholine receptors and acts as a powerful activator of dopaminergic pathways. Administration for even a few days results in a severe withdrawal syndrome.

Nicotine withdrawal is characterized by depression, dysphoria, and anxiety; decreased sleep and restlessness; irritability; poor concentration; and increased appetite.

Nicotine dependence is treated pharmacologically either with nicotine replacement in patches or gum, or with the dopaminergic antidepressant bupropion (in Wellbutrin or Zyban).

Inhalants

Inhalants are the aerosolized organic compounds found in adhesives, solvents, paint and paint thinners, gasoline, and many other products. Their primary mechanism of action is either through interaction with inhibitory GABA receptors or through the fluidization of cell membranes (much as the halogen anesthetics). Inhalant intoxication results in a syndrome characterized by mood changes (irritability, apathy, or euphoria); nystagmus, incoordination, impaired gait, and slurring of the speech; sedation, decreased reflexes, and psychomotor slowing; weakness; blurred vision; and tremor.

Inhalant withdrawal is rare, but dependence may develop. Persistent use often results in dementia.

Key points

- *Substance abuse* is the use of a substance in ways that cause re-peated detrimental consequences.

- *Substance dependence* is loss of control over use of a substance.

- There is a strong biological contribution to addictive behavior involving genetics and alterations in dopaminergic functioning.

Personality disorders 9

The disorders discussed so far typically are perceived as superimpositions on an individual's usual state of functioning. People with depression, for example, often see themselves during the course of a depressive episode as different from their usual selves. It is as if an outside force has invaded them, and is making them think and feel in ways quite distinct from the ordinary. In other words, the disordered state is *ego-dystonic*.

A "usual self" is described by the APA as "enduring patterns of perceiving, relating to, and thinking about the environment and oneself that are exhibited in a wide range of social and personal contexts" (American Psychiatric Association, 1994). This is the *DSM-IV* definition of personality traits. *Personality* is one's usual style of understanding the self and engaging the world. When depression strikes, it is not the "enduring pattern of perceiving, relating to, and thinking about the environment and oneself" that has gone awry, it is the additional state of depression that causes distress and dysfunction.

For some individuals, however, the enduring pattern of personality itself is the cause of troubles. Obviously, anyone's personality is liable to cause difficulty at some point. Character traits that are adaptive in some contexts may be counterproductive in others. Perfectionism and orderliness may be adaptive for an accountant, whose work requires attention to detail, a willingness to postpone gratification (so that she can stay late at the office during tax season), and organization in the midst of chaos. However, if the accountant is unable to enjoy time with her family due to excessive perfectionism—perhaps she cannot appreciate a vacation because she is excessively preoccupied with unimportant details—her perfectionism is maladaptive in the context of her family life.

The adaptive personality is flexible. If orderliness isn't working in a particular situation, can it be given up for a different pattern, even temporarily? When a pattern of engaging the world becomes predominantly inflexible and maladaptive in many contexts, psychiatrists recognize a *personality disorder*.

Personality is a person's usual style of understanding the self and engaging the world.

DSM-IV general diagnostic criteria for a personality disorder

A. An enduring pattern of inner experience and behavior that deviates markedly from the expectations of the individual's culture. This pattern is manifested in two (or more) ways.

    (1) cognition (i.e. ways of perceiving and interpreting self, other people, and events)

    (2) affectivity (i.e., the range, intensity, lability, and appropriateness of emotional response)

    (3) interpersonal functioning

    (4) impulse control

A personality disorder is a pattern of engaging the world that is predominantly inflexible and maladaptive in many contexts.

B. The enduring pattern is inflexible and pervasive across a broad range of personal and social situations.

C. The enduring pattern leads to clinically significant distress or impairment in social, occupational, or other important areas of functioning.

D. The pattern is stable and of long duration and its onset can be traced back at least to adolescence or early adulthood.

E. The enduring pattern is not better accounted for as a manifestation or consequence of another mental disorder.

F. The enduring pattern is not due to the direct physiological effects of a substance (e.g., a drug of abuse, a medication) or a general medical condition (e.g., head trauma).

Reprinted with permission from the *Diagnostic and Statistical Manual of Mental Disorders,* Fourth Edition. Copyright 1994, American Psychiatric Association.

Case example

Mr. H was a man who looked angry most of the time. When asked what was troubling him on any given day, he invariably responded by implicating the world at large. He never said, for example, "I had a fight with my daughter, and I'm feeling so sad and angry it makes me give up hope that life is worth living." Instead, he would say, "I just can't go on. It's that goddamn government. They're slowly taking away our liberties, one by one, and people can't even see it."

When the psychiatrist pushed hard enough, by telling H that it didn't seem like the reason he was suicidal could really be the government, H would eventually reveal what the true problem was. But initially he couldn't look at himself so piercingly. In fact, he genuinely believed the government was really why he was feeling bad, until the gentle but firm inquiries of the psychiatrist helped him to lower his guard. Once H became assured of the safety, understanding, and stability of the psychiatrist, he could finally examine what really troubled him.

Insight and self-examination were not how H led off. His emotions were always predominant, as if they were immutable. If something upset him—and he was exquisitely sensitive, particularly in interpersonal situations—he immediately reacted with an intense swelling of emotion, often hurt followed by rage, which he was unable to examine at the moment. He simply knew he was angry. It was not a state to be questioned or altered.

As a result, the problems in H's life always appeared to him to be external. If he felt bad, something must have caused it, and that cause almost always lay outside him. It took the first 40 years of H's life for him to begin to realize that many of his problems were a direct result of his own actions. For example, he would display bumper stickers with provocative political slogans and then wonder why strangers seemed antagonistic toward him. Usually, after his rage at rejection quieted, he would become profoundly suicidal. He drank, despite knowing how adversely drinking affected his life, particularly his marriage, and he came close to making attempts on his life. Only the encouragement of others could carry him through these times.

H's problems were long-standing, and they pervaded every aspect of his life. They caused trouble at work, in his marriage, with his children, with his doctors, and with the police, and they had since he was a teenager. H had a personality disorder with features of mood and self-image instability, extreme interpersonal sensitivity with resultant instability of interpersonal relationships, and self-destructive impulsiveness.

When H developed a major depressive episode, he experienced it as a pronounced change from his usual state—which often involved depressed mood and feelings of worthlessness and hopelessness, but in which his mood changed rapidly, even hourly, and seldom included difficulties with sleep, appetite, energy, or concentration. In other words, H was often depressed, but it was a very circumscribed emotion, without the duration and associated physical symptoms usually seen with the syndrome of major depression. When H finally developed a major depressive episode, it was a distinctly different experience from his usual moodiness, and included the expected changes in sleep, appetite, energy, and concentration that accompany a major depressive episode. H's primary problem was a pervasive personality disorder called *borderline personality disorder*.

Case example

Ms. A, on the other hand, was remarkably reserved. She was so quiet and diffident, in fact, she was practically invisible. When attention did turn toward her, people were likely to see a small woman who never took off her coat and who looked at others with a frightened blink, almost as if she expected to be struck. A was chronically unable to generate relationships because, as she eventually revealed in treatment, she was terrified of rejection. As a result, she made it virtually impossible for anyone to become close to her by passively sabotaging her relationships before they could get started. Her character style of avoiding interpersonal risk, her intense fear of rejection, and her feelings of worthlessness, which had persisted since early childhood, were the result of *avoidant personality disorder*.

The current diagnostic system recognizes 10 different personality disorders, divided into three subgroups, or clusters. Each personality disorder is described briefly in the following pages. (Cluster designations are used with permission from the *Diagnostic and Statistical Manual of Mental Disorders*, Fourth Edition. Copyright 1994, American Psychiatric Association.)

Cluster A: odd and eccentric

Paranoid

The paranoid personality style is characterized by pervasive suspiciousness but lacks frankly delusional paranoia. Paranoid personalities usually are hostile and angry, and assign blame entirely to others rather than to themselves. The prevalence of the disorder varies from 0.5% to 2.5% of the population (American Psychiatric Association, 1994). The pathophysiology is not well-understood beyond theories for the personality disorders in general.

Case example

Ms. R was referred by her primary care physician for relentlessly incorrigible behavior. She constantly questioned the motives of the office staff and seemed to take offense at the most minor inconveniences, such as a brief wait at the scheduling desk. She assumed that tests were ordered not for her benefit, but only to generate revenue for the clinic. R was single, and unemployed. She had been released from her work as a police officer because she could not get along with any of her coworkers. R interpreted this as persecution by evil and incompetent superiors. When asked if she had any friends, R said no, claiming they would "only screw me."

Schizoid

Schizoid personalities are socially aloof, with little or no interest in relationships or sexual experiences. They have difficulty experiencing pleasure. Reciprocal social interaction is difficult for individuals with schizoid personalities. The prevalence of schizoid personality disorder is not well-established, but may be higher than the other cluster-A personality disorders.

Case example

Mr. V, age 20, was brought for an evaluation by his parents. Although he had finished high school, graduating with average grades, he continued to live with his parents and seemed disinclined to want to move out. He had no stated goals for his future. His parents were concerned that he seemed to have no friends, and they worried that perhaps he was depressed, since he rarely seemed to enjoy anything to the same degree as the rest of the family. V himself denied depressed mood and said that he had plenty of friends. However, his parents confirmed that what he called friends were simply acquaintances whom he greeted in passing. He had never been involved in any romantic relationships and expressed a lack of sexual interest toward women or men.

On interview, V was quiet and uncomfortable and rarely made eye contact. His speech tended to be monosyllabic, and he rarely spontaneously offered information, although when talking about cars, his favorite topic, he became slightly more animated.

Schizotypal

Individuals with schizotypal personality disorder often have odd mannerisms and beliefs that typically include magical thinking (a style of thinking characteristic of children, in which events are not connected through observable cause-effect relationships but rather through magical means, such as believing that having a bad thought about someone might actually be physically harmful). They also may have illusional experiences and a sense of derealization. Schizotypal personality disorder is thought to occur in about 3% of the population (American Psychiatric Association, 1994). It is more common in the relatives of individuals with schizophrenia and shares some of the same subtle neurological deficits (Sadock & Sadock, 2000; Siever et al., 1990). For that reason, schizotypal personality disorder has been hypothesized to be a reduced-penetrance form of schizophrenia.

Case example

Mr. H was referred for work related problems. He had been suspended from his job after pushing one of his coworkers. When interviewed, Mr. H was calm and seemed to trust the interviewer, but he was extremely disturbed that he had been suspended, since he viewed his action as a just retaliation for abuses he felt he had received at the hands of his coworkers. His coworkers' offenses had been playing music too loudly and "causing trouble." It was difficult for H to specify how they caused trouble, but it was clear he felt they were somehow conspiring against him. When a coworker happened to be in the same restaurant as H, he wondered how the man had known he would be there.

H led an extremely isolated life. He desired friends, but he had no idea how to make conversation. His eye contact was normal, but his expression was quite lacking in expression (flat affect).

Cluster B: dramatic, emotional, and erratic

Antisocial

Antisocial personalities repeatedly commit criminal acts and show a lack of empathy or remorse. About 75% of the prison population has antisocial personality disorder (distinguishing it from criminality in general). Antisocial personality disorder occurs in perhaps 2% of the general population, with males predominating 3:1 over females (American Psychiatric Association, 1994). Of all the personality disorders, antisocial personality is the least controversial, and is considered to be both valid and reliable (Guze, 1997). Although the pathophysiology of antisocial personality disorder remains elusive, it may be associated frequently with neurological disorders. A recent study has shown that individuals with antisocial personality disorder have reduced prefrontal gray matter and decreased autonomic activity (Raine, Lencz, Birhrle, LaCasse, & Colletti, 2000). Thus, they may be prone to aggression due to a phenomenon known as *frontal disinhibition*, a condition seen in trauma patients with injury to the prefrontal cortex (Damasio, Grabowski, Frank, Galaburda, & Damasio, 1994). Individuals with reduced autonomic response may be less fearful, since the fear response is mediated by the autonomic nervous system (see Chapter 6). Because of their decreased autonomic activity, antisocial individuals may be less responsive to social conditioning, a phenomenon also seen in head trauma patients (Damasio, Tranel, & Damasio, 1990).

Case example

Mr. Q was initially evaluated for complaints about his excessive gambling. He often lied to his wife about his whereabouts, and then took long trips to a casino in a nearby town. Although he regretted losing the money for purely practical reasons, he appeared to have no remorse about how either his lying or losing the money might affect his wife. In the course of the interview, during which he was extremely charming and pleasant, it became apparent that Q had a long history of neglecting the needs of others. As a youth, he often had provoked fights so that he would have an excuse to assault people. At times, he injured others severely. He did not regret this at all and, in fact, expressed satisfaction about it. He also had tortured animals and been involved in a number of robberies. When interpersonally stressed, such as when his boss fired him for pushing a customer, Q reacted initially with threats. However, he quickly became depressed and suicidal, and required a brief hospitalization.

Borderline

Borderline personality is marked by impulsivity, unstable moods and self-image, repeated suicide attempts or self-mutilation, and fear of abandonment. Borderline personality disorder is thought to occur in about 2% of the population, with females accounting for twice as many cases as males (American Psychiatric Association, 1994). Mr. H is an example of borderline personality disorder.

Narcissistic

Individuals with narcissistic personality are preoccupied with a sense of their own specialness, have fantasies of unlimited success and power, require constant admiration from others, and are interpersonally exploitative. Narcissistic personality disorder occurs in less than 1% of the population, but that number is thought to be increasing.

Case example

Ms. C was a charismatic woman who nevertheless found it difficult to sustain relationships. In conversation, she relentlessly shifted the topic back to her own accomplishments, and she had an overwhelming sense of their importance. Although she thought of herself as a spiritual healer and boasted of performing spectacular healing miracles, she was not successful in maintaining a clientele and so worked as a bookkeeper. She quickly attempted to take control of any social situation and seemed to assume that others would naturally abide by her wishes. When they bridled, she had no understanding of what had gone wrong.

Histrionic

Histrionic individuals are excessively emotional and self-dramatizing. Their cognitive style is impressionistic rather than precise (the opposite of obsessive-compulsive personality disorder; see later section). The prevalence of histrionic personality disorder appears to be 2% to 3% of the population (American Psychiatric Association, 1994).

Case example

Ms. V always dressed provocatively. She worked as an artist, but she had a difficult time making a living, since she could not keep appointments. She had married her current husband, who was more than a decade her senior, after knowing him for 3 weeks. When Ms. V was asked how her week had been, she invariably responded with an exclamation, either "Great!" or "Terrible!" However, she had difficulty relating any specifics about how her mood had come to be that way. Ms. V talked about the future almost as if she was unable to conceptualize it. She made no plans and seemed to live on whim. This caused her financial difficulties and often led to stress in her marriage.

Cluster C: anxious and fearful

Avoidant

Avoidant personalities are socially inhibited, preoccupied with fear of criticism, and have pronounced feelings of inadequacy. Ms. A is an example of avoidant personality disorder. Avoidant personality disorder is thought to occur in 0.5% to 1% of the population (American Psychiatric Association, 1994).

Dependent

Individuals with dependent personalities need excessive caretaking from others, dread separation, and are submissive. They are preoccupied with the fear that they will have to care for themselves and will be unable to do so. The prevalence of dependent personality disorder is not well-established.

Case example

Mr. K was in a marriage he disliked intensely. His wife was abusive and unpredictable, and K despised her, but he found it impossible to conceptualize life without her and so remained. K shunned responsibility at work, preferring to take a supportive role. The only relationship K had found consistently comforting was with his mother. When she died, K became suicidal and required hospitalization. In therapy, K tended to dwell on a litany of complaints, but he seemed interested mainly in the comfort and compassion of the therapist and could not be engaged to make changes. A change in therapists, necessitated by the therapist leaving practice, proved nearly as devastating to K as the death of his mother.

Obsessive-compulsive

Those with obsessive-compulsive personality disorder (OCPD) are preoccupied with details (losing the forest for the trees), order, and control. OCPD is an overall cognitive style, as opposed to obsessive-compulsive disorder (OCD), in which the individual's personality is assailed by obsessive thoughts that he perceives to be intrusive. Those with OCPD approach life in a rigid, overly controlled manner. OCPD is not thought to be etiologically related to OCD. The prevalence of OCPD is about 1% (American Psychiatric Association, 1994).

Case example

Mr. D was referred for an evaluation at the request of his wife. She was quite emotional and found his controlled style intolerable. D was highly disciplined; his life was scheduled nearly to the minute. He rose at 4 A.M. to engage in a specific routine of reading and physical exercise. He was extremely efficient at work, but had difficulty if his routine was disturbed. Deviation from usual patterns often led to frantic feelings of chaos and to late hours repetitively searching for errors. D tended to believe that most of his problems were related to the inefficiencies and emotionality of others.

The pathophysiology of personality disorders

Current theory holds that personality is the confluence of biologically based temperament with life experience. Individuals have an inborn temperament that is then influenced by the experiences and environments they encounter in life. That individuals have constitutionally different temperaments is supported by common experience and infant research. We are all familiar with people who have seemed destined for their distinctive adult personalities since early childhood, even infancy. The quiet infant becomes the shy toddler becomes the socially inhibited adult; or the lively infant becomes the toddler who is always on the go and eventually has problems with impulsiveness as an adult. Critical features of personality such as chronic mood state, thinking style, and behavior patterns are built on biological propensity. Some individuals are biologically more energized to seek novelty, for example, others less so. It seems likely that biological temperament has some genetic component and is present at birth.

Temperament is a person's inborn characteristic inclination of emotional response.

When Jerome Kagan and his colleagues (Kagan, Reznick, & Snidman, 1988) followed a cohort of children representing the extremes of timid shyness and sociable extroversion, they found that these differences persisted from 21 months up to even 5 years later. Up to half of severely inhibited children remained so by age 7½. Kagan et al. found that measures of norepinephrine metabolism correlated moderately with social inhibition. More impressive was the correlation between heart rate and inhibition. Those infants with the highest heart rates were most likely to remain severely inhibited. Kagan et al. thus argued that inhibited children had greater sensitivity to arousal than unininhibited children. This research was subsequently replicated in nonhuman primates.

It is clear, however, that the "personality trait" of social inhibition is the result of more than inborn temperament. Only about 5% of the group of infants originally selected as inhibited remained clearly so at the study's endpoint. Many who began as inhibited eventually functioned indistinguishably from their peers. Thus, biological temperament alone is not sufficient to explain personality.

One interesting model of personality disorders comes from the work of C. Robert Cloninger (1986, 1987). Following animal models, Cloninger proposed that there are three essential traits which determine personality: reward-dependence (regulated by norepinephrine), harm-avoidance (regulated by serotonin), and novelty-seeking (regulated by dopamine).[1] Each individual has characteristics that lie on a spectrum in each of three dimensions. That spectrum can be plotted on the axes of a three-dimensional graph (Figure 9.1). The noradrenergic axis, for example, which sets the level of reward-dependence, will determine whether an individual is shy and reserved or brash and insensitive—in other words, how sensitive they are to social rewards such as praise or criticism. Thus, an individual who is at the extremes of high novelty-

---

1. The term "reward-dependence" may be confusing in light of the research linking dopamine to addictive states. In Cloninger's model, reward-dependence refers to the trait of social inhibition, in which reward-dependent indi-

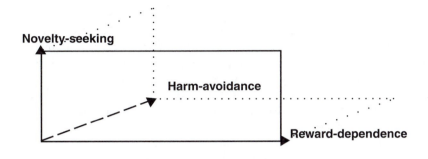

FIG. 9.1.
Three-dimensional
model of character
and temperament.

seeking, low harm-avoidance, and low reward-dependence might have antisocial personality disorder.

Cloninger's model is open to criticism. Is temperament really composed of only three dimensions? Given the complexity of the human brain, might there not be an infinite variety of possible dimensions to human personality? Cloninger's model argues that these are the dimensions seen in animals in general, and thus reflect a cluster of core traits common to all animal species, including humans.

But there is by no means universal agreement about what exactly constitutes a personality disorder, or even that personality disorders are actually valid diagnostic categories. Some claim that all personality disorders are actually variations of other disorders. H's borderline personality disorder bore a suspicious resemblance to very rapid-cycling bipolar disorder, and individuals in the midst of episodes of depression often look like they have personality disorders until the mood disorder is successfully treated, at which point they no longer look personality-disordered. Such resemblance has led some to speculate, for example, that borderline personality is a variant of bipolar disorder rather than a disorder of personality. The diagnostic criteria for the personality disorders are quite nonspecific. While the diagnostic agreement of clinicians assessing for other psychiatric disorders, such as schizophrenia or major depression, approaches 95%, for personality disorders diagnostic agreement is only about 60% (Guze, 1997). Although H probably best fit the description of borderline personality disorder, he also had symptoms of narcissistic and paranoid personality disorders. Most individuals diagnosed with a personality disorder meet criteria for more than one. Thus, it may be argued, personality disorders are perhaps not discrete disorders at all, but are unusual manifestations of other known psychiatric syndromes or possibly unknown entities altogether.

An opposing argument is that personality disorders usually do not respond to the typical treatments for other mental disorders. De-

---

viduals are inhibited and need predictable social rewards, while novelty-seeking is regulated by dopamine. Thus, the substance-addicted individual would be seen as seeking high novelty stimulus through dopaminergic substances.

spite the resemblance of borderline personality disorder to bipolar disorder, for example, attempts to treat borderline personality disorder with therapies such as lithium—a very successful treatment for bipolar disorder—have been disappointing. This may prove nothing more than that borderline personality disorder is an extremely unusual variety of bipolar disorder and so lacks the same robust response to medications like lithium. But it might also mean that borderline personality is a different disorder entirely.

These difficulties do not make the diagnosis of a personality disorder a trivial matter. Specific treatments for personality disorders, usually in the form of psychotherapy, do exist. But despite intriguing evidence of a biological basis for personality, consistently useful biological interventions for disorders of personality remain elusive.

Key points

- *Personality disorders* are disorders in characteristic patterns of understanding the self and interacting with the world.

- Personality disorders are divided into three clusters: Cluster A, the odd and eccentric; Cluster B, the dramatic, emotional and erratic; and cluster C, the anxious and avoidant.

- *Cluster-A personality disorders* are the paranoid, schizoid, and schizotypal.

- *Cluster-B personality disorders* are the borderline, antisocial, narcissistic, and histrionic.

- *Cluster-C personality disorders* are the avoidant, dependent, and obsessive-compulsive.

- Personality diagnoses are controversial, but there is clearly a biological substrate to personality.

Other psychiatric disorders 10

The previous chapters have reviewed the most common and best understood mental disorders. But there remain several groups of disorders that are less common and less well-understood neurobiologically.

Eating disorders

The eating disorders include anorexia nervosa—which is characterized by caloric restriction, disturbed body image, and low body weight—and bulimia nervosa, characterized by episodes of binge eating with compensatory behavior.

Anorexia nervosa is characterized by caloric restriction, disturbed body image, and low body weight.

Anorexia nervosa

The cardinal feature of anorexia nervosa is a preoccupation with weight and a conviction that one is overweight (a type of body dysmorphism, the conviction that one's body is severely defective in some way), resulting in a failure to maintain 85% of ideal body weight. Anorexia nervosa occurs in about 4% of the U.S. population, with a 10 to 20:1 female-to-male ratio (American Psychiatric Association, 1994). It is much more common in developed countries than in developing nations.

DSM-IV criteria for anorexia nervosa

    A. Refusal to maintain body weight at or above a minimally normal weight for age and height (e.g., weight loss leading to maintenance of body weight less than 85% of that expected; or failure to make expected weight gain during period of growth, leading to body weight less than 85% of that expected).

    B. Intense fear of gaining weight or becoming fat, even though underweight.

C. Disturbance in the way in which one's body weight or shape is experienced, undue influence of body weight or shape on self-evaluation, or denial of the seriousness of the current low body weight.

D. In postmenarcheal females, amenorrhea, i.e., the absence of at least three consecutive menstrual cycles. (A woman is considered to have amenorrhea if her periods occur only following hormones, e.g., estrogen administration).

Reprinted with permission from the *Diagnostic and Statistical Manual of Mental Disorders,* Fourth Edition. Copyright 1994, American Psychiatric Association.

Anorexic behavior may be limited to caloric restriction (restricting subtype), or may include binge eating and compensatory purging (by vomiting, diuretic or laxative use, or severe exercise—the binge eating/purging subtype). Anorexia nervosa is commonly comorbid with other psychiatric disorders, with a mood disorder prevalence of up to 84%.

It is important to distinguish anorexia nervosa from *anorexia secondary to general medical conditions.* Tumors, including hypothalamic tumors, can cause weight loss, as can endocrine disorders (particularly diabetes mellitus, hyperthyroidism, and Addison's disease); gastrointestinal disorders, such as malabsorption syndromes; and infections, such as HIV and tuberculosis. Weight loss caused by these conditions, however, is rarely associated with a desire to lose weight or with the body dysmorphism of anorexia nervosa.

Endocrine abnormalities usually are evident. The starvation of anorexia nervosa results in amenorrhea, hypercortisolemia, suppression of thyroid function, and reversible enlargement of the cerebral ventricles. Mortality is high (5%–18%), usually from arrhythmias resulting from hypokalemia (Sadock & Sadock, 2000).

The pathophysiology of anorexia nervosa is not well-understood. Genetic studies have been largely equivocal. However, serotonergic neurotransmission has been implicated. Serotonin is crucial in regulating animal feeding. High doses of serotonergic antidepressants (such as fluoxetine at 80 mg. a day) have demonstrated efficacy in reducing the symptoms of anorexia nervosa. Some evidence for the effectiveness of amitriptyline in doses of 160 mg. per day also has been found (Biederman et al., 1985; Halmi, Eckert, LaDu, & Cohen, 1986).

Case example

Ms. K, age 28, was admitted to the hospital weighing only 58 pounds. At 5 feet 7 inches, this represented a life-threatening degree of malnutrition. Despite this, K persisted in the belief that she was overweight. She had long since stopped menstruating and was so thin she could no longer walk. Hair loss was advanced, and her serum potassium level was 2.7 mEq/L. Even after regaining a satisfactory weight, K continued to regard herself primarily through the dimension of her weight. Any other qualities she might possess were meaningless if she failed to keep her weight below an arbitrary upper limit.

Bulimia nervosa

Bulimia nervosa is characterized by episodes of binge eating, usually of carbohydrates. This is accompanied by compensatory efforts such as vomiting, laxative use, diuretic use, severe exercise, and dieting.

Bulimia nervosa is characterized by episodes of binge eating followed by compensatory behavior such as purging, severe exercise, and dieting.

DSM-IV criteria for bulimia nervosa

A. Recurrent episodes of binge eating. An episode of binge eating is characterized by both the following:

   (1) eating, in a discrete period of time, (e.g., within any 2-hour period), an amount of food that is definitely larger than most people would eat during a similar period of time and under similar circumstances

   (2) a sense of lack of control over eating during the episode (e.g., a feeling that one cannot stop eating or control what or how much one is eating)

B. Recurrent inappropriate compensatory behavior in order to prevent weight gain, such as self-induced vomiting; misuse of laxatives, diuretics, enemas, or other medications; fasting; or excessive exercise.

C. The binge eating and inappropriate compensatory behaviors both occur, on average, at least twice a week for 3 months.

D. Self-evaluation is unduly influenced by body shape and weight.

E. The disturbance does not occur exclusively during episodes of Anorexia Nervosa.

   Reprinted with permission from the *Diagnostic and Statistical Manual of Mental Disorders*, Fourth Edition. Copyright 1994, American Psychiatric Association.

As in anorexia nervosa, medical complications of bulimia nervosa are common and include parotitis, dental erosion, hypokalemia, hypomagnesemia, and metabolic alkalosis.

It is estimated that between 1% and 3% of women experience bulimia nervosa in their lives (American Psychiatric Association, 1994). However, perhaps 40% or more of college women have experienced binge eating and purging (Sadock & Sadock, 2000). The pathophysiology of bulimia nervosa is poorly understood but seems to involve disturbances in sertonergic neurotransmission. Like anorexia nervosa, bulimia nervosa responds to serotonergic antidepressants, such as fluoxetine (Fluoxetine Bulimia Nervosa Collaborative Study Group, 1992). Evidence for the effectiveness of trazodone, TCAs, and MAOIs also has been found (Pope, Keck, McElroy, & Hudson, 1989; Walsh, Gladis, Roose, Stewart, Stetner, & Glassman, 1988).

Case example

Ms. F, a college student, was preoccupied with her weight and watched her diet carefully. Despite this, she remained somewhat overweight. More disturbing to her, she began to experience periodic urges to ingest large amounts of carbohydrates. This often occurred at night or during times of stress. During these episodes, F would eat entire boxes of cookies, a quart of ice cream, or perhaps an entire pizza. Overcome with shame, she would then induce vomiting. The next day, she would redouble her efforts to lose weight, restricting her caloric intake and exercising heavily.

Insomnia is the prolonged abnormal inability to obtain adequate sleep.

Sleep disorders

Normal sleep

Normal sleep is 6 to 9 hours in length. Normal sleep architecture is described using EEG findings from the polysomnogram:

Stage 1	5% of sleep	3–7 hertz (theta waves)
Stage 2	45% of sleep	12–14 hertz (beta waves)
Stage 3	10% of sleep	1–3 hertz (delta waves)
Stage 4	15% of sleep	1–3 hertz (delta waves)
REM	25% of sleep	low-voltage sawtooth, rapid eye movements, dreams

Dyssomnias

Primary insomnia. This diagnosis is arrived at after eliminating general medical causes of insomnia, substance-induced insomnia, and other psychiatric disorders that cause insomnia (particularly mood and anxiety disorders). Primary insomnia usually is treated first with sleep hygiene measures, and then with hypnotic agents such as benzodiazepines if required.

Sleep hygiene includes being in bed only for sleep or sex; regular bed and rising times; no naps; no alcohol or caffeine of any kind; quiet activities in the evening; smaller meals in the evening; regular exercise, but not within 2 hours of sleep time; and using relaxation techniques.

Primary hypersomnia. Primary hypersomnia consists of excessive daytime somnolence with periods of unrefreshing sleep and shortened sleep latency (time to sleep after lying down). The primary treatment is stimulant medication such as methylphenidate (Ritalin) or dextroamphetamine (Dexedrine) (Janicek et al., 1997).

Primary hypersomnia consists of excessive daytime somnolence with periods of unrefreshing sleep and shortened sleep latency.

Narcolepsy. Narcolepsy involves daytime attacks of refreshing sleep that can occur even in dangerous settings, with either cataplexy (sudden loss of muscle tone) or hypnogogic (falling asleep)/hypnopompic (awakening) hallucinations. Like primary hypersomnia, narcolepsy is treated primarily with stimulant medications.

Parasomnias

Nightmares. Nightmares are terrifying dreams produced during REM sleep. They are not usually treated pharmacologically.

Sleepwalking. Sleepwalking is the occurrence of walking and other habitual activities (driving, cooking, etc.) during stage 3–4 sleep. Sleepwalking can be treated with the benzodiazepine *diazepam*.

Narcolepsy involves daytime attacks of refreshing sleep that occur even in dangerous settings.

Sleep terrors. Sleep terrors are unremembered episodes of screaming during stage 3–4 sleep. Sleep terrors can be treated with diazepam.

Disorders of childhood

Attention-deficit hyperactivity disorder

Attention-deficit hyperactivity disorder (ADHD) is thought to occur in about 3% to 6% of the population. Although ADHD always appears in early childhood, perhaps 25% of individuals with the disorder will have persistent symptoms into adulthood. It is more common in boys (by a 3 to 5:1 male-to-female ratio, according to the American Psychiatric Association, 1994). The characteristic symptoms are inattention, hyperactivity, or both.

DSM-IV criteria for ADHD

A. Either (1) or (2):

   (1) Six or more of the following symptoms of *inattention* have persisted for at least 6 months to a degree that is maladaptive and inconsistent with developmental level:

   ### *Inattention*

   (a) often fails to give close attention to details or makes careless mistakes in schoolwork, work, or other activities

   (b) often has difficulty in sustaining attention in tasks or play activities

   (c) often does not seem to listen when spoken to directly

   (d) often does not follow through on instruction and fails to finish schoolwork, chores, or duties in the workplace (not due to oppositional behavior or failure to understand instructions)

   (e) often has difficulty organizing tasks and activities

   (f) often avoids, dislikes, or is reluctant to engage in tasks that require sustained mental effort (such as schoolwork or homework)

   (g) often loses things necessary for tasks or activities (e.g., toys, school assignments, pencils, books, or tools)

   (h) is often forgetful in daily activities

   (2) Six (or more) of the following symptoms of *hyperactivity-impulsivity* have persisted for at least 6 months to a degree that is maladaptive and inconsistent with developmental level:

   ### *Hyperactivity*

   (a) often fidgets with hands or feet or squirms in seat

   (b) often leaves seat in classroom or in other situations in which remaining seated is expected

(c) often runs about or climbs excessively in situations in which it is inappropriate (in adolescents or adults, may be limited to subjective feelings of restlessness)

(d) often has difficulty playing or engaging in leisure activities quietly

(e) is often "on the go" or often acts as if "driven by a motor"

(f) often talks excessively

Impulsivity

(g) often blurts out answers before questions have been completed

(h) often has difficulty awaiting turn

(i) often interrupts or intrudes on others (e.g., butts into conversations or games)

B. Some hyperactive-impulsive or inattentive symptoms that caused impairment were present before age 7 years.

C. Some impairment from the symptoms is present in two or more settings (e.g., at school [or work] and at home).

D. There must be clear evidence of clinically significant impairment in social, academic, or occupational functioning.

E. The symptoms do not occur exclusively during the course of a Pervasive Developmental Disorder, Schizophrenia, or other Psychotic Disorder, and are not better accounted for by another mental disorder (e.g., Mood Disorder, Anxiety Disorder, Dissociative Disorder, or a Personality Disorder).

Reprinted with permission from the *Diagnostic and Statistical Manual of Mental Disorders*, Fourth Edition. Copyright 1994, American Psychiatric Association.

ADHD was first described after a wave of viral infections in the 1920s led to a syndrome known as "minimal brain disorder." The symptoms of this disorder are now recognized to be ADHD. Although structural abnormalities are not evident on brain imaging or post-mortem studies, functional imaging such as positron emission tomography (PET) has demonstrated that individuals with ADHD have decreased regional blood flow and hypoactive metabolism in the frontal lobes (Rubia, Overmeyer, Taylor, Brammer, Williams, & Simmons, 1999). It is thought that frontal hypometabolism may cause failure of the frontal lobes to inhibit indiscriminate behavior and to focus attention. The decrease in frontal lobe activity seen in individuals with ADHD may be the result of alterations in dopaminergic neurotransmission. The addition of stimulant medications—such as methylphenidate (Ritalin), dextroamphetamine (Dexedrine), dextro/levoamphet-amine (Adderall), and pemoline (Cylert)—increases the activity of the dopaminergic tract in the brain, since all stimulants either block the reuptake of dopamine or increase the rate of its release. Some benefit also has been obtained through the use of dopaminergic antidepressants such as bupropion (Wellbutrin).

Some have questioned whether diet, parenting, or other environmental factors may be implicated in the pathogenesis of ADHD. Diet—especially a diet high in sugar—has been studied extensively and has not been shown to be associated with symptoms of ADHD (Wolraich et al., 1995). Although environmental factors undoubtedly play a role in the development of ADHD, heritability has been shown in twin studies to be 80% (Farone & Biederman, 1999). Although behavioral psychotherapy is useful in treating ADHD, studies have shown medications to be more effective (MTA Cooperative Group, 2000).

Case example

Ms. B came to treatment at the age of 40. She reported a lifetime of problems with organization. She was always late, and no matter what she set out to do, she seemed to accomplish little. If she decided to work on the computer, in a matter of minutes, having just started the first task, she would become distracted by a second, and then a third. Ultimately, she would start several projects and finish none of them. Reading was difficult; despite her obvious intelligence, B could hardly finish a page before her mind was elsewhere. Sitting through a movie was impossible for her. As a child, B had been a daydreamer. Her report cards from that period remarked on her inattentiveness. Neither B nor her parents recalled any symptoms of hyperactivity as a child.

B's symptoms led to severe difficulties with her husband, who found her behavior frustrating and considered her lack of accomplishment a sign of laziness. When treated with the stimulant medication dextroamphetamine, however, her symptoms improved miraculously.

Mental retardation

Mental retardation is defined as intelligence in the lower first percentile, which corresponds roughly to an IQ of less than 70, appearing before adulthood. An IQ of roughly 70 to 85 is considered borderline intellectual functioning.

DSM-IV criteria for mental retardation

A. Significantly subaverage intellectual functioning: an IQ of approximately 70 or below on an individually administered IQ test (for infants, a clinical judgment of significantly subaverage intellectual functioning).

B. Concurrent deficits or impairments in present adaptive functioning (i.e., the person's effectiveness in meeting the standards expected for his or her age by his or her cultural group) in at least two of the following areas: communication, self-care, home living, social/interpersonal skills, use of community resources, self-direction, functional academic skills, work, leisure, health, and safety.

C. The onset is before 18 years.

Reprinted with permission from the ***Diagnostic and Statistical Manual of Mental Disorders***, Fourth Edition. Copyright 1994, American Psychiatric Association.

Mental retardation is defined as intelligence in the lower first percentile appearing before adulthood.

The *DSM-IV* distinguishes between four degrees of mental retardation.

Mild (85%): IQ of 55 to 70; education to late grade school; may be self-supporting, but often require guidance.

Moderate (10%): IQ of 35–40 to 50–55; education to early grade school; usually live in supervised situations, can perform some work under supervision.

Severe (3%–4%): IQ or 20–25 to 35–40; limited communication.

Profound (1%–2%): IQ below 20–25; often nonverbal with severe sensorimotor impairments.

Pathogenesis of mental retardation.   The causes of mental retardation are many, and include:

Chromosomal abnormalities, such as Down's syndrome (trisomy 21), Turner's syndrome (XO), and Kleinfelter's syndrome (XXY).

Genetic disorders, such as neurofibromatosis and tuberous sclerosis.

Metabolic disorders, such as phenylketonuria, galactosemia, and Wilson's disease.

Trauma, including perinatal trauma, cerebral palsy, infections, accidents, and tumors.

Autism and Asperger's syndrome

Autism.   Autism is a relatively rare developmental syndrome (prevalence 4 in 1,000) that is characterized by impaired communication, inhibited social interaction, and impoverishment of behaviors and interests. Language acquisition is delayed and communication often is characterized by idiosyncracy, echolalia (repetition of others' words), errors in prosody (tone and inflection that carry emotional valence), and grammatical errors such as pronoun reversal. Parents often notice that the autistic child seems disinterested in social interaction. The autistic child may appear to be unattached to the parents and usually avoids eye contact. Empathy and social reciprocity are lacking. Interests tend to be nonhuman and idiosyncratic, such as a preoccupation with lists or numbers. About 75% of autistic children are mentally retarded (American Psychiatric Association, 1994).

Autism is characterized by impaired communication, inhibited social interaction, and impoverishment of behaviors and interests.

The cause of autism is not known. Autistic individuals have high levels of perinatal complications, but as yet no definitive causal link has been described. The concordance of autism is greater in monozygotic twins than in dizygotic twins, and nonautistic relatives of autistic individuals may show some evidence of linguistic impairment.

Neuroanatomically, autism is associated with abnormally decreased numbers of Purkinje's cells in the cerebellum (Ritvo et al., 1986), and autistic states have been described in individuals who have incurred damage to the temporal lobes. In animals, destruction of the temporal lobes may lead to repetitive behaviors and loss of social interaction skills.

Biochemically, disordered metabolism of both dopamine (as evidenced by increased cerebrospinal fluid levels of the dopamine metabolite homovanillic acid, or HVA) and serotonin have been observed (Fein, Joy, Green, & Waterhouse, 1996).

Asperger's syndrome.   Asperger's syndrome is similar to autism in that individuals with Asperger's syndrome evidence impaired social interaction skills (characterized by a lack of social reciprocity and empathy and a seeming inability to comprehend nonverbal communication) and idiosyncratic, nonhuman interests. Verbal communication, however, is intact, and individuals with Asperger's syndrome may show any level of intellectual ability, from mental retardation to superior.

The cause of Asperger's syndrome is not known. Because individuals with Asperger's syndrome have intact semantic linguistic ability but impaired nonverbal communication skills, it is hypothesized to be a nondominant hemisphere disorder; as the dominant hemisphere processes semantic language, nonverbal communication such as prosody is a nondominant hemisphere function (Fein et al., 1996). Individuals with Asperger's syndrome may respond to serotonergic agents, which can reduce social anxiety.

Case example

Mr. C was brought in by his parents at the age of 19. The purpose of the evaluation was to determine why C seemed to have no friends and little ambition. He seemed content to spend all his time watching television, often for 16 hours a day or more. Indeed, television was one of only two topics that C felt like discussing. He also was obsessed with license plates, and he spent a great deal of time carefully cataloguing license plate numbers he observed. C was superficially friendly and was of average intelligence. He had finished high school, although he had not performed exceptionally. However, he evidenced severe deficits in nonverbal communication and social awareness. When asked to stand what he considered a comfortable speaking distance from the examiner, C stood across the room and seemed oblivious to the oddity of this distance for social interaction. He lacked any empathy whatsoever, and even with coaching could only barely be coaxed to ask what another person was feeling. He admitted that the concept seemed alien to him. C quickly became anxious in social situations and would immediately turn the topic back to television programs.

Asberger's syndrome is characterized by impaired social interaction skills and idiosyncratic, nonhuman interests.

Conduct disorder

Conduct disorder is characterized by repeated transgression of the rights of others and the violation of social norms. Individuals with conduct disorder have a repetitive history of violence toward others, damage to property, theft, and rule violation.

The neurobiology of conduct disorder is not well-understood. ADHD is more common in conduct-disordered children (American Psychiatric Association, 1994). Lower levels of noradrenergic functioning may be associated with the disorder. Low cerebrospinal fluid levels of the serotonin metabolite 5-hydroxyindolacetic acid (5-HIAA) have been correlated with aggression (Brown et al., 1979; Linnoila et al., 1983) and may be found in some conduct disordered children.

Somatization disorder is characterized by multiple simultaneous physical symptoms that lack a definitive general medical etiology.

Somatoform disorders

The somatoform disorders are characterized by the presence of physical symptoms that lack a definitive medical explanation. The primary cause

Conversion disorder is the unconscious production of a physical symptom to solve an unconscious conflict.

is thought to be psychological, and somatization will be discussed further in Part 3 of this book. The somatoform disorders respond primarily to psychological treatment and the minimization of unnecessary medical care. Several somatoform syndromes are described below.

Somatization disorder

Somatization disorder is characterized by the presence of multiple simultaneous physical symptoms lacking a definitive general medical etiology. The *DSM-IV* requires four pain symptoms, two gastrointestinal symptoms, one pseudoneurological symptom, and one sexual symptom to diagnose this disorder.

Conversion disorder

Conversion disorder is the unconscious production of a physical symptom (often neurological) to solve an unconscious conflict. (The concept of the unconscious will be discussed in detail in Part 3.) For current purposes, in conversion disorder the symptom is not intentionally produced but, instead, is the result of anxiety that cannot be managed except by the production of a physical symptom. For example, someone with aggressive impulses might become unable to walk, ostensibly because of a stroke. However, upon examination, the strength deficits do not fit known neurological patterns. It is critical to thoroughly evaluate the patient for possible medical etiologies before diagnosing a conversion disorder.

Somatoform pain disorder is disporportionate distress and disability in response to a given disorder.

Somatoform pain disorder

Somatoform pain disorder is characterized by distress and disability that are disproportionate to the pain that could be produced by a given disorder. Since pain is an entirely subjective phenomenon, this diagnosis can be difficult to make.

Hypochondriasis

Hypochondriasis is the preoccupation that one has a particular illness. Hypochondriacal fears cannot be assuaged by unrevealing medical workups. (If the preoccupation becomes frankly delusional, then delusional disorder is diagnosed.)

Hypochondriasis is the preoccupation that one has a particular illness.

Body dysmorphism

Body dysmorphism is the preoccupation that a particular body part is defective. It often is comorbid with eating disorders.

Factitious disorder

In factitious disorder, symptoms are intentionally feigned so that the individual may assume the role of one who is sick. In this role, the individual is exempted from usual expectations and is cared for.

Malingering

Malingering is the intentional feigning of symptoms so that a secondary objective—such as staying out of jail or collecting insurance—may be met.

Dissociative disorders

Dissociation is a phenomenon in which the usual sense of the self as a single, well-structured state of consciousness is lost, so that the individual becomes confused about his or her identity. In dissociative states, the self is not perceived as integrated into a unitary personality. Dissociation often is the result of general medical conditions. The biological cause of primary dissociative disorders is not well understood. Descriptions of several primary dissociative disorders follow.

Dissociative amnesia

Dissociative amnesia is the loss of recall for personal information. The areas of loss are not accompanied by other cognitive deficits usually seen in the cognitive disorders such as dementia.

Dissociative fugue

In a fugue state, a person will travel and assume a new identity while forgetting her formal identity. Fugue states typically are transient, but occasionally they last for years and involve the formation of an entirely new life.

Dissociative identity disorder

This controversial disorder, formerly called "multiple personality disorder," involves the formation of more than one personality within a single individual. Typically, the primary (or host) personality does not have conscious awareness of the presence of other personalities. Some researchers believe this disorder to be either factitious/malingered or the result of inappropriate psychotherapy with suggestible subjects. Other

Body dysmorphism is the preoccupation that a body part is defective.

Factitious disorder is an intentional feigning of symptoms to assume the role of someone who is sick.

Malingering is the feigning of symptoms to obtain a secondary objective.

In *dissociation* the usual sense of self as a unitary state of consciousness is lost.

Dissociative amnesia is the loss of recall for personal information.

investigators find that distinct personalities clearly emerge in some individuals, to the point that eyesight and handedness may change (Sadock & Sadock, 2000). When dissociative identity disorder is present, there is almost always a history of childhood abuse (Steele, 1990).

Case example

Ms. V presented with complaints of depression and was successfully treated with an antidepressant medication. However, as treatment progressed, she revealed a lifetime history of unusual complaints. V would lose periods of time and often found herself in unfamiliar locations, unsure of how she got there. She would find items of clothing in her wardrobe that she did not recall buying. Her handwriting would change considerably in the course of a paragraph. Her husband and friends reported that she often abruptly changed, usually acting either as a small child or as an angry, defensive woman. V had no recollection of these shifts, which were also confirmed by her therapist.

In a dissociative fugue state, a person may travel and assume a new identity while forgetting his formal identity.

Depersonalization disorder

Depersonalization, the sense that one is unsure who one is, is a common phenomenon, but may become pervasive and cause severe disturbances.

Dissociative identity disorder is the formation of more than one personality in a single individual.

Sexual disorders

The sexual disorders may be categorized as either disturbances in sexual functioning or disturbances related to sexuality (parasexual disorders).

Sexual dysfunction

Broadly speaking, there are four phases of sexual functioning. Disturbances in these areas often are related to the effects of general medical conditions (particularly neurological disorders such as multiple sclerosis and stroke, endocrine disorders such as diabetes, peripheral vascular disease, and medication side effects), but they may also be primary. Dysfunction may been seen the first three stages of sexual functioning.

Depersonalization is the sense that one is unsure of who one is.

1. ***Excitement.*** This involves erection or vaginal vasocongestion and lubrication. The disorders of sexual excitement include *hypoactive sexual desire, erectile dysfuntion,* and *female arousal disorder.*

2. **Plateau**: Sexual stimulation leads to increased excitement and preparation for orgasm. *Dyspareunia* is pain with intercourse, whereas *vaginsimus* is the contraction of the outer third of the vagina, preventing penetration.

3) **Orgasm**: This involves either male ejaculation or female orgasm. Disorders of orgasm include *premature ejaculation, delayed ejaculation*, and *anorgasmia*.

4) **Resolution**: This is the quiescent phase after orgasm. Females remain sexually responsive, while males enter a "refractory period" during which arousal is impossible.

Paraphilias

Individuals with paraphilias require the presence of a nonsexual object in order to achieve sexual arousal. The paraphilias include these:

Exhibitionism is the need for exposure of the genitals to strangers for sexual arousal.

Fetishism is the need for stimulation using nonliving items.

Pedophilia is sexual attraction to children, either heterosexual or homosexual.

The biological basis of the paraphilias is not known.

Impulse-control disorders

The hallmark of the impulse control disorders is the experience of an irresistible impulse to act in a certain manner that leads to impairment.

Kleptomania is characterized by repetitive stealing of unnecessary objects.

Pyromania is characterized by repetitive fire setting.

Trichotillomania is characterized by repetitive hair-pulling.

Pathological gambling is characterized by repetitive gambling despite serious adverse outcomes.

Exhibitionism is the need to expose one's genitals to strangers for sexual arousal.

Fetishism is the need for stimulation using nonliving items.

Pedophilia is sexual attraction to children.

Kleptomania is the repetitive stealing of unnecessary items.

Pyromania is repetitive fire setting.

Intermittent explosive disorder is characterized by impulsive aggression toward others or objects.

The impulse-control disorders are not well-understood. There is some evidence that they may be related to OCD (Cohen, Simeon, Hollander, & Stein, 1997). Trichotillomania has an animal analog in compulsive parrot feather-pulling and, like OCD, responds to serotonergic antidepressant medications. There is growing evidence that pathological gambling and kleptomania also may respond to serotonergic antidepressants (Sadock & Sadock, 2000).

Trichotillomania is repetitive hair pulling.

Key points

- *Anorexia nervosa* and *bulimia nervosa* appear to result from dysfunction in serotonergic neurotransmission, and may respond to serotonergic medications.

Pathological gambling is repetitive gambling, despite serious adverse outcomes.

- *Attention-deficit hyperactivity disorder* may arise from an underactive prefrontal cortex and responds to stimulant medications such as methylphenidate and dextroamphetamine.

- *Autism* and *Asperger's syndrome* result in deficits in social functioning, idiosyncratic nonhuman interests, and (in the former) language deficits.

- The neurobiology of *somatoform* and *dissociative disorders* is poorly understood.

Intermittent explosive disorder is impulsive aggression toward others.

- The *impulse control disorders* may be related to obsessive-compulsive disorder and may respond to serotonergic medications.

Psychological models III

Introduction to psychological models 11

We have examined the neurobiology underlying the mental disorders. The psychological models of mental illness propose that mental states arise from antecedent mental states. Thus, earlier states of thought, feeling, perception, behavior, and cognition lead to future states. The psychodynamic psychologies examine how pathological mental states arise from unconscious wishes, fantasies, and beliefs. The cognitive-behavioral models focus on how conceptual assumptions and patterns of behavior shape psychopathology.

Psychodynamic psychologies examine how pathological mental states arise from unconsious wishes, fantasies, and beliefs.

Case example

Mr. F was 23 years old and complained of obsessions and compulsions. He worried constantly about the possibility of contamination and went to great lengths to avoid circumstances that seemed to present this risk. He could not touch garbage. Boxes in storage remained unpacked, since he worried that opening them would release mold or fungus.

F was highly intelligent and widely read, and in an anthropology class had come across the story of the Egyptologists who had unwittingly become exposed to aspergillous fungus after opening ancient tombs, subsequently succumbing to what was then thought to be "the curse of the mummy." F could not touch many things, including payphones (who knew what germs lurked on the mouthpiece?) and coins (who knew where they had been?). Public restrooms were out of the question, and he endured many excruciating hours delaying toilet use until he could reach the safety of his home.

F had been treated with the drug clomipramine, with some success. However, his level of functioning had gradually deteriorated over the years. F had finished high school and then become involved in a lengthy relationship with an older woman. When she left him, his life began a downward spiral. He dropped out of college, lost his job, and financial difficulties forced him to live with his mother again. This was a strained relationship. F had always

Cognitive-behavioral psychologies focus on how conceptual assumptions and patterns of behavior shape psycho-pathology.

experienced his mother as having what he called (in an intellectu-alized way) "poor boundaries." She had involved F in the intimate details of her emotional life since he had been a small child. F viv-idly remembered hearing of his mother and father's marital diffi-culties, including sexual problems, at the age of 4. His parents were now divorced, and F's mother was lonely and looked to him for companionship in a way that seemed to lack reciprocity. Their con-versation was never about F's thoughts and feelings, he said, and so he felt used by his mother. This left him feeling enraged, al-though he usually disavowed that this was so.

F only gradually admitted to angry feelings, and then with great shame. After becoming angry with his psychiatrist during a session, he returned for the next appointment afraid the psychia-trist thought he was "a pain in the ass" and might not want to continue treating him. In other words, the expected penalty for expressing anger in F's mind was abandonment.

F had extreme difficulty with relationships in general. He was nervous and shy. He looked scared much of the time, almost as if he expected to be struck. Upon first meeting F, the psychiatrist felt afraid of disrupting his equilibrium. Immediately, F expressed a fear of what clomipramine, despite its benefits, might be doing to his brain, even though he had been taking it with apparent good effect. "Who knows what could happen after 20 years?" he said. "It might be safe so far, but . . . "

Switching medications proved difficult, since every choice aroused in F the same fear. When taken off all medications, he be-came even more anxious and depressed and his obsessions wors-ened. Concerned, he agreed to try a new medication, but he took only one dose before expressing a wish to return to clomipramine. Attempts at a form of psychotherapy called *behavioral therapy* (the psychological treatment of choice for OCD, which requires expos-ing the patient to what he fears) were started. But F abandoned this treatment after only one session, even though that session pro-duced immediate benefits. Gradually, F began to miss treatment sessions, despite a staunch avowal that he wanted to "get my life turned around."

When confronted with his pattern of missing appointments and foregoing beneficial treatment, F began missing even more, usually canceling at the last moment. His bill went unpaid. Gradu-ally, the psychiatrist found himself angry with F. The situation came to a head when he insisted that F attend sessions regularly or treat-ment could not continue. F took offense at this, ostensibly on the grounds that his disorder (OCD) made it impossible that any de-mands be placed on him, since his brain was not reliable.

It then dawned on the psychiatrist that F was exquisitely sen-sitive to anyone using him for their own purposes, even the apparently benign requirement that he participate in a treatment plan designed by him for his own benefit. Realizing he had to relinquish all control if treatment was to proceed, the psychiatrist told F that he could come as he wished, and the two of them would deal with the consequences on a day-to-day basis. F agreed, and for the next months he never missed a session.

Together they reviewed his treatment plan. Behavior therapy was not what he needed, F said. Instead, his loneliness and sense of claustrophobia at his mother's house necessitated that the therapy hour be spent simply talking, so as to ground him in reality, which he felt at times was slipping away from him in a sea of anxiety and depression. As the therapist worked with F in this manner, further details of his obsessions came to light. F's greatest fear, the therapist discovered, was that he would fail to maintain certain rituals and that, as a result, something catastrophic would befall his mother. As is often the case with OCD, F had no worries about the dangers of contamination to himself. Reinstituting the clomipramine provided some relief from this obsession and its resulting compulsion to avoid contamination.

Amazingly, total relief came abruptly one day when F's mother was hospitalized with severe food poisoning. With his mother in the hospital, F suddenly found himself entirely free of his obsessions, and indeed of all depression as well. F seemed to have been using obsessive worry about harming his mother as a defense against a destructive rage, a wish to destroy his mother that percolated constantly inside him. Because F believed that his anger, if expressed, would result in abandonment, he kept it carefully sequestered from conscious awareness by obsessing about harming his mother inadvertently. Now that his unconscious wish that his mother be harmed had come true, he no longer had to defend himself against the awareness of that wish by using obsessions and compulsions. Predictably, when F's mother recovered, F was again besieged by obsessive worry and depression.

The examination of F's case forces us to reconsider what it means to say someone has a "biological" illness. F had an obvious pathological dysfunction of his central nervous system—OCD. Yet he was only partially responsive to medication. The true treatment successes occurred primarily from interpersonal interactions that led to a shift in his mental state. For example, his mother's hospitalization led to a change in conflicts about angry feelings toward her, which resulted in symptom resolution. Unfortunately, his relief lasted only as long as the change in circumstances. As soon as his mother came home, he began to suffer again.

This in no way implies that what F was thinking and feeling did not have a biological underpinning. In the biopsychosocial model, mental states always have an organic substrate underlying them. The very treatment F rejected—behavioral therapy—has been shown to result in the same functional anatomical changes visible on PET scans (which measure blood flow and energy metabolism) as the administration of a drug like clomipramine (Baxter et al., 1992). These are profound results. They imply that changing psychological states can itself be a biological intervention.

But the neuroanatomical basis of mental states is not known in detail. It is apparent that the process of having a mental state is vastly complex, occurring not at a specific anatomic location but diffusely across the nervous system, involving many neural networks, including those we have already talked about such as the dopaminergic, serotonergic, noradrenergic, and cholinergic pathways. It may never be known in precise detail exactly what is transpiring at the cellular and tissue levels in a given individual's immediate thoughts and feelings. This lack implies that we need a different vocabulary than the purely biological to describe psychological states.

In addition, it is clear that the biological interventions available to F were capable of doing him only as much good as he would allow. F's biological problems (i.e., dysregulation of serotonergic neurotransmission, resulting in OCD) and psychological problems (i.e., unconscious conflict) combined to resist attempts to intervene directly at the cellular level with medications and behavioral therapy. Until F could be engaged in treatment—for example by proving to him that the psychiatrist was willing to relinquish control of the therapy to him—he could not participate to his own benefit.

Psychological models operate on the presumption that mental states cause other mental states. Sigmund Freud's drive theory, as we will see, proposes that anxiety arises from dangerous wishes and fantasies. Cognitive psychology holds that depression is the result of our interpretation of the meaning of events. Behavioral psychology claims that all behaviors are learned from previous behavior. In each case, one mental state is presumed to cause another. No mention is made of the biology underlying the mental states in question.

There are virtually as many psychologies of the mind as there are human beings. We all operate with a sense of what makes other people tick and so, in a sense, we each have our own psychological theory about minds. Sometimes this is explicitly stated; other times it may simply be an intuitive response to others that is never articulated but that underlies and informs our thoughts and actions. Human history, particularly in the twentieth century, is replete with attempts to systematically elucidate what it is that makes human psychology operate. The psychologies of Sigmund Freud, Alfred Adler, Carl Jung, Eric Erikson, Melanie Klein, Anna Freud, Margaret Mahler, Donald Winnicott, and Heinz Kohut—as well as various other behavioral and cognitive psychologies—are all twentieth-century attempts at a scientific explanation. If we include religious psychologies such as Christianity, Islam, Judaism, Hinduism, and

Buddhism and the work of philosophers, sociologists, and anthropologists across time, the list grows long indeed.

Certain common features among the psychologies greatly simplify the task of choosing among them. And, as was the case in the previous discussion of models of the mind in general, choosing among psychological models to attempt to find the "right" one is unnecessary and, in fact, counterproductive. The comprehensive psychiatric assessment takes this into consideration by requiring a formulation using several psychological models at once. Realizing that any given psychological model presents only one perspective that may ignore useful information, we can choose among them to select the most useful. Better still is to understand the clinical data by using several different psychological models at once. Because many psychologies may be relevant to a particular case, the psychiatric assessment typically will include formulations in, for example, Freudian drive theory, ego psychology (following Anna Freud), object relations theory, and Heinz Kohut's self-psychology, as well as cognitive and behavioral formulations.

There is, however, a unifying theme in all the psychologies. Without exception, they propose that psychopathology occurs when people are motivated to think, feel, cognate, perceive, and behave in ways of which they are largely unaware and do not consciously control, and which are maladaptive in some way. Although often well-aware that a problem exists, the pattern of the problem eludes the sufferer. When the lack of awareness allows functionally disruptive events to occur, it becomes simultaneously the source of the problem and the problem's potential solution. For once conscious awareness of patterns is achieved, conscious control may follow, such that the individual may become the shaper of her life, rather than an object shaped by forces beyond her awareness and control. The point of contention between the psychologies is how awareness and control are to be achieved. The techniques through which change is instituted differ from model to model. This contention does not mean that some psychologies are "right" at the expense of others. Their various solutions increase the clinical armamentarium of the psychiatrist, so that more than one solution is always available. This greatly increases the chances of successfully solving a patient's difficulties.

Key points

- *Psychological models* conceptualize mental states as arising from other mental states.

- *Psychodynamic models* look for unconscious drives, expectations, fantasies, and wishes as precursors for mental states.

- *Cognitive-behavioral models* focus on observable patterns of thinking and behaving and their resultant mental states.

- All psychological models propose that patients fail to perceive psychodynamic or cognitive-behavioral patterns that lead to psychopathology, and that *conscious awareness* of these patterns is the route to change.

Sigmund Freud 12

Drive theory

The structural model

All living organisms share a single potent characteristic—the drive toward life. The maintenance of life is the force behind the self-organizing structure of all living beings. Without this force there could be no life, and this force must be surpassingly strong. The obstacles against life are monumental and ultimately fatal for every living thing.

Living organisms require raw materials with which to maintain their structure against the entropy that continually threatens erosion. These materials must be either generated de novo or consumed from the external environment. The former is the method of plants and some single-cell organisms. All other creatures, including human beings, must consume. Since other life forms present the raw materials of life admirably concentrated, consumption is, in significant proportion, consumption of other life. Thus, the maintenance of life for all animals requires the consumption of other life. This is fundamentally aggressive. Since all life is striving to maintain itself as its organizing principle, consumption by another organism is the greatest violence that can be done to it.

In addition to maintaining themselves, living organisms seek to reproduce. This principle is coextensive with the first, and may even supplant it. Many animals will sacrifice their own lives for the safety of their young. The most primitive of living organisms, the virus, lacks any metabolic capability. Yet, despite this absence of metabolism, it reproduces its kind by plundering the machinery of host organisms.

Consumption and reproduction thus are the two fundamental behaviors of living organisms, behaviors so basic they inform every action each organism undertakes. Sigmund Freud saw human beings as no exception to this rule. Like all living things, human beings have aggressive and reproductive (or libidinal) drives.

According to Freud, the aggressive and reproductive drives motivate every cell in every organ of the body. Since the conscious mind is aware of only a small portion of the overall state of the body and the activity of the nervous system, the drives are largely unconscious. The drives are there at every moment of existence, yet we are only transiently aware of them. In this sense, these drives reside in "the unconscious," that domain of the body operating out of conscious awareness. The workings of the immune system, for example, are unconscious, not available to the conscious mind. Likewise, the drive to consume may lie largely out of conscious awareness, only occasionally becoming a conscious motivator.

Left untethered, these drives would make any society of human beings impossible. Our unregulated drives would leave us in a world of aggression, rape, animal consumption, and libidinal discharge based on what Freud called the "pleasure principle"—that which is immediately pleasurable is good and to be pursued regardless of other factors. In the case of most animals, the pleasure principle is the only principle. When the libidinal drives press for expression, they are expressed.

But human adaptation to the world is subtle. Reason has allowed human beings the capacities of foresight and planning. What is immediately pleasurable may have adverse consequences in the long run. Delaying gratification now may lead to greater pleasures in the future. And we face dangers. To children, parents are all-powerful, the sources of food and love, and physically capable of destruction. Displeasing a parent in the interest of short-term gratification may prove dangerous or even fatal. Furthermore, individuals live in a society, and society has proscriptions against behavior detrimental to its functioning. What threatens our parents and society is not only dangerous to individuals and society, it is wrong. That which society deems helpful, it sanctions as "the good."

The human organism is possessed by aggressive and libidinal drives, which it regulates to achieve greater pleasure, to avoid danger, and to appease a sense of right and wrong that develops through the influence of parents and society.

This is Freud's *structural model* of the "mental apparatus" (Freud, 1923/1964c). With modifications, this remains the dominant "drive theory" even today. According to this model, the drives are located (metaphorically) in the *id*. Overseeing these drives in a regulatory manner is the *ego*, which is synonymous both with the self and with that agency that acts to discharge the drives. And, finally, the ego acts in concert with an internalized sense of morality: the *superego*.

> Freud's *structural model* says that people are possessed by aggressive and libidinal drives which they regulate to achieve greater pleasure, to avoid danger, and to appease a sense of right and wrong.

The id

Freud identified the aggressive and libidinal drives as fundamental motivating forces even from infancy. In fact, there probably are other primary motivators that we will look at later, including socialization, curiosity, and mastery. For the purposes of drive theory, however, the id comprises two libidinal drives: aggression and sexuality. These drives are largely unconscious. Most of the activities of the nervous system are not accessible to consciousness, given the enormous complexity of the brain and the relative simplicity of our conscious state, and the libidinal drives are no different.

The drives are more than simple motivators. They are wishes and fantasies. These wishes and fantasies, Freud believed, first arise in the preverbal period—they are there from birth. Thus, they are essentially nonverbal and predate the development of adult "consciousness," the self-consciousness that talks to itself and is able to construct a narrative of its own history, observe its own actions, plan, and consciously recall.

Conflict and repression.   Later in life, with the development of the ego and the superego, the drives are capable of causing great conflict. If the id's wishes and fantasies are inappropriate for immediate gratification or are in conflict with the morality of the superego, then they are diverted by the ego from conscious awareness, a process Freud called *repression*. The control of drives by repression is a function of the ego, and serves to protect the ego from anxiety.

The id comprises two libidinal drives: aggression and sexuality.

Strictly speaking, this presentation of the aggressive and libidinal drives comes from Freud's early hypothesis, when he hoped to have a biological explanation for the drives. Freud and his followers subsequently abandoned this hypothesis in favor of an explanation based purely on clinical material. It is not, according to Freud's later work, the fact that living organisms universally possess aggressive drives to consume that proves human beings have similar motivation. Instead, what we see in children and adult patients is evidence of such motivation. As Freud's patients talked, they gradually became comfortable. In the accepting atmosphere of Freud's consulting room, they began to remember events and, more important, thoughts and feelings from early childhood. These thoughts and feelings often had an aggressive or sexual character, which was unpleasant because of shame or anxiety. Freud's patients felt discomfort in recalling them (often for the first time in many years). Freud came to believe that, since these thoughts and feelings were distasteful or even dangerous, they were actively kept out of conscious awareness until the psychoanalytic process allowed the censorship to be removed (Freud, 1914/1958).

Case example

Mr. J was in therapy for some time before he recalled, for the first time in many years, an episode that occurred when he was about 5 years old. He was sitting in the living room, where his mother was drawing at a table. J recalled watching her hands with fascination for a time, and then going to his room, where he began to trace with crayons on paper the image of his own hands. He remembered an illicit thrill at doing this, and then terror and shame when his mother knocked on the door, forcing him to hide the drawings so she would not see them. As an adult, he had a fascination with women's hands—they were sexually attractive to him. In remembering this scene, J was recalling something that he had remembered at times, but which he had not thought about for many years. The memory still triggered feelings of shame.

This is clinical evidence that what is remembered by a person is edited to exclude those memories which make him or her uncomfortable. Freud found that often such memories contain aggressive or sexual themes that are their source of discomfort. In J's case, the shame came both from the discovery of sexual feelings (he likened the experience of having his mother discover him drawing to being found naked) and, worse, that the sexual feelings were directed toward his mother, a universal taboo in all societies.

The sequestering of aggressive and sexual thoughts and feelings in the unconscious, safely out of conscious awareness, was, Freud believed, an activity of the ego. This repression is one of the ways the ego defends itself from anxiety.

The ego

The ego is the segment of the mental apparatus that is concerned with achieving the gratification of drives. Freud also uses the term as synonymous with *self*, the sense of ourselves as independent entities in the world, with an organized thought process that is consistent over time. In early development, prior to the acquisition of language, the ego appears in the form of motor control and simple learning. The ego effects the activity of nursing to discharge aggressive and libidinal drives. As the infant matures, it begins walking and using its hands, so that exploration and more elaborate drive discharge becomes possible. Later, the ego is responsible for the exquisitely intricate manipulation of the environment made possible through the vehicle of language. The developed ego also allows gratification to be delayed. It accomplishes this either by repressing the drives from conscious awareness or by diverting them into indirect avenues that can be satisfied.

The ego is concerned with achieving gratification of the id's drives.

Freud explained it this way:

> We have formed the idea that in each individual there is a coherent organization of mental processes; and we call this his *ego*. It is to this ego that consciousness is attached: The ego controls the approaches to motility—that is, to the discharge of excitations into the external world; it is the mental agency which supervises all its own constituent processes, and which goes to sleep at night, though even then it exercises the censorship on dreams. From this ego proceeds

the repression, too, by means of which it is sought to exclude certain trends in the mind not merely from consciousness but also from other forms of effectiveness and activity. (*The Ego and the Id*, 1923/1964c, p. 630)

When F was first confronted with the apparent anger that he had toward many people in his life—for example, toward his psychiatrist, which he expressed by not arriving for appointments—he adamantly denied that anger was possible for him. He viewed himself philosophically as a man of peace and claimed that he could not exercise control over his promptness because of the very problems that brought him in for treatment. Yet later, when he had become comfortably assured that the therapy was nonthreatening, F was able to admit verbally that he was greatly angered at times, and he demonstrated that his behavior was under his control after all, since he could then attend all of his sessions regularly.

The drive theory interpretation of this situation is that, for F, his aggressive drives proved too anxiety-provoking to be allowed into consciousness. Since he was attached to his psychiatrist, becoming openly angry and defiant was too risky—his previous developmental experiences had proved that important figures in his life really would withdraw their love if he openly displayed aggression, neediness, or any other requirement. Thus, any aggressive or needy feelings had to be repressed from consciousness to avoid anxiety. Ultimately, however, these feelings were too strong for repression alone to regulate them, and they found expression in an alternative form, of which F was entirely unaware—he "found" himself unable to keep his appointments. This put him in control, since only he knew whether he would actually arrive for a session, and it inconvenienced the psychiatrist, who felt simultaneously irritated and inadequate (he had the feeling that if only he were a competent therapist, the patient would come to treatment). But F kept himself unaware that his behavior placed him in control and satisfied his aggressive impulses. He did not consciously choose to do this. Rather, the choice occurred outside his awareness. Repression is a function of the ego that operates unconsciously. One is not aware that repression is occurring until after the fact, when repressed material returns to consciousness. As in J's case, it was only in suddenly remembering an event from his childhood that he realized he had forgotten it in the first place.

A similar process occurred with F's obsessions. F's hostile feelings toward his mother proved intolerable, since he was both emotionally and financially dependent on her. Thus, he obscured his aggressive feelings toward her through a series of obsessive thoughts and compulsive behaviors. When his unconscious wish to destroy his mother was actualized by her illness, he no longer needed the obsessions and compulsions to defend against the wish. Thus, when his mother became ill and nearly died, the obsessions and compulsions disappeared, only to return when she regained her health. We might say that the aggressive drive had been gratified by the mother's illness.

The psychosexual stages

Freud's *Three Essays on Sexuality* (1905/1964f) established his reputation for oversexualizing, which remains to this day. In this landmark paper, Freud presented his belief that many forms of pleasure other than genital pleasure are the results of sexual energy displaced through other organs. One of Freud's examples is that people derive sexual pleasure from kissing, even though the mouth is part of the digestive tract rather than a sexual organ per se. Freud believed that the mucus membranes of the mouth, in this case, display a remnant of libidinal energy that was present in infancy and so is available to be revived in adulthood through tactile stimulation. In psychoanalytic terms, the object of the mouth is *cathected*, or invested, with libidinal energy. During human development, there is a progression of cathexis from one organ of the body to another in a sequence called the psychosexual stages.

Oral stage.   The earliest manifestation of this oral cathexis appears at birth, when the child is primarily absorbed in the task of nursing, to the exclusion of most other awareness. Freud proposed that this oral stage was the first in a series of libidinal cathexes that progressed through childhood.

Anal stage.   The second psychosexual stage is the anal stage, arrived at after about 18 months of orality. Around this time, the child develops growing motor and language capacities that allow for some autonomy from the caregiver. Parents utilize the child's growing ability to begin toilet training. Pleasure at mastering the time and place of elimination grows. And the child finds that, just as her parents use her growing motor mastery to control her, so her parents can be controlled through her choice of the time and place of elimination. Aggression can be expressed by refusing to defecate in the toilet. Thus, issues of autonomy and control are the paramount conflicts surrounding the anal stage of development.

Freud held that the conflicts of each psychosexual stage must be substantially resolved in order for the libido to transfer its primary focus (cathexis) to the next object in the developmental sequence. According to drive theory, this is never a completed task—some libido will always remain attached to the oral and anal orifices throughout life. Nevertheless, classic drive theory holds that the conflicts can and must be largely processed or "worked through." Otherwise, those conflicts remain even into adulthood.

F serves as a good example of anal fixation. His predominant themes revolved around cleanliness and control. He was enthralled by powerful aggressive impulses, which threatened to override his fragile attempts to control them. Thus, he turned to obsessions—with cleanliness—as a method of drive control. His relationships all followed a similar pattern. Intimacy for F was not a matter of degree, but one of kind. He was alternately distant and inscrutable or overly enmeshed. This happened in his relationship with his mother, as well. His tendency was to desire enmeshment with her—so he lived at home, financially and emotionally dependent on her. But because such dependency threatened the loss of his autonomy, he was overwhelmed by aggressive impulses. The same thing happened in the course of his therapy. Initially, his entry into treatment was cold, distant, wary, and controlling in a passive way. F could not talk about his conflicts with treatment up front, because they were too dangerous and needed therefore to be repressed. Instead they were "acted out"—he skipped treatment despite avowing how much he needed it. When this conflict was finally resolved in the treatment—by the therapist relinquishing control of the therapy—F could suddenly enter wholeheartedly into treatment, to the point of marked dependency.

Control and autonomy are the central themes mastered in the anal phase. Successful completion of the stage leaves the individual not completely free of issues around control and autonomy, but at least with a general and pervasive sense that he or she is an autonomous actor in control of much. If development becomes stymied, then the adult may act out issues of control and autonomy as if still a young child.

What contributes to fixation is not clear. Freud supposed it could be the result of over- or undercontrolling parents during toilet training. Yet child development research has generally not found that adult character can be definitively linked to early childhood events. We will also see later that newer theories of development provide evidence that the themes of the psychosexual stages are not definitively mastered at a particular point in development, but are continuously reworked throughout life.

Genital stage.   In the third to fifth years, the libido cathects the genitalia. The sex of every person becomes a matter of fascination for the genital-stage child. For example, a 3-year-old caused surprise and some shock when he was allowed to say Thanksgiving grace for the first time. He said, "Daddy has a penis and Mommy doesn't. Amen." This family was not sick or oversexualized. The boy had recently learned about the genital differences between males and females, and he was fascinated by this information. In keeping with the as yet poorly developed ego of the toddler years, he was not able to restrain his expression of his interest in this knowledge.

The transfer of libido primarily to the genitalia, where it remains for adult life, is preparatory for the now-famous culmination of the early psychosexual stages in the oedipal phase.

The oedipal phase.   Around the fourth or fifth year of life, children universally develop a deepening awareness that they are not the center of every relationship. Whereas before they had perceived the world always in relation to themselves, they now realize that other people have relationships that do not include them. This is a shocking discovery. Mother and father have a relationship independent of the child. This discovery is the beginning of the oedipal period, named for Sophocles' tragic hero Oedipus, who was blinded and disgraced after he unwittingly killed his father and married his mother.

The oedipal-age child has sexual feelings, and they are directed toward the opposite-sex parent, as was seen in the case of Mr. J. During the oedipal phase, the child becomes aware that mother and father have an independent relationship, and that the child is therefore not the only important figure in the life of each parent. The child's nascent sexual desires are focused on the opposite-sex parent. But the child realizes now that he or she has a rival in the same-sex parent for the love of the opposite-sex parent.

This rivalry engenders aggressive wishes to destroy the same-sex parent, which is readily apparent to even casual observers. A son will suggest that Daddy move away so that he can live alone with Mommy. A daughter will react with guilty fear when Mommy comes upon her reading a book with Daddy.

The oedipal stage is characterized by a child's rivalry with the same-sex parent for the attention of the opposite-sex parent.

But the oedipal child recognizes his or her relative powerlessness compared to the same-sex parent, who has at once vast prowess physically, genitally, and mentally, and who also is an object of love for the child. This makes any rivalrous feelings intensely conflictual. The urge to destroy the same-sex parent in order to win the rivalry is unrealizable and dangerous. The parent might retaliate or withdraw love.

Since the rivalry cannot be won, the child successfully maneuvers through the oedipal phase by repressing the amorous impulses toward the opposite-sex parent and identifying with the same-sex parent. This identification leads to the taking on of the parent's values as one's own. The young boy learns that if he cannot have his father's wife, he might win a similar wife of his own by becoming like the father. These internalized values are, according to Freud, the moral sense that is the mature superego.

The superego

In addition to the id and the ego, Freud proposed a third intrapsychic structure: the superego. The superego is the moral conscience that regulates acceptable ways for the ego to discharge the drives of the id. The superego is made up of the internalized values primarily of the child's parents, as well as those of society in general as reflected through the parents.

The superego makes its appearance in the first year of life, as an imitation of the parents. Later, the values of the parents become internalized—that is to say, the child makes them his or her own, so that they seem to come from within—in a series of stages which co-occur with the psychosexual development stages. In the first 2 years of life (the oral phase) identification with the parents is primarily based on imitation of them. Since the oral child cannot predict the comings and goings of objects in the world, objects may disappear arbitrarily. Freud believed that loss of the object is the primary fear of the early superego.

Identification gives way to a harsh and punitive primitive superego in the anal phase, when parents become disciplinary and demand certain behaviors, such as control of the bowels and bladder. This superego is rigid and inflexible, and tends to divide the world into black and white opposites, without shades of gray. That which is wrong is very, very wrong, and the child feels—rightly or not—that transgressions threaten loss of the parents' love. In F's case, this appeared as extreme shame and fear after apparent transgressions. For example, in one session F might vent anger at his mother. In the next, he would come in looking whipped and afraid, asking if the psychiatrist found him tiresome and annoying. The penalty for transgression in the anal phase is severe—it is, according to Freud, the loss of the love of one's parents, which for a young child is literally a matter of life and death. Young children do not yet have a sense of themselves or others as entities that exist across time. They live in a perpetual present. So, faced with a parent who is angry, the child cannot assuage feelings of fear and abandonment by consciously remembering previous good experiences and imagining that the anger will pass and good experiences return. An angry parent seems angry in a timeless and therefore terrifying way.

The superego is the moral conscience that regulates the ego and the id.

During the oedipal phase, the identification with the same-sex parent produces a "consolidated" superego. Transgressions against the proscriptions of the consolidated superego do not carry the same dire consequences as in early developmental stages. Whereas before the fantasized punishment is abandonment or loss of love, now guilt and fear of punishment predominate. Even though unpleasant, guilt is a more tolerable emotional state to a child than the terror of abandonment. Guilt implies that the individual is capable of alternative behavior, and that so doing might subsequently win the desired approval. The child who has passed successfully through the oedipal phase has made great strides in developing autonomy. The world is no longer savagely black and white—shades of gray can be tolerated. Parental disapproval is no longer starkly bad but, rather, a disagreeable sensation that can be managed by alternative action, which in turn can be consciously planned. The oedipal-age child has the capacity to see the environment as complex. Parents get angry, but anger fades and love reemerges.

Case example

Ms. E felt nervous and anxious much of the time. She was something of a perfectionist, and she feared failure. As a result, she
tended to deal poorly with criticism, whether at work or home.
Wracked with guilt and feelings of inadequacy whenever she performed below the impossibly high standards she set for herself,
she would lapse into depression. Her husband and others attempted to reassure her, and she could be comforted in this way,
but her fear of failure always returned. In treatment, E revealed
that her father had placed a high premium on work and was highly
critical. It gradually dawned on E that she was attempting through
her current actions to please her difficult father, although he no
longer scrutinized her every move as he had during childhood.
Relaxing meant coming to terms with displeasing him, and with
the ultimate futility of trying to please his internalized voice.

In the drive model, Ms. E evidenced a more mature ego and superego development than F. Relationships with other people presented difficult but not insurmountable challenges for her, so that she was able to
sustain interpersonal exchanges that were moderately satisfactory to her
in an enduring way. Yet she was plagued by perfectionism and a fear of
judgment. The disapproval of others was painful enough to elicit damaging compensatory maneuvers when she believed it would be forth-
coming. But her relationships were stable enough that she could, for
example, enter into treatment without conflict substantial enough to
threaten that treatment. Thus, she could make use of and gradually as-
similate alternative perspectives so that, with time, she might eventually abandon her sense that she is "not a failure" only if she keeps her
weight below an arbitrarily prescribed point. This is the work of an ego
that has developed greater tolerance for anxiety and greater adaptive
flexibility, and a superego that punishes primarily by guilt rather than
terror.

Psychodynamic psychotherapy

Transference

One of Freud's greatest contributions to psychiatry is his concept of *transference* (Freud, 1912/1964b). Freud saw that patients often would behave in ways that were not reflective of the actual relationship between
himself and them. One day a patient would see him as warm and kindly,
the next as harsh and domineering, while little had changed in Freud's
demeanor. This suggested that the patient was responding to the thera-

peutic relationship in a way that reflected unconscious factors more than the qualities of the actual relationship. Freud thought that, since repression often kept uncomfortable ideas and feelings out of conscious awareness, those ideas were repeated nonverbally and unconsciously instead of remembered consciously. Unconscious material thus came to be acted out in various relationships in the patient's life, with the result that relationships became disturbed. Freud found that the therapeutic relationship became an arena for repetition no less than any other relationship, and he called this phenomenon transference.

Transference is the redirection of feelings and desires unconsciously retained from childhood toward a new object.

Case example

Ms. A came to treatment for anxiety at the workplace. She was perfectionistic and driven, and she found herself becoming increasingly panicky when anything seemed out of control in her life. A's father had been domineering, and A had succeeded both in her relationship with him and in the rest of her life by watching others carefully and then molding herself to meet their needs. She was, therefore, extremely uncomfortable when the psychiatrist waited silently for her to begin her sessions with whatever she wished to discuss. What she desired was for him to give her direction about how the session was to proceed that day by starting her off with an inquiry.

A's response to the psychiatrist was thus a transference response— her feelings for her father were transferred to the psychiatrist. After all, there is nothing necessarily anxiety-provoking about being given the opportunity to talk about what you want—in fact, some people love it. The question is not whether a given response is right or wrong, but why it happens, whatever it is.

Transference is ubiquitous in every relationship. The difference between transference in treatment and transference in the rest of the patient's life is that the therapist can accept the patient's transference and then interpret the meaning of these events back to her. The patient then can access the unconscious material and express it verbally rather than repeating it in unconsciously motivated behavior. Finally, conflictual thoughts and feelings are remembered instead of repeated, and so they can be worked through, to use Freud's term, so that they no longer cause inappropriate behavior in other relationships.

Interpretation

Psychodynamic psychotherapy achieves this aim primarily through interpretations. Interpretations are the psychiatrist's verbal explanations to the patient of the unconscious processes observed in the course of treatment. The repetition of unconscious processes can be seen in past relationships and in present relationships, including the therapeutic relationship (through transference). Interpretations make the unconscious process available to consciousness so that it can be "remembered." Once unconscious patterns of repetition are available to consciousness, the hope is that they can be relinquished in favor of behavior based on clearly defined goals.

We will discuss other psychodynamic psychotherapy techniques in further chapters.

Caveats

When it fits a case, the drive model is extremely convincing. It is no wonder Freud believed it was *the* explanation for all of human behavior. As he was educated as a scientist, however, this very hope should have struck him not only as unrealistic but as undesirable. The application of drive theory, like any other model of the mind, must occur as a hypothesis. There must exist the possibility that drive theory could be disproved if the model is to be a scientific-critical theory.

Unfortunately, clinical material is prone to severe bias. Unless one works assiduously, it is difficult to avoid allowing drive theory to become a self-fulfilling prophesy. For example, since sexual behavior is obvious in children, Freud and his followers thought that anyone who couldn't see it must be repressing the data because of conflicts with his or her own childhood sexual feelings, thus proving that drive theory is correct even if it is refuted. This might be true; but it might not be, and Freud's approach violated the principle of scientific inquiry, which states that a hypothesis must have conditions under which it could be shown to be true or not.

Fortunately, this situation can be remedied by research, if research is done with an open mind as to whether children are aggressive and sexual beings. It turns out that they are, but this is not something that should be determined independently of experimentation.

Thus, we can never approach a case knowing in advance that drive theory will be relevant. Only if there is evidence of drives in conflict can drive theory become relevant. The symmetry of drive theory is beautiful enough that it can make any set of symptoms seem consistent with it. Only if the model leads to clinical predictions that are subsequently verified and result in clinical change, however, does the model become relevant. Whether the model is ever "true" remains a matter for speculation. The patient comes to treatment seeking relief. If application of the model provides relief, then the model is vindicated. If not, then a different model must be sought. As Stern said, "one works with whatever reconstructive metaphor offers the most force and explanatory power, even though one cannot get at the 'original edition' of the metaphor" (1985, p. 257).

As the patient presents his or her story, the psychiatrist listens for themes of wishing and fantasy, their aggressive and libidinal content, how conscious these drives and fantasies are, how they are defended against, and how symptoms enact compromise between wish and defense. When such themes emerge in a manner convincing to both patient and psychiatrist and the result is symptom relief, the drive model has proved its relevance.

Lately, cognitive research has lent some credence to the structures of the "mental apparatus" Freud proposed. It seems self-evident that many of the workings of our nervous systems at any given moment are not available to our conscious awareness. This may establish the existence of an "unconscious," those operations of the nervous system which are outside conscious awareness, but what Freud's theory really implies is that human beings can learn and think unconsciously, for this would be how unconscious conflicts might develop. Can this happen? We now have more formalized knowledge that unconscious learning and thinking do occur.

Research has revealed two types of memory, explicit and implicit. *Explicit memory* is what we usually think of as memory, the conscious semantic awareness of information. Explicit memory is at work when we learn a new name, study for a test, recall a day in the fourth grade, or remember where we put the checkbook. It is language-based, and the images are conscious.

Implicit memory is the memory responsible for learning skills, such as playing the guitar or bicycling. Whereas reading information works well for storing explicit memories, implicit memory primarily organizes around activity. You can't learn to ride a bike by reading about it. Some authors have argued that implicit memory is analogous to "the unconscious." Such a model offers an explanation for the common finding that psychodynamic psychotherapy takes time to work. Although several sessions may suffice for relief of symptoms, often years of therapy are required to achieve a lasting change. Simply explaining the cause of symptoms is not enough for dynamic therapy to be effective. The truth of interpretations must be lived by the patient in therapy and in his or her life outside of therapy.

The reason for this may have its explanation in the differing characteristics of explicit and implicit memory. Explicit learning and memory would be the operant mechanism in learning through explanation. Explicit knowledge can be gained rapidly. It often takes only a few trials to learn new information. Yet explicit memory tends to fade without constant revisiting.

Conversely, implicit memory takes more repetition to achieve. Learning to play the guitar, for example, takes a great deal of time and practice. The action must be performed repeatedly. Reading or talking about it doesn't help much. Once learned, however, implicit memory is tenacious. You never forget how to ride a bike once you know how. And

Explicit memory is the conscious semantic awareness of information.

Implicit memory is responsible for learning skills, such as riding a bike.

implicit learning tends to be difficult to express explicitly. Walking occurs with ease once you've learned how. Describing the process in any detail, however, is quite difficult. Implicit knowledge tends to defy explicit description.

Some have suggested that if relationship patterns are mostly learned implicitly, this may account for why they tend to be largely unconscious and resistant to change. It also explains why it takes a lot of practice to learn new patterns. Drive theory–based psychotherapy is therefore about making unconscious thoughts and feelings conscious, so that the therapy can be a new relationship freed of unconscious conflict. This model relationship is then hoped to generalize to other relationships outside of therapy.

Drive theory has undergone decades of elaboration. Several major schools of psychodynamic theory have subsequently developed, including ego psychology, object relations theory, and self-psychology. Current psychodynamic practice incorporates these theories with drive theory for a comprehensive psychodynamic psychology. The next chapters will discuss these theories in detail.

Key points

- The structural apparatus comprises the id, the ego, and the superego.

- The *id* consists of drives toward aggression and reproduction (the libido).

- The *ego* actualizes the demands of the id.

- The ego protects itself from anxiety by the use of ego defenses, particularly repression, which sequesters uncomfortable impulses from conscious awareness.

- The *superego* is an internalized moral framework.

- *Libidinal energy* cathects with various organs of the body in a developmental sequence that goes from oral to anal to genital to oedipal.

- The *oral phase* is concerned primarily with oral consumption (e.g., nursing).

- The *anal phase* centers around emerging volitional control of the body.

- The *genital phase* is characterized by growing awareness of one's own genitalia and the sexual identity of others.

- The *oedipal phase* occurs around ages 4 to 5, and is marked by the growing awareness that others (particularly the parents) have a relationship that does not involve the child.

- The child's sexual impulses toward the opposite-sex parent engender feelings of rivalry with the same-sex parent.

- Resolution of this conflict through the repression of sexual impulses toward the opposite-sex parent and identification with the same-sex parent furthers the developmental process.

- Consolidation of the superego occurs with the resolution of the oedipal phase through identification with the same-sex parent.

The ego 13

Mechanisms of ego defense

The pragmatic requirements of clinical practice gradually led to the expansion of Freud's original theories. In 1936 his daughter, Anna Freud, published *The Ego and the Mechanisms of Defense* (A. Freud, 1936/1946). This work maintained that the ego of every human being, even of healthy individuals, is constantly engaged in the process of modulating drives to decrease anxiety.

As we saw in the discussion on drive theory, one of the functions of the ego is to protect itself from anxiety. Anxiety may come either from the external world, through direct threats, or from the internal world, through conflict. Internal conflict arises between the structures of the mental apparatus. The ego seeks to actualize the drives of the id within the constraints of reality and the moral confines supplied by the superego. If, for example, the impulses of the id are producing urges that are morally incompatible with the superego, anxiety results. In that case, the ego represses awareness of those impulses. This action is known as *repression*, and repression is classified as an *ego defense.*

Ego defenses are the means by which the ego protects itself from anxiety.

The ego can use a number of tactics to accomplish the defense against anxiety, and Anna Freud and her followers produced a classification of ego defense mechanisms based on the order of their appearance in the developmental sequence.

A very young child has an immature ego that is just beginning to effectively interact with the world. One of the ego's most important tasks in this regard is a skill Freud termed *reality testing*. Reality testing is the ability to distinguish those stimuli that are generated within the subjective psyche from those that come from outside.

In the first year of life, the infant's drives are relatively unopposed. Thus, wish and fantasy constitute a large proportion of the mental apparatus. The infant has no capacity to distinguish wish from reality. The breast is not distinguishable to the infant as a separate entity, nor can the infant predict its comings and goings. The breast will not appear immediately when wished for, so the wish of the hungry infant for the breast may be frustrated. Though uncomfortable, the resulting distress is in-

Reality testing is the ability to distinguish between stimuli generated from within and those coming from outside.

structive for the infant. Through frustration, the infant learns that his internal mental life may generate stimuli, and that these stimuli are distinct phenomena from external, or "reality-based," stimuli. This capacity is extremely useful, for therein lies the seed of the mature ego's capability for delayed gratification. Without a sense of reality, wish and fantasy are indistinguishable from reality.

Thus, the ego defenses present during the oral stage (which also are known as the *psychotic* or *narcissistic defenses*) involve gross failures in reality testing. Freud believed that the hallucinations and delusions of psychotic individuals represent a return to this primitive ego functioning as a last-line defense against total disintegration of the ego. Use of psychotic defenses involves significant distortion of reality. As the child matures, her reality testing improves, and so more mature ego defenses allow for greater degrees of reality testing.

In general, the ego defenses are arranged hierarchically to parallel the developmental sequence: Thus, the ego defenses are classified as psychotic, immature, neurotic, and mature. The *psychotic ego defenses* are seen in infants. *Immature ego defenses* appear in early childhood. *Neurotic ego defenses* develop with the resolution of the oedipal phase. Finally, *mature ego defenses* generally appear during adolescence.

More mature ego defenses allow the individual to adapt to the demands of external reality while reducing anxiety. It is important to note, however, that early ego defenses can appear in adults when they are stressed. This was a process Freud termed *regression*. Virtually anyone can become severely regressed if compromised sufficiently. For example, a drug overdose may so stress the nervous system that the individual can make sense of the world and reduce anxiety only by conjuring paranoid delusions.

The ego defenses are defined in detail in the following pages (Vaillant, 1971).

Psychotic defenses

Projection

Projection is the attribution of internal events to the outside world.

Projection is the attribution of internal events to the external world. For example, believing that internally generated voices belong to the outside world is a form of projection. Paranoia is another variation of projection, in which intolerable feelings about the self are attributed to the outside world.

Rather than perceiving their subjective distress as arising—at least partly—from within themselves, paranoid individuals project all of the blame for their distress onto the outside world, which they perceive as malevolent and persecutory. The reason for this is simple: The infantile ego is incapable of tolerating the idea that its distress arises from internal sources. It is much simpler and less anxiety-provoking to believe that all such feelings are brought on by outside others. Psychotic levels of paranoia and distortion involve frank delusions of persecution.

Distortion and denial

Distortion radically alters one's perception of reality, whereas denial rejects the very existence of troublesome events. Distortion is the misapprehension of external reality to make it congruent with internal states. Delusional thinking, such as the idea that the television is broadcasting special messages that only certain individuals can perceive, is an example of psychotic distortion. Denial is the refusal to acknowledge external realities that are anxiety-provoking. When a woman who is diagnosed with cancer refuses to believe the diagnosis, despite adequate demonstration, she is in denial.

Distortion is the altered perception of external reality to make it congruent with internal states.

Immature defenses

Nonpsychotic projection and distortion

Individuals who have progressed from the psychotic to the immature level of ego-defensive functioning lack the extreme impairment in reality testing characteristic of the psychotic ego defenses. As a result, they are not frankly delusional or hallucinatory. Nevertheless, as we saw in Mr. H's case, they may rely on nondelusional projection and distortion to cope with anxiety. For example, H severely distorted the role of the government in his malaise, without becoming frankly delusional.

Splitting

Splitting reduces the world to polar opposites, in which good and bad are incompatible qualities that cannot ever exist simultaneously. Mr. H was not dissatisfied with just some activities of the federal government; he believed it was pure evil, entirely hateful in every conceivable way. When questioned empathetically but persistently, he could eventually admit that it was not the government per se, but rather some of the government's activities he disliked, and that there were things the current government did that were even desirable. This took some effort, however. During moments of stress, H's ability to see the world in shades of gray disappeared.

Freud believed that splitting is a natural act of the early ego as it attempts to differentiate between what is acceptable for consumption and metabolism, and therefore good, and what is unsuitable and therefore bad. Anyone watching a young child eat knows that she takes in what is good with unreserved gusto, whereas what is bad is rejected

Denial is the refusal to aknowledge external realities that are anxiety-provoking.

uncompromisingly. It is very difficult to coax a child into orally accepting an item once he has rejected it. Thus, splitting tends toward absolutism. The good is taken in, the bad kept out; the two are therefore *split*.

Splitting reduces the world to polar opposites, in which good and bad are incompatible qualities that cannot exist simultaneously.

While this is a fine strategy for a young child, its persistence into adulthood is problematic. Most things in the world have a mix of good and bad features. Relationships with other people are unlikely to be completely harmonious and satisfying or entirely without redeeming qualities. The persistence of splitting for an adult will likely lead to wild swings between overvaluation and devaluation. If every disappointment is interpreted as an action of malign intent, relationships tend to deteriorate. This is particularly problematic if the person who lets you down is yourself. If splitting is one's predominant coping mechanism, this situation is likely to result in suicidal thoughts and even actions.

Acting out

Acting out is the discharge of impulses without regard to their consequences. When toddlers do not get what they want, they may have temper tantrums. In such a state, they are unable to use cognitive skills to cope with a situation. Instead, they blow into action, discharging their rage and frustration through action. Since they possess as yet poorly defined self-regulatory capabilities, acting out is a natural defense for children. In such situations, the adult must act as an external "auxiliary ego" who places limits on the child's acting out and soothes her by encouraging a calm, linguistic, rational approach to the conflict. Children gradually learn such abilities themselves. If they do not—possibly because of the lack of a regulating caregiver—then acting out may persist as a coping strategy into adulthood. Suicide attempts and drinking bouts are examples of acting out, as is becoming abruptly enraged and storming off the job when criticized at work. In acting out, the individual acts on impulses without regulating them, often with deleterious consequences.

Acting out is the discharge of impulses without regard to their consequences.

Somatization

Somatization is the presentation of psychological distress as physical distress. Somatization occurs when individuals are unable to define their internal feeling states, whether because of attempts to keep them unconscious or because they lack the skill to do so (a problem known as *alexithymia*). As a result, their emotional distress is interpreted not as a psychological state but as a physical state, since physical distress is localizable, separate from the psyche, and possibly treatable by medicine or physical removal. Thus, anxiety in somatizing individuals presents not as anxiety about a conflict but as anxiety over a worrisome physical symptom such as pain, constipation, or dizziness.

Somatization is hypothesized to be a cause of hypochondriasis, which typically is the result of an overinterpretation of normal bodily sensations. We know that minor fluctuations in bodily function naturally occur over the course of the day in healthy individuals. In somatization, a person's brief awareness of the feeling of his own heart beating allows his anxiety to be about that physical symptom rather than about his conflictual thoughts and feelings. In a sense, it is easier for him to worry that something is wrong with his body than to experience anxiety about his unconscious conflict. With worried energy focused on the state of his body, his unconscious conflict can remain unconscious.

Somatization is the presentation of psychological distress as physical distress.

Passive-aggression

Passive-aggression is a mechanism whereby aggressive impulses are expressed without the intolerable anxiety of consciously experiencing them. Mr. F presented an example of passive-aggression when he canceled appointments at the last moment, on the ostensible grounds that he was "unable to make it." Later evidence revealed that this was not true and that, if he wanted to, he could make every appointment without fail.

F needed the conscious belief that his behavior was not aggressive and controlling, because the anxiety triggered by his aggression was too terrible to be allowed into consciousness. Nevertheless, the aggression "leaked through" his apparently cooperative demeanor and frustrated his psychiatrist.

Passive-aggression is a mechanism whereby aggressive impulses are expressed without the intolerable anxiety of consciously expressing them.

Undoing

Undoing is the attempt to neutralize dangerous thoughts and feelings by reversing them. When F washed his hands repeatedly for fear of carrying germs back to his mother, he was undoing the unconscious wish to harm her.

Neurotic defenses

Neurotic defenses are evidence of greater ego strength than the early ego defense mechanisms. They protect from excessive anxiety while retaining a significant capacity for reality testing. The neurotic defenses therefore evidence greater long-term adaptive capacity than the early ego defenses, which tend to be effective only in the short term. The development of neurotic ego defenses usually is thought to occur in the third to seventh years, concurrent with the resolution of the genital and oedipal phases.

Undoing is the attempt to neutralize dangerous thoughts and feelings by reversing them.

Repression is the submerging of anxiety-provoking conflict from one's conscious awareness into the unconscious.

Repression

The classic neurotic defense—the first mechanism of ego defense characterized by Freud—is repression. Repression is the submerging of anxiety-provoking conflict from one's conscious awareness into the unconscious. It is the "forgetting" of anxiety-provoking thoughts. Since repressed ideas are not available to conscious awareness, the conscious experience of repression happens after the fact, when a repressed memory resurfaces after long absence. Repression is lifting when one says of a painful childhood memory, "Oh. I just remembered. I hadn't thought of that for a long time." Repression occurs unconsciously. It simply happens before we are aware of it. Only later do we realize it has occurred.

The intentional choice to ignore information is not repression but *suppression*, which is a mature defense. In suppression, one makes a conscious choice to put the information out of mind temporarily. If you are at work and receive bad news, it may be necessary and adaptive to say, "I can't think about that until after work," and forget the bad news until work is finished. Once work is over, however, the anxiety-provoking material will be attended to rather than forgotten. Repression is useful, but it has the effect of creating significant distance between awareness and the emotionally laden material. On the other hand, because it is done through conscious decision, suppression leaves the emotionally laden material more accessible to consciousness. With suppression, the trouble can be attended to at a more convenient time, whereas with repression, the material may not be returned to at all.

Suppression is the conscious choice to put information out of mind temporarily.

Intellectualization and isolation-of-affect

Intellectualization and isolation-of-affect hold emotionally laden material at bay by acknowledging the facts while withdrawing any emotional value to them. When someone discusses something that should be painful in a matter-of-fact way, intellectualization and isolation-of-affect are at work.

Imagine someone dryly recounting the death of a loved one. "I was devastated," he says, but his face is composed and neutral. Perhaps he even smiles wryly. The facts of the event are not distant, but the corresponding emotion is—in other words, the affect (or, more accurately, the mood) is isolated from the thought. Intellectualization occurs, for example, when an individual develops a keen intellectual insight rather than an emotional understanding of anxiety-provoking material. This might be manifested in a cancer patient as endless research on cancer treatments to the exclusion of feelings of grief and anger. The person does gain knowledge and, through knowledge, a certain power over her circumstances. However, important emotions may not be attended to, but are instead eliminated from conscious awareness through a focus on an intellectual task.

Intellectual-ization is the attempt to develop rational, rather than an emotional, understanding of a problem.

Intellectualization and isolation-of-affect do not distort reality to the same degree as denial. The capacity to focus on facts to the exclusion of emotion may be highly adaptive in certain circumstances. A surgeon who dryly and methodically categorizes the extent of damage to a trauma victim will be more effective than one who is overwhelmed by the horror of the injuries. Keeping overwhelming emotion at a comfortable distance can be critical to coping. If it becomes too rigid, however, an overly intellectualized and affect-isolated style may lead to problems. An inability to access emotions may lead to increasing conflict in which one's external life is not true to one's emotions.

Isolation-of-affect is the attempt to keep overwhelming emotions at a comfortable distance.

Reaction formation

Reaction formation occurs when an anxiety-provoking urge is transformed into its opposite. For example, as we saw in the case of F, his aggressive impulses toward his mother became an obsessive worry about harming her, and F went to debilitating lengths to prevent this from happening.

Displacement

Displacement is sometimes called the "kicking the dog" phenomenon. When impulses toward an object are frustrated because they are unacceptable, they may be displaced onto an object toward which the impulse is acceptable. Thus, repressed aggressive impulses toward the boss at work are displaced and manifest as irritability toward the family (and perhaps an irritable strike at the family dog).

Reaction formation transforms an urge into its opposite.

Mature defenses

The primary purpose of the ego, Sigmund Freud said, was to find a route to satisfy the drives of the id. As the child develops, his ego becomes increasingly skillful at navigating a complex world to find satisfying outlets for these drives. One of the main regulators of the id drives is society, as Freud well knew. The free expression of raw aggressive and libidinal drives threatens the maintenance of an orderly society. Mature ego defenses permit long-term delay of gratification and the use of anxious energy to promote useful and desirable activity.

Sublimation

The mature ego defenses are useful to society, and usually are seen as virtues. One of the best examples is sublimation, in which drive energy is diverted into socially useful goals. Thus, drives to aggressively con-

Displacement is the transfer of impulses from an unacceptable object to an acceptable object.

quer might be used to write poetry or become a physicist, a top athlete, or president of a bank. The outcome of this diversion of drive energy is useful both to the individual and to society. Since society is one of the greatest forces the individual encounters, it generally is adaptive to channel drive energy in directions that are socially useful and sanctioned.

Sublimation is the attempt to divert drive energy into socially useful goals.

This is not to suggest that simple, mindless obedience to societal norms is the desirable end. Rather, it is to say that society plays a crucial role in the life of any individual. Even adaptation that rejects the norms of a given society completely is, in some sense, shaped by that society. Goal achievement is highly adaptive. In the most basic sense, it is how organisms successfully manipulate the world to achieve the ends of living, whether in simply foraging for food or in designing a skyscraper to obtain money to purchase food. Long-term goals are derived largely by way of society. The language that makes abstract thought—and thus long-range planning—possible is a societal phenomenon, and society provides the context within which most of human life occurs.

Anticipation

Anticipation of future problems, particularly anxiety-provoking stimuli, generally is extremely adaptive. It allows for the attainment of long-term goals through the lengthy delay of drive discharge. It also allows for planning and choosing between multiple strategies to avoid anxiety-provoking situations. The immature ego must deal with anxiety as it arises, and in the throes of emotion will do what is necessary to protect itself, not always to its long-term benefit. But if anxiety can be anticipated, it can be avoided.

Anticipation is the ability to visualize a future event or state, and thus deal with it in advance.

This requires that our anxiousness not lie too far from our consciousness. A certain amount of anxiety must be tolerable and accessible for the individual to know what future events might be anxiety- provoking. Take the example of a man who is overweight and smokes who is told he must alter this situation or face an early demise. If the anxiety of dying is tolerable to him, he may see that eventually having a heart attack is undesirable, both functionally and emotionally. Thus, he may undertake modifications to alter this outcome. If the anxiety of dying is too severe (or if other, conflicting emotions such as anger at authority arise) the man cannot live consciously with this anxiety and examine alternative behaviors which might avert the feared outcome of death. The result might be a complete repression of the fear of death—the man simply forgets to stop smoking and overeating—or acting out—his food and cigarette intake increases to assuage the anxiety.

Humor

Humor is the capacity to step back from one's situation and laugh at it. This requires that one not be completely immersed in what is happening, but instead place the event in a larger perspective. Humor allows us to see that what seems terribly important at the moment may not be so crucial after all. Humor requires an ego that can take other perspectives, particularly that of one existing not just in the here and now but over a long lifetime, when what seems important now will eventually recede into the past.

Altruism

Altruism is the ability to place the interests of another above one's own momentarily, an ability that (as with humor) requires appreciating other perspectives than one's own immediate situation. Altruism is a mature ego defense not because giving is a virtue, but because the mental flexibility required to appreciate the concerns of others and consider placing them above one's own is adaptive.

Mature defenses thus allow for a high degree of adaptive flexibility. Using mature defenses, the individual has the greatest capacity to consciously choose and actualize the course of her life.

Humor is the capacity to step back from one's situation and laugh at it.

Treatment

Every human being uses ego defenses to regulate anxiety. How do we know that one defense is pathological and another is not? Who is to say that paranoia about the government is pathological and that becoming a novelist is not? There is, of course, no wholly objective measure by which to categorize defensive functioning. The name "ego defense" has an unfortunate pejorative quality unintended by psychoanalytic writers. Defending the ego is a good thing, since the alternative is its disintegration—a decidedly poor outcome for an organism that must interact with the world for survival. If psychotic projection is the best one can muster to keep intolerable anxiety at bay, then it must (and inevitably will) be used to do so.

Some defenses, however, cause as many problems as they solve. The psychotic and immature defenses may spare the ego from intolerable anxiety, but they usually result in other difficulties. Paranoia tends to cause poor interpersonal interactions, which leads to social isolation, failure to achieve desired goals, and more paranoia. Over the long run, a person's adaptation is compromised by the use of the early ego defenses, and this usually is noticed by others. Mature defenses, on the other hand, often generate byproducts that are seen by others as useful and desirable. If I am besieged by sexual fantasies and as a result I carve a great sculpture or become a scientist who finds a cure for cancer, the results not only reduce my anxiety but also make the world a better place.

Altruism is the ability to place the interests of another above one's own.

Adaptation to life

There is scientific evidence that the use of early ego defenses leads to poorer outcomes for people. In his landmark study presented in ***Adaptation to Life*** (1977), George Vaillant followed a cohort of Harvard students into late middle age. The findings were striking. Not only did those who typically used immature defenses have impoverished interpersonal lives and poorer occupational and economic accomplishments, but they also had more chronic illness and shorter life expectancies. Social life and occupational functioning may be debatable measurements of good versus poor outcome, although they are basic human functions worldwide—all human beings are social creatures who must manipulate the environment to sustain life. Such values thus tend toward being universally valid. Vaillant's findings of poorer health and decreased longevity in those using early ego defenses are even more difficult to dismiss. They suggest, as psychiatry has long believed, that physical and mental functioning are so intimately intertwined as to be indistinguishable. If health and longevity mean anything to people, then early ego defenses, although better than nothing, are poorly suited for adaptation over time.

Psychodynamic theory originally proposed that ego defensive style was a result of childhood development. One's ego defenses, it was thought, were the result of development. The persistence of immature defenses into adulthood was then a symptom of developmental arrest. Modern ego psychology, however, takes a different perspective. It holds that any insult to the brain leads to disruption. The brain under stress must cope in any way it can. The use of immature ego defenses does not necessarily imply a developmental problem. A person who is postoperatively delirious may be hallucinating and paranoid. In the language of ego defense psychology, this person is using the psychotic defenses of projection and distortion. In such situations, however, this means simply that the stress has overwhelmed the patient's normal coping strategies, so that he is reduced to whatever he can muster to make sense of the world. It does not necessarily imply a developmental defect.

Most individuals use immature (although not psychotic) ego defenses from time to time. The assessment of ego defenses obviously takes into consideration acute strategies, which may include immature ego defenses in stressful situations. Ego assessment also should include an attempt to understand the individual's pattern over time. What type of defensive functioning has predominated? Faced with a stress, does the person lead off with early ego defenses, or are they strategies of last resort?

For some people, the use of immature ego defenses is the routine coping strategy. This is typical of those with personality disorders. In many others, the appearance of early ego defenses is the result of an unusual stress on the nervous system, such as a bout of depression or anxiety, a delirium, substance intoxication, or a schizophrenic break. Many people who have used mature defenses for most of their lives become regressed in the face of a major depressive episode. When the depression is adequately treated, their ego functioning is restored to its former level.

Ego psychology has the virtue of being largely observable. Although the initial formulation of ego psychology was conceived in terms of managing unconscious conflict, it is not necessary to invoke the concept of the unconscious to make ego psychology a workable clinical psychology. The acts are there to see, whether they are paranoid or the creative accomplishments of sublimation. Paranoiac behavior is almost invariably a source of long-term problems for the individual who engages in it, regardless of whether unconscious conflict is the cause of that behavior. The concept that paranoia is the result of unconscious conflict may not be required to achieve the desired clinical end. Early ego defensive acts often are the cause of trouble, and they can be pointed out as such and modified. Thus, acting-out individuals can be helped to build skills in consciously observing their feeling states and delaying the discharge of impulses. As we will see, ego psychology in this regard bears a close resemblance to behavioral psychology.

Interpretation

Therapy in the ego psychology model revolves around identifying ego defense mechanisms to the patient. The majority of these defenses, particularly the early defense mechanisms, operate unconsciously. The individual is seldom aware of her ego defenses, but this can change. The therapist can point out ego defenses as they occur. For example, when Mr. H rambled incessantly about the horror of the federal government rather than talking about his personal problems, the therapist could point this out to him. Then H could gradually see that ruminating about the government was not just a case of seeing things "the way things are," but had a distinct cause. It was easier when H became anxious for him to think that the government had all the problems, rather than admit to himself that his problems were largely of his own making. Since conscious awareness of anxiety is a hallmark of the mature ego defense mechanisms, this interpretation of ego defenses to the patient tends to result in the patient gradually using those mature defenses. Psychodynamic psychotherapy thus moves the patient in the direction of more mature ego functioning.

Interpretation is the act of pointing out ego defenses as they occur.

Such defense interpretations—the pointing out of ego defense mechanisms to the patient—must be done judiciously, in a setting of empathy and under conditions in which other coping strategies are available. Otherwise, the patient may stiffen her defenses to ward off the anxiety provoked by the interpretation. In H's case, this meant he had to build up a lot of trust in the therapist so he could willingly relinquish his paranoia for more mature ego defenses. Without that sense of support to bolster him through his anxiety, he would never have been able to face that anxiety.

Key points

- *Ego defenses* protect the ego from anxiety.

- Ego defenses gradually develop along with the capacity to distinguish the internal world from the external world.

- Ego defenses may be organized developmentally, from psychotic to immature to neurotic to mature.

- The more mature ego defenses reduce anxiety while increasing reality testing, and allow for more successful interaction with the external world.

- *Psychotic ego defenses* appear in infancy and cause gross distortions in reality testing.

- Psychotic ego defenses include psychotic projection, distortion, and denial.

- *Psychotic projection* is the attribution of internal states to the external world.

- *Distortion* is the severe misapprehension of external events to make them compatible with internal states.

- *Denial* is the refusal to acknowledge external realities that are anxiety-provoking.

- *Immature ego defenses* include nonpsychotic projection, distortion, denial, splitting, acting out, somatization, passive aggression, and undoing.

- *Nonpsychotic projection, distortion*, and *denial* alter the characteristics of the external world without frank delusions or hallucinations.

- *Splitting* separates the world into polar opposites of good and bad.

- *Acting out* is impulsive activity without regard to future consequences.

- *Somatization* is the presentation of psychological distress as physical distress.

- *Passive-aggression* is action that communicates aggression while appearing superficially nonaggressive.

- *Undoing* is action that attempts to reverse dangerous thoughts and feelings.

- *Neurotic defenses* allow greater reality testing than do the immature and psychotic ego defenses.

- Neurotic defenses include repression, intellectualization, isolation-of-affect, reaction formation, and displacement.

- *Repression* is the unconscious process of sequestering anxiety-provoking material from conscious awareness.

- *Intellectualization* and *isolation-of-affect* separate emotions from anxiety-provoking facts.

- Reaction formation transforms and urge into its opposite.

- Displacement is the transfer of impulses from an unacceptable object to an acceptable object.

- *Mature ego defenses* allow a high degree of reality testing and minimal distortion of external reality.

- Mature ego defenses include sublimation, anticipation, humor, and altruism.

- *Sublimation* is the use of anxiety as a motivator for productive activity.

- *Anticipation* is the ability to foresee future causes of anxiety.

- *Humor* is the ability to distance oneself from the immediate situation and to find humor in it.

- *Altruism* is placing another's interests before one's own.

- Ego defenses always are adaptive to some degree, but mature defenses are more adaptive than immature defenses.

- Ego defenses can be changed by interpretation and conscious modification.

Object relations theory 14

Introduction

Drive theory holds that relationships with people are a secondary effect of drive discharge. Our desire to be with other people, Sigmund Freud believed, is caused by the need of our aggressive and libidinal drives for objects that can fulfill them.

The object relations theorists modified this position by proposing that human beings have an innate drive for sociability. Human infants are born social creatures. Melanie Klein (Caper, 1988; Gabbard, 1994) observed that after about 2 months, human infants are actively involved in developing complex interactions with the mother that go beyond simply satiating appetite ("mother" is used here as a catchall term for any primary caregiver). Part of what such interactions involve is the development of an internalized sense, or *representation*, of the mother—an image of her that is both cognitive and emotional. This is called an *object representation*. The word object in this sense refers to the person who is the object of the representation.

Object relations are repetitions of old relationship patterns in current relationships.

This developing bud of representation eventually will expand and form one of the paradigms for later interpersonal relationships. When relationships are in any degree influenced by object representations, *object relations* are at work. Object relations are our sense of how things usually go in relationships. They are the patterns we expect (usually unconsciously) to see, and the patterns we repeat in our relationships. At times we may act as ourselves in the pattern; at other times we may assume the role of another.

Melanie Klein

Melanie Klein's belief was that very early object representations coalesce around the process of splitting. As we discussed in Chapter 13, splitting arises in early life, when the infant's world is split into events and objects that satisfy drive demands and those that do not. Nursing is entirely satiating when available, and the infant experiences the breast as a blissful source of pure goodness. On the other hand, when the infant becomes hungry and the breast is absent even momentarily, the image of the breast is one that is withholding, denying fulfillment, and therefore bad. Thus, the image of the breast oscillates between pure goodness and pure badness. At this early stage of development, the images cannot be integrated, for both cognitive and emotional reasons. The early ego is capable neither of conceiving that the two breast images are one and the same nor of tolerating the anxiety that entails from seeing the same object as a source of both bliss and pain. Also, the infant does not distinguish between the fantasized image and external reality. The fantasy of the breast is reality.

> The *paranoid–schizoid position* is characterized by splitting—the ego cannot see the same object as a source of both bliss and pain.

Klein termed this the *paranoid-schizoid position*, wherein the infant lives in a world of alternating salvation and terror. When caregiving is available, it succors all anxiety and satisfies all drives completely. When it is not available, even momentarily, pain and terror become overwhelming—the infant has no ability to modulate such feelings except by satisfying its drives through its caretaker.

Only later does the child begin to develop and integrate a sense that objects have both good and bad properties, and that the fantasized object is distinct from the real object. This latter ability is never completely developed, however. Even mature adults interact with the world through object representations and are not always able to distinguish between fantasy and reality. Is the boss really overbearing? Or is the perception of the boss influenced by previous experiences with authority, so that sensitivity to authority is determined both by the actions of the boss and by how we have acted and perceived ourselves in previous interactions with authority?

According to the object relations theorists, adults may become arrested in the early stage of object-relations development—the paranoid-schizoid position. This developmental arrest results in psychotic and severe personality disorders. The world of an adult fixated at the paranoid-schizoid position threatens annihilation when it is not completely gratifying. The frustrating acts of others are incompatible with their good qualities. Conversely, gratifying objects cannot have any bad aspects. Thus, paranoid-schizoid adults view the world not as an integrated, linear experience across time but as disorganized, as one or another object representation predominates and the object correspondingly garners idealization or devaluation.

Case example

When Mr. L was pleased with his therapeutic relationship, he became quite effusive, showering the psychiatrist with praise. "You are so good," he said repeatedly. "No one else has ever understood me before."

Although such compliments seem gratifying, they obviously are wildly magnified, no matter what the skills of the psychiatrist. In L's case, they were a warning knell for the devaluation that must eventually arrive.

If L called between sessions with trouble, he inevitably up-braided the psychiatrist if he could not or would not give L more than 15 minutes of telephone time outside of scheduled sessions. When asked how much time L thought was sufficient, L could not say. He thought the psychiatrist should "just know."

When a change in the psychiatrist's practice required termination of treatment, L lamented the end, saying, "You're the only thing in my life I have to live for." Finally, the therapy ended in total devaluation. "You're the worst psychiatrist I have ever known. I hate you."

A key feature of reality testing is the ability to distinguish the characteristics that actually belong to objects of the external world from our own projections of object representations (Kernberg, 1980). When L believed the psychiatrist had failed him, it was very difficult for L to perceive any quality in the psychiatrist other than withholding and neglecting. Of course, it is all too common in the world for people to hate one another, and sometimes such hatred may be based in reality. But L's shifts from overwhelming love to absolute hatred and back again are evidence of a different phenomenon, that of a poorly developed ego attempting to make sense of a world that is sometimes gratifying and other times disappointing.

In many ways, Klein's theory is another way of describing the ego defense of splitting. However, in the model of ego psychology, splitting is a purely defensive maneuver designed to protect the ego from anxiety. As seen by object relations theory, splitting is a developmental failure in (or regression from) the ability to conceptualize relationships with emotionally important individuals in an emotionally mature and realistic way.

Klein believed that if children successfully traverse the paranoid-schizoid position, they attain a mature phase of object relations called the *depressive position*. In the depressive position, the child becomes aware that her actions can impact another. The child is no longer focused only on what impact the world has on her, but on how she can impact the world. Since the child has aggressive and libidinal drives that may be dangerous and uncomfortable, she (in the depressive position) realizes that objects are potentially injured or destroyed by her actions or even by her fantasies, and this realization allows for the guilt characteristic of depression.

The *depressive position* is characterized by the realization that one's actions can impact others.

Margaret Mahler

Separation–individuation

Margaret Mahler proposed a somewhat different formulation of object relations development, based on intensive observations of young children and mothers going through a process (or phase) she called *separation–individuation* (Gabbard, 1994; Mahler, Pine, & Bergman, 1975). Mahler saw that after a *symbiotic* period, the young child at around 5 months begins to crawl and explore his environment independent of his mother. This is the subphase of *differentiation*, when the child begins to distinguish what in the environment is distinct from his mother. *Stranger anxiety*, the fear reaction of the infant to unfamiliar individuals, becomes prominent during these months.

By about 10 months, in the *practicing* subphase, the child has begun to crawl actively, which allows for greater distance from the mother. The child typically experiences euphoria at his newfound abilities, but also fear of separation from his mother. So, he will explore, then return to mother for comfort.

At 18 months, the child has a deepening sense of separateness from his mother, brought about by his improving ambulation and linguistic ability, and is no longer intoxicated with this sense of separateness. The separateness now brings about at once a desire for autonomy and a fear of abandonment. Reunions with mother no longer are unambivalent—they are conflictual. The child both desires and loathes his mother. Typical reunions during this *rapprochment phase* are fraught with these split emotions. Yet this phase is necessary. The splitting must be overcome by the child, so that more mature and stable object relations can develop, in which the child is secure in the belief that his mother will be there and he uses the environment for alternative sources of soothing. This is the final subphase of separation–individuation, known as *consolidation*. Failure to develop these mature object relations leads to the perpetuation of splitting as a characteristic style into adulthood.

Object constancy

It is not unusual for adults such as L to have difficulty with what is termed *object constancy*. This is the stable sense that emotionally significant others still exist even when they are absent, an ability Mahler believed developed as the rapprochement subphase was resolved. Libidinal object constancy develops at roughly the same time as general object constancy, a capacity first described by Jean Piaget (Sadock & Sadock, 2000). Piaget discovered that young children at first behave as if objects that move out of their immediate field of awareness simply cease to exist. Thus, a ball that bounces out of sight is immediately ignored as if it no longer existed. Between 18 months and 2 years of age, however, children show a developing ability to track objects even if they disappear from immediate perception. Thus, the child will follow and search for the absent ball. Very young infants are perpetually surprised at the reappearance of people and other objects after they have been absent from the perceptual field.

Similarly, emotionally significant others, or *libidinal objects,* cease to exist for the young child when they are out of sight (Fraiberg, 1969). If caretaking is reasonably stable, the child eventually will develop the sense that these others continue to exist as caretakers even when they are absent from the immediate environment. In later life, this appears as the ability to pull to mind images of absent "others" in order to modulate anxiety, as a man might say to himself, "Well, I just got chewed out by the boss, but my wife still loves me."

Adults who lack this ability cannot sustain a sense of others as stable libidinal objects when they are physically absent, and so they are said to lack *libidinal object constancy.* This deficit often appears in otherwise cognitively intact or even high-functioning individuals.

Case example

Mr. O was an attorney who had done very well both academically and occupationally, but who had persistent relationship difficulties that brought him to psychiatric treatment. Part of the problem turned out to be a deficit in libidinal object constancy. When his psychiatrist left on vacation, O became overwhelmed by a fear that the psychiatrist had ceased to exist. He could calm this fear only by calling the psychiatrist's answering machine to hear his voice. When this was explored in treatment, O revealed that he was unable to visualize or "feel" the psychiatrist, and so he could create this sense of the psychiatrist as a stable object only when some concrete reminder, such as his voice on an answering machine, was available. Later, O and the psychiatrist arranged for O to carry a pen from the psychiatrist's office during such absences; this small token functioned in a similar capacity as the answering machine message.

Transference

Object relations theory gives another explanation of the clinical phenomenon of transference. Recall that, according to drive theory, *transference* is the repetition of unconscious conflict in the therapeutic relationship between doctor and patient, wherein it manifests itself as responses by the patient to the doctor that are inappropriate simply based on their current interactions. The actions of the psychiatrist—so long as they are within the limits of typical social interactions and not so extreme that anyone would be uncomfortable, of course—produce different responses in different people. Observing and interpreting these responses with the patient, rather than simply assuaging them (by, for example, talking more so that the patient becomes less anxious) is one of the common techniques of psychodynamic psychotherapy.

According to object relations theory, the explanation for transference is that it is the manifestation of old object relations. For example, if Mr. L was the victim of an absent and withholding mother, we would expect that this object relationship might be repeated in the current therapy relationship. The psychiatrist would then appear to L as the withholding mother, and L would experience the psychiatrist as withholding. This might explain why no amount of time on the phone between sessions was satisfying to L. The real amount of phone time had little bearing, since the issue was a repetition of an object relationship—anything the psychiatrist did was likely to become entwined in this pattern, since it was L's habitual way of seeing the world, largely independent of external reality. L's psychiatrist was withholding to some extent, of course—he could not spend hours on the phone with L—and this provided the nidus around which the object relations repetition condensed. But L had to get used to people being somewhat unavailable to him if he was to succeed in relationships, since everyone was destined to disappoint his needs sooner or later. The psychiatrist might therefore interpret the object relationship L was experiencing, perhaps saying, "I notice you become extremely upset when I'm not available to you," and then exploring L's responses with him.

It is important to note that in the unconscious drama of object relations, a person can play any role. Although the individual often acts as herself, she might equally play the role of the parent, friend, lover, or any other person. Thus, when L turned frosty, he might have been playing the withholding mother in his object relationship pattern, while the psychiatrist became the rebuffed child.

Case example

Ms. U was the daughter of an extremely volatile woman, who was alternatingly adoring and abusive. As an adult, U sought out leadership roles but found it difficult at times to carry out some of the responsibilities of leadership, particularly if the job required confrontation. When one of U's employees persistently violated her expectations, U was faced with a quandary. Confronting the employee made her so uncomfortable she could hardly tolerate the thought. In exploring this with her therapist, it became apparent that U saw herself in the role of the benevolent leader who would handle underlings kindly. This fantasy was so powerful it threatened to render her ineffective in her leadership role.

In this fantasy, U played several roles at once. First, she was her own mother, but who was now treating her children in the kindly manner in which U wished to be treated. Thus, for her to act aggressively to correct her employee would have been to recapitulate the treatment she had received from her mother, which would have been intolerable. Second, she played herself in two other roles: In one role U identified with the rebellious employee who stood up to authority. In the other, she and the employee reversed roles, so that U became the child who was frightened of the wrath of the employee. All three of these themes coalesced to make U terrified of confronting the employee. But in talking through these object relations, she was able to take a more realistic view of her relationship with her employees, and she finally was able to properly and humanely intercede to correct the problem.

Today, older theories of object relations (in which object relations are formed at an early age through interactions with parents) are being supplanted by empirical research showing the powerful effect of peer relationships, both in early childhood and during the teenage years, on personality development. It is apparent that object relationships continue to form throughout the lifespan and are constantly readjusted.

Case example

Mr. T often had felt somewhat distant from his peers, and this was particularly true during adolescence. Although not unattractive, he found it difficult to muster the courage to ask for dates. As the years went by, his general opinion of himself was that he would never share in the intimacy others enjoyed. However, he eventually married. As the years passed, his marriage began to experience difficulties. T's wife was not nearly as affectionate as he was. T was unable to adjust to her more reserved style, and whenever she failed to exhibit the affection he longed for, he felt injured. Although ostensibly T related his displeasure as the result of marriage to a "frigid" woman, he admitted during therapy that he often experienceed fantasies of intimacy that brought flooding back the feelings of his teenage years, which he remembered as filled with isolation and loneliness.

Key points

- *Object relations* are repetitions of old relationship patterns in current relationships.

- In psychoanalytic theory, this process is thought to be due to unconscious expectations about the patterns of relationships. It is the explanation for the phenomenon of *transference*.

- Melanie Klein proposed a developmental process for object relations, in which the child traverses first the *paranoid-schizoid position* (characterized by splitting), followed by the *depressive position*.

- Margaret Mahler observed a sequence of object relations, termed *separation–individuation*, that appears in early childhood and includes *differentiation, practicing, rapprochment*, and *consolidation*.

- Change in object relations occurs therapeutically through interpretation, conscious change, and the living of new relationships that do not confirm old object relations expectations.

- Object relations continue to be formed throughout childhood and probably throughout the lifespan.

The self 15

Self-psychology

Sigmund Freud used the term *ego* to include the sense of self, not simply the agency that affects the realization of drives. Each human being has a sense of him- or herself as a separate and autonomous entity, a "who I am" that is maintained across time and events. Freud left this aspect of the ego relatively unexplored, concentrating his efforts on the mechanisms by which the ego regulates drive discharge. *Self-psychology* first appeared in the work of the American psychiatrist Harry Stack Sullivan. Sullivan believed that the experience of the self was primarily a social one (Sadock & Sadock, 2000). In part, this belief came from that fact that the only self that is observable is in interaction with others. Sullivan believed that the earliest sense of self is created by the bond between mother and infant, a bond characterized by empathy and attunement. This *self-system* later becomes a rich network of relationships and is used by the self to modulate anxiety. For Sullivan, the personality is the "relatively enduring pattern of interpersonal relations that characterize human life" (Sadock & Sadock, 2000, p. 633).

Case example

Ms. J was prone to using immature ego defenses, particularly somatization, and had a poorly integrated sense of self. She often was unable to define her feeling states with accuracy. She simply felt "bad" at times. Whether this feeling was anxiety, fear, depression, or something else, J could not say, because she could not identify her thoughts at the time. Instead of thinking, "I'm worried about my relationship with my boyfriend because it's very dissatisfying," she would simply become disorganized in a nameless, terrifying way.

J had a remarkably poor sense of herself as a consistent entity over time and multiple situations. Introspection was difficult for her—she had little skill in observing her own internal states, of generating a dialogue with herself that connected the events of her internal life to the external world in a meaningful way. Thus, J might feel bad after a fight with her boyfriend, but she could not connect her feelings with the fight. Instead, she simply found herself feeling bad and could provide no explanation for the feeling. If asked what had happened immediately before she felt bad, J could only haltingly and with great difficulty reconstruct her thoughts and feelings.

J's sense of self was not a reliable phenomenon with predictable characteristics. Instead, her life seemed a disjointed, fragmentary experience that shifted from moment to moment with extreme intensity and without apparent cause. She remembered little of her childhood; she could recount a few events she knew had occurred because others had told her about them.

Now contrast J's situation with Mr. B's.

Case example

Mr. B began to be depressed when he moved in with his girlfriend. Although he was unsure exactly why this was the case, B could causally connect the events. He also had a definite sense that he was different from his usual self, the person he had been for the first 40 years of his life. He was able to name his "self's" characteristics—outgoing, energetic, tending to get his own way although sometimes ruffling feathers en route. "It's not like I was a gem, but I'd like to be my old self again," he said when he came to treatment. Although he was not without problems, B's emotional state tended to be relatively stable and predictable, partly because he understood who he was and therefore how external events might impact him.

Heinz Kohut

Self-objects

Heinz Kohut believed that the sense of self grows through developmental stages, much like the growth of the psychic structures hypothesized by Freud and the object relations of Klein and others (Baker & Baker, 1987; Kohut, 1971, 1977). Kohut thought the sense of self consolidated in childhood, in a timeframe roughly consistent with the consolidation of the ego and superego in the oedipal phase. Like the object relations theorists and Sullivan, Kohut believed that relationships are a crucial element in the formation of the self. As we have seen, the early infant has no ability to distinguish between what is internal and what is external. An infant only gradually experiences her mother as a discrete object. It is easy to observe an infant discovering the boundaries of her body. At very early ages, the infant's hand will come across her visual field as if it was a separate object. Conversely, the infant may not experience the walls of the crib as a separate object until she bumps into them. Later, these experiences of separateness condense into the toddler who understands what part of the world belongs to her "self."

No matter how autonomous the self becomes, it always is partly defined by objects in the external world. We derive much of our sense of who we are, even as adults, by the objects to which we attach ourselves. To use an example, the experience of having one's house broken into is more than simple disappointment and anger at material damage. It involves a sense of personal violation, the feeling that one has somehow been invaded and abused, because one's residence is a defining characteristic of oneself. In other words, a residence may be one of the ways people define a sense of self. This is one reason for why moving to a new location is disconcerting until it becomes familiar.

Self-objects are those we use to define our sense of self.

Winnicott (1953) described a special relationship young children have with important objects in their environments. According to Winnicott, *transitional objects* help the young child bridge the gap between an infantile world in which he is entirely unable to distinguish himself from outside objects and the well-developed ego of older years, which has a clear sense of such distinctions. Young children typically develop close relationships with special objects, such as a blanket or teddy bear, and they invest those objects with a great deal of emotional attachment. Such a transitional object serves as a tool with which the young child can explore the emotional and cognitive differences between himself and the object; this is one of the first important self-object relationships. Eventually, the transitional object is relinquished when it no longer is necessary and the child can enter into more complex self-object relationships.

Interpersonal relationships generally are more important than material objects in defining the self. Kohut termed the network of objects—both material and interpersonal, including people, things, ideas, and memories by which we define the self—as *self-objects*. Note here that *define* is not usually a conscious process. The formation of self-object fields is largely unconscious. Whereas we may choose with whom we want to be, unconscious processes largely determine how another person will be incorporated into our self-object fields.

Transitional objects are items children invest with emotional attachment.

Development of the self

Developmentally, the first self-object is the primary caretaker. Kohut believed that the infant derives much information about herself from interacting with her caretaker. Subsequent infant research has borne this out. In caretaking relationships of adequate quality, mother and infant quickly develop rapport and attunement. Infants appear to be hard-wired for social interaction from birth and almost immediately prefer to look at humans rather than other objects. The mother also is instinctively attuned. Across all cultures, mothers hold their infants at a distance which is optimal for an infant's visual acuity. Mothers also repeat a small set of phonemes, vocalizations such as "Ah" and "Ooh"—the universal building blocks of language—in a sing-song voice that allows for optimal processing by the infant. An infant's emotional attunement also is in evidence at an early age. Mothers reflect the emotional states of their babies, smiling, frowning, or staring wide-eyed when the baby does. Kohut called the infantile sense of self *dissociated*, since it scattered and primitive.

At some point the toddler begins to discover that his subjective world is in part isolated from others. This is particularly because of his deepening linguistic abilities. The child discovers that not everything is expressible to others, and thus there are parts of his self that will remain isolated. Furthermore, there are some inner experiences that would be destructive to share, such as aggressive impulses or sexual fantasies. As months and years pass, the subjective sense of the self in relation to others becomes increasingly complex, with a greater sense of individual autonomy and an experience of the self as a unique entity which is distinct from others. Yet that autonomy is never absolute. Throughout the lifespan, the subjective sense of self continues to be defined to a significant degree by the self-objects that populate our worlds. During the toddler years, the sense of self coheres into what has been termed a *nuclear cohesive self.*

Narcissism

Kohut believed that a person's experience of the self can fail to develop successfully, leading to psychopathology, depending on the degree of developmental arrest. Defects in self-experience are both cognitive and emotional. Ms. J, for example, had a cognitive experience in which she was unable to conceive of herself as an individual distinct from her mother. Of course, she knew intellectually that she was a different and distinct person, but she did not live this knowledge. Her subjective experience was that she could not conceive of life without intimate involvement with her mother. Thus, when facing her mother's death, J reacted first with denial and, when that failed, she became suicidal. The emotional experience of poor self-development is one of wild swings from ecstasy to terror, depending on the fluctuations in the self-object field. Notice that this parallels the phenomenon previously described as splitting.

J's self-psychology manifests itself in an extreme form. Kohut formulated his theory of self-psychology from treating and observing a less disturbed group of individuals who had "narcissistic" disturbances, individuals who oscillated between feelings of inferiority and envy, on one hand, and a sense of grandiose self-importance (although not of psychotic proportions), on the other. In turn they tended to either devalue or idealize others, depending on how well others fulfilled their needs.

Kohut believed that narcissistic psychopathology was the result of a specific developmental defect. He observed that children in the genital developmental period, before the consolidations of the oedipal period, pass through a phase in which their relationships with their caregivers are characterized by a need to idealize and be idealized. This need is appropriate at that age and must be met empathetically by caregivers. Thus, the child who comes to his mother saying "I'm Superman today, Mommy!" needs to be met by a mother who plays along with the game and allows the child to be Superman. Time and reality will teach the child that he is not Superman, and the game will die away over the day. But the bolstered sense of self derived from a self-object (the mother) who idealizes the child persists and, when it is eventually consolidated, becomes healthy and realistic self-esteem. Kohut believed that the child needs to see the "gleam in the mother's eye" (Baker & Baker, 1987, p. 3) to internalize a sense of self-esteem, since so much of the self is defined by others.

Those with narcissistic disturbances oscillate between feelings of inferiority and grandiose self-importance.

If the grandiose approach of the child is met by a mother who precipitously lets down his need for idealization (perhaps by saying brusquely, "You're not Superman. Don't bother me, I'm working.") the child is crushed, and the need for idealization and validated grandiosity persists into adulthood (if this is a repetitive pattern throughout childhood). The result is an adult left with unconscious wishes to be idealized and feel omnipotent.

Case example

Mr. M was a young man who came into treatment for depression. Even as his depression lifted with antidepressant medication, however, he continued to have a very volatile relationship with his wife, and he had difficulty maintaining a stable mood. M was extremely sensitive to even the slightest misattunement between himself and others. This sensitivity manifested itself in displeasure with his wife when she failed to empathetically perceive his needs. If M wanted physical closeness—usually cuddling, and in large quantities—and his wife was distant or absorbed in other activities, he became momentarily despondent and then angry, so that a fight ensued. After fights, M felt worthless and unlovable, even sometimes suicidal.

M also had trouble holding down a job. Typically in his view, the issue was that his coworkers did not appreciate his specialness. He became offended and refused to participate in educational sessions if they were about something he felt he had mastered already, with the result that he was often reprimanded. M felt he was tremendously talented, yet he was underachieving because his talent went unrecognized. At times he felt like a failure; at other times he externalized the blame onto others.

In therapy, M could not tolerate even a semblance of conflict. If the psychiatrist pointed out that M looked angry or down, he became extremely uncomfortable, so that the psychiatrist found himself hesitant to say or do anything that might disrupt M's fragile equilibrium. M overidealized his psychiatrist, and also sought to identify with him through a fascination with science. This was pronounced enough that M spent hours daydreaming over books about being a scientist (or even a physician), while his real work went undone.

In mirror *transference individuals seek a state of complete empathic attunement, in which their need to be idealized is mirrored back to them.*

Kohut proposed that individuals who had narcissistic self-system deficits would continue to seek the sort of childhood experiences they had originally missed. They sought, he believed, a *mirror transference*—a state of complete empathic attunement in which their need to be idealized is mirrored back to them by another. Furthermore, they would evidence a grandiose sense of their own importance and continually seek validation of their specialness. And, just as a child views the parent with an idealizing awe, so the narcissistic adult continues to see others in an idealized way, an *idealizing transference*. When denied these experiences, the adult experiences narcissistic rage, involving extreme anger and total devaluation toward those who have not mirrored his need to feel special or remained idealizable. Occasionally, this rage erupts into destructive acts.

In Kohut's model, treatment for such narcissistic pathology is the provision of the missing childhood experiences. The therapist largely empathizes with the patient's need for specialness and mirrors to the patient a sense that she is special. As this empathy decreases narcissistic needs, more traditional interpretation of unconscious conflict, ego defenses, and object relations can occur.

In idealizing *transference individuals see others in an idealized way.*

Individuals with narcissistic disturbances sometimes form cohesive groups based on their mutually interlocking narcissistic needs. This dynamic commonly is seen in charismatic leader-follower groups (such as cults). In such groups, the charismatic leader typically is an individual seeking a mirroring transference. As such, the leader seeks out those who will mirror to him a sense of specialness. This is likely to happen when the group consists of individuals who are hungry for a figure to idealize (an idealizing transference). The mirror hungry leader and the ideal hungry followers thus form a commensal unit that meets the needs of both.

Key points

- *Self-psychology* proposes that human beings define much of who they are based on their relationships, both real and imagined, to animate and inanimate objects.

- Objects that define the sense of self are termed *self-objects*.

- Heinz Kohut's self-psychology views the self as developing through a phase of narcissistic needs for validation (*mirroring*) and the *idealization* of others. Failure to have these needs met results in *narcissistic psychopathology*.

- As in ego and objects psychology, change in self-psychology occurs through interpretation and replacing habit with conscious choice, as well as through living new self-object relationships.

Psychodynamic psychotherapy and other dynamic psychologies 16

Four psychodynamic psychologies

The four models of psychodynamic psychology—drive, ego, object, and self—have overlapping features (Pine, 1988). For example, the phenomenon of splitting may be conceptualized as the experience of orality/anality in drive psychology, as an early ego defense mechanism, as an immature form of object relations, or as an immature self-object relationship. Although these four models have different theoretical reasons for why splitting occurs, they all recognize splitting as a clinical phenomenon.

The four models have parallel developmental lines as well. Splitting in each of the models is an immature experience. In drive theory it occurs in the oral/anal stage—the earliest psychosexual stages—as one of the immature ego defenses used by young children. Ego psychology sees splitting as an attempt to defend the ego against anxiety by keeping good and bad as separate qualities. Object relations theory conceptualizes splitting as the early form of object relations that later consolidates into mature object relations. Self-psychology also views splitting as an early self-object experience in which the distinction between self and object is poorly developed and is at times precariously maintained in adulthood by violently splitting the two.

This parallelism has happened in part because the psychodynamic models appeared somewhat sequentially. Anna Freud built on her father's work. Kohut formulated his self-psychological model to dovetail with drive psychology. But it also is because different clinical observers saw the same phenomona occurring developmentally, even though they had different explanations for why they occurred. Klein had no allegiance to Anna Freud (indeed, their rival schools remain political adversaries in Britain), but she nevertheless observed splitting as an important clinical phenomenon.

This parallelism can be visualized graphically (Table 16.1). The result is a pictorial representation of developmental issues. Drive issues are laid next to ego defense mechanisms, which in turn are next to object relations and self-systems. This does not imply, however, that a given psychodynamic picture necessarily represents developmental problems. It is common for stress upon the central nervous system to impair functioning—whether that stress is due to a brain tumor, serious depression, alcohol abuse, or a developmental problem. As we saw in Part 2, the

TABLE 16.1   Stages of psychodynamic development

Age/ Drive Stage	Erikson	Ego Defenses	Object Relations	Self
1 Oral	Trust vs. mistrust	***Psychotic*** Projection Disortion Denial	Schizoid- paranoid position	Dissociated self
2 Anal	Autonomy vs. shame and doubt	***Immature*** Projection Denial Distortion Splitting	Depressive position	Nuclear cohesive grandiose self
3 Genital	Initiative vs. guilt	Somatization Acting out		Idealized parent imago
4 Oedipal		***Neurotic*** Repression Isolation-of-affect Intellectualization Reaction formation Displacement		Consolidation
6 Latency	Industry vs. inferiority			
11 Adolescent	Identity vs. role diffusion	***Mature*** Suppression Sublimation Anticipation Humor		
20 Mature	Intimacy vs. isolation	Altruism		
40	Generativity vs. stagnation			
70	Wisdom vs. despair			

The sequence of human psychological development as described by the various psychodynamic psychologies are listed in parallel. Adapted from Kaplan, Sadock, and Grebb (1994, p. 249).

problem at issue may result from a number of causes. Depressed people often are impaired in their psychodynamic functioning. Treat the depression, and psychodynamic functioning may improve dramatically, so that it no longer appears as if there is a developmental problem. On the other hand, if the depressed mood is successfully treated, say with antidepressant medication, and the psychodynamic impairment persists, this suggests that developmental difficulties may be present.

The important question is not whether a patient "really" has developmental psychodynamic problems but, instead, whether using a psychodynamic assessment and intervention is helpful in alleviating the problem. Psychodynamic psychotherapy can be successful in treating depression. Antidepressant medication and behavioral therapy also improve symptoms. Which model we use is more a matter of evidence than of a search for absolute truth.

The obvious question is how to choose among the various psychodynamic psychologies during assessment and treatment. If they all are correct, how is one to know which to apply in a given case? As is the case for psychiatric models in general, the answer is they should *all* be applied, particularly during the assessment phase, when a psychological formulation of the case is developed in each of several psychologies. Applying the psychologies in treatment is a process of weighing the advantages and drawbacks of each for a given patient.

This approach might draw the criticism that, if there is no single correct psychological explanation for a case, then there is none. How can we say that conflicting theories may both be correct and useful? As the patient and psychiatrist work together to solve problems, the hope is that, with so many models available, one will "speak louder" to the problems, with greater explanatory power and utility, than others. Helping this to occur is the practice and the art of psychotherapy. In the case of Mr. F, who had OCD, behavioral psychology was not "incorrect" in its formulation of his symptoms—in fact, he benefited from his treatment using behavioral techniques. But at some points in the treatment process, dynamic issues were more relevant and so needed to be addressed before another form of therapy could provide its maximum benefit. Later, it might be hoped that the consolidation of dynamic issues would make a course of behavioral therapy the treatment of choice for his OCD symptoms.

For a single psychological model to be correct requires individuals to remain static entities. Of course, they are not. Individuals are in a constant state of flux. What is important at one time is succeeded by something else the next. This should not be surprising. Although human beings universally require food, they are not hungry all the time. Sometimes, eating may be my most important goal, the primary issue in my life. Once this need is satiated, however, other concerns arise. Finding the route among psychological models eventually requires using them all.

Psychodynamic psychotherapy

The psychodynamic psychologies all have one important characteristic: *They are dynamic in that they hold all psychological processes to be the dynamic results of previous thoughts and experiences that are largely unconscious.* Freud believed that every mental state was derived from an antecedent mental state. Thus, discovering the cause for psychological distress in psychodynamic psychotherapy lies in uncovering the antecedent mental states. This is the essential process of psychodyanamic psychotherapy, wherein unconscious processes—whether drives, ego defenses, object relationships, or self-system deficits—are uncovered through the conversation and relationship between the therapist and patient.

Free association is the process of allowing the patient to say anything that comes to mind, without censoring the material.

Psychodynamic assessment.   Freud and subsequent psychodynamic therapists used the therapeutic relationship for two purposes. First, the patient directly gives the therapist material with which to make a psychodynamic assessment. The patient relates her emotional state and associated thoughts. She also provides information though a process called *free association*. At various points in the conversation, the patient has the option of choosing what to say next. What is chosen may have meaning. If she speaks of her depression and then quickly segues into an apparently irrelevant discussion of a particular relative, it may be that there is something in that relationship that bears on the depression, even if the patient is not consciously aware of it. For example:

Patient: . . . and so I've just been feeling so down, I finally decided to make an appointment.

Therapist: I see.

Manifest content is the overt meaning of the words a patient speaks.

Patient (After a pause, looking unsure what to say next): You know, my wife works just down the street from here.

The therapist immediately makes a mental note to further explore the relationship of the wife to the patient's depression. In this vignette, what Freud termed the *manifest content* of the conversation superficially reveals no connection between the relationship and the depression. However, the *latent content* indicates a possible connection, since the patient apparently was led to discuss his wife immediately after talking about his depressed mood. The psychiatrist therefore hypothesizes a connection, and then uses subsequent clinical material to confirm or refute the hypothesis.

Case example

Ms. A was referred by her psychiatrist to a social worker for psychotherapy treatment for her complaints of anxiety and irritability. She found herself chronically frustrated and irritable at work, where she frequently yelled at coworkers. She also was plagued by perfectionism, worry, and social avoidance. The psychiatrist diagnosed generalized anxiety disorder and prescribed a medication for her.

When the psychiatrist saw the patient again, she asked A about the progress of psychotherapy. A replied that she had met the social worker once, but she was not too sure about him. His demeanor, she thought, was overly sympathetic, and she wondered if he pitied her because he thought she was "crazy." The psychiatrist inquired why she assumed this. "He must have been revolted by me," A replied.

Far from being a simple statement about not liking her new therapist, A's report was filled with information. First, A had made a number of unjustified conclusions based solely on the initial handshake. She assumed that the social worker's concern stemmed from his being repelled by her. She thought he was repelled because he might think she was "crazy." In fact, any number of reasons could account for his limp handshake. Perhaps he was nervous because he was unsure of himself as a therapist. Or maybe he wasn't feeling well. Or he simply miscued when reaching for her hand. Any number of possibilities existed, but A had latched on to the one which fit her preconceived beliefs. This was evidence of a *transference* reaction. A might have been repeating an object relations theme: In A's unconscious, was the social worker an angry, judgmental parent? Or was A the judgmental parent, and he the helpless, limp child?

Here also was evidence of the ego defense of *projection* at work. A projected her own fear that she was crazy onto her therapist— neither he nor any other mental health professional had ever called her crazy or implied that she was so. Her suspicion reflected her own fear that she was tremendously defective, a fear which she vocalized.

From a drive perspective, A was having problems with aggression. She was often irritable or openly angry. She attempted to regulate her aggressive impulses by projection, so that the judgment and anger seemed to her to be coming from others, rather than from herself. Her sense of self was shaky, so her tendency was to view herself in a derogatory manner, as someone deserving of judgment. She was unsure of herself.

The psychiatrist pointed out the nature of the distortion, that there were many possible interpretations of the handshake, and that A had selected a negative one without data to support her conclusion. A then agreed that her assumption was unwarranted. "I always assume other people are going to hurt me." Despite this insight, A did not seem much comforted.

Latent content consists of the associations, nonverbal cues, and unspoken connections of a conversation.

But A's statement had provided new data. It strongly suggested that she had been judged or even abused in the past and so had learned to associate meeting someone new with an adverse consequence. She expected to be judged negatively because she had been in the past.

Judgment by others was a familiar paradigm in A's life, but in this case A was actually the one doing the judging. She had a negative impression of the therapist for his failure to properly shake her hand. The psychiatrist therefore asked what it would mean if someone thought she was crazy. "That I was weak," was A's reply.

The psychiatrist wondered—how was A weak? Her statement that she expected to be hurt carried the connotation that she had tried to have relationships in the past, and they had ended in pain. The psychiatrist suddenly found herself imagining a child desperately seeking nurturing and meeting only rebuff and hurt.

"I wonder if, deep down, you really liked Mr. Smith, but liking someone has often led to pain, and so you want to keep him away by assuming he didn't like you?" she asked. This interpretation was both a defense interpretation—the projection was pointed out—and an object relations interpretation—A has assumed the role of judge to avoid the role of one who is judged.

A looked thoughtful and nodded. Her demeanor of haughty suspiciousness diminished. As she relaxed, A began to talk about how her relationship with her schizophrenic mother had led her both to fear that she would turn out "crazy" like her mother and also to loathe weakness. Her mother's illness had led to so much distress in her own life, that the only way A could tolerate it was to denigrate her mother.

Thus, A's reaction to the social worker could be explained as (a) engendering aggressive impulses and (b) derived from an object relationship in which she loathed weakness both in herself (because it might be a sign of "craziness") and in others (because it reminds her of her mother's illness), so that (c) these feelings had to be projected onto the therapist as a defensive measure in order to protect herself from anxiety.

In working through this dynamic, A eventually was able to return to the social worker and continue therapy.

Insight is the act of consciously recognizing previously unconscious processes.

Confrontation is pointing out what the patient may not want to face.

Interventions.   In the example of A, we see both psychodynamic assessment and therapy occurring at one time. Since every encounter between people is potentially healing, therapy is always occurring, even in what might formally be called the assessment phase. In A's case, the primary intervention of psychodynamic psychotherapy is evident: the interpretation of transference.

The psychiatrist was able to interpret A's transference to the social worker on two levels: (a) as an ego defense and (b) as an object relationship. *Interpretation* is merely the act of pointing out unconscious processes that are evident to the therapist but not to the patient. This process makes the unconscious material conscious and thus available for modification. This is called *insight.*

Psychodynamic interventions may be more or less aggressive in how deeply they penetrate unconscious material. Interpretation, as seen above, is the most aggressive of the psychodynamic interventions, since it reveals unconscious material directly. A number of other psychodynamic interventions have been described (by the Menninger Clinic Treamtent Intervention Project; see Gabbard, 1994), ranging on a spectrum from expressive (or insight-oriented) to supportive. At the expressive end of this continuum lie interventions designed to precipitate insight into unconscious material. Supportive interventions emphasize the social support available in the therapeutic setting and seek to strengthen coping.

Somewhat less expressive than interpretation is *confrontation.* Confrontation is not necessarily blunt and aggressive, but simply serves to point out to the patient what he may not want to face. For example, if a patient frequently shifts the discussion from himself and onto others—by talking about a relative's psychology, for example—the therapist might confront this behavior by saying gently, "I notice you seem to prefer talking about your family to talking about yourself."

Still less expressive is *clarification*, in which the therapist attempts to summarize information so that it is clearer to the patient. Clarification typically is used when the patient evidences less denial. As an example of clarification, a therapist might say, "I think what you're trying to get at is how, when you make a mistake, you end up feeling that no one likes you."

In the middle of the expressive–supportive continuum is *encouragement to elaborate*. This device simply consists of asking the patient to say more about a particular topic. This of course communicates that the therapist sees the material as important and wants to hear what else the patient thinks about it and what associations occur with it.

Empathic validation occurs when the therapist expresses an understanding of and empathy for the patient's internal state. A therapist using an empathic statement might say, "I can see why you would feel that way."

Advice and praise lie even further toward the supportive end of the continuum. Advice might be phrased, "The next time your child disobeys you, I think you need to make sure and follow through on your threat to ground her." Praise would include remarks such as, "You did a great job setting limits with your child this time. I know that wasn't easy for you."

Finally, *affirmation* is the most supportive therapeutic technique, and consists of registering the patient's situation. It may take the form of nodding and saying "Mm-hmm," or "I see."

In *clarification* the therapist summarizes information so it is clearer to the patient.

Encouragement to elaborate consists of asking the patient to say more about a particular topic.

Empathic validating occurs when a therapist expresses understanding and empathy for a patient's internal state.

Advice and praise are techniques at the supportive end of the supportive–expressive continuum.

It must be remembered that unconscious material, according to psychodynamic theory, is unconscious for a reason: The material is too anxiety-provoking to be allowed to rise to conscious awareness. So, psychodynamic interventions are potentially destabilizing as well as potentially healing. Whether an intervention with a particular patient should tend toward the expressive or the supportive depends on that patient's strengths and weaknesses. In general, more expressive therapy is indicated with patients who have good ego functioning and a history of positive responses to trial interpretations. Patients who evidence poor ego functioning and lack psychological mindedness, or who are under severe social stress, are usually better served by supportive therapy, especially in the early stages of treatment.

The other crucial element in psychodynamic therapy is the *healing relationship* between therapist and patient. Therapy is not merely an intellectual exercise of the patient gradually coming to consciously understand the unconscious motives that have driven her. It also is a process of learning new relationships. As we have seen, transference is an inevitable part of any interpersonal interaction. The patient attempts to draw the therapist into reenacting old patterns. What therapy provides is a forum in which a relationship can be different. When transference inevitably occurs, it can be interpreted rather than simply lived out. This does not occur in most relationships outside of therapy, so the therapeutic relationship is a unique opportunity. As the transference is worked through, the patient is able to make use of the therapeutic relationship in relationships outside therapy.

Affirmation consists of simply registering the patient's situation.

Psychoanalysis

Psychoanalysis is the original psychodynamic treatment modality. It is designed for patients who are appropriate for maximally expressive psychotherapy. In psychoanalysis, patient and therapist meet 3 to 5 times a week for an hour. The duration of the therapy is open-ended but typically takes years. The purpose of this intensive undertaking is to allow transference to become maximally apparent. To this end, an intense relationship between patient and therapist is deliberately fostered by the frequency of meeting and by a reliance on *free association*. The patient is encouraged to say anything that enters his mind, without attempts to censor the material. It is hoped that through free association, unconscious material will freely emerge to conscious awareness, where it can then be interpreted. The goal of psychoanalysis is a restructuring of character and a resolution of mood and anxiety symptoms through improvements in ego functioning, object relationships, self-system, and drive gratification.

The *healing relationship* between therapist and patient allows the patient to learn new ways of relating to others.

Despite its long history, there is little systematic data supporting the efficacy of psychoanalysis beyond case reports and case series. Because of the highly specific nature of the individual therapeutic relationship, it is difficult to standardize treatment among therapists so as to conduct clinical trials. It also is difficult to design an appropriate placebo condition. This does not mean that psychoanalysis is not effective. However, its efficacy remains to be rigorously demonstrated.

Psychoanalytically-oriented psychotherapy

Psychoanalytically-oriented psychotherapy is modeled after psychoanalysis, but it places less emphasis on the development of transference and restructuring the character. Meetings typically occur every 1 to 4 weeks for an hour, and the focus can range anywhere on the supportive–expressive continuum. Duration of treatment is indefinite, but is typically less than for psychoanalysis.

In short-term anxiety-provoking psychotherapy the patient moves rapidly from assessment to interpretation of unconscious material.

Brief psychodynamic psychotherapy

Brief psychodynamic therapy is structured so that the client completes the course of treatment in a specified number of sessions, typically 6 to 20. Rather than aiming for restructuring of the character, brief psychodynamic psychotherapy seeks to resolve a particular problem or set of symptoms. This focus of treatment is spelled out in advance. The therapy may be supportive (such as helping someone through a crisis) or expressive (with the aim of resolving a specific unconscious conflict that is causing symptoms). An example of the latter is *short-term anxiety-provoking psychotherapy*, or STAPP (Sifneos, 1972), which is used with patients who have good ego strength and who can withstand a rapid transition from assessment to interpretation of unconscious material.

Brief psychodynamic therapies often make use of a concept called the *core conflictual relationship theme*, or CCRT (Crits-Cristoph, Luborsky, Dahl, Popp, Mellon, & Mark, 1988). Brief therapy attempts to elucidate this theme, which gets quickly to issues of ego defenses, object relationships, self-system, and transference. The focus of the therapy is on quickly understanding the CCRT, with limited attention paid to peripheral themes.

The core conflictual relationship theme is used in brief therapy to get quickly to problem issues.

Other dynamic psychologies

The four psychologies represent the predominant schools of dynamic psychological thought used in psychiatry today. However, they are not all-inclusive. Although they have proved useful in clinical practice, other dynamic psychologies may be equally useful.

Erik Erikson

Erik Erikson improved on Freud's concept of psychological stages of development by extending it throughout the lifespan (Erikson, 1980). Freud implied that the most crucial developmental stages occur in childhood. Erikson held roughly to the stages of childhood development elucidated by Freud, but he added other stages, believing that crucial developmental tasks are posed to adults as well as to children and that these stages must be mastered sequentially—the *epigenic principle*.

During the oral stage, Erikson believed, the infant is primarily concerned with issues of basic trust versus mistrust. In the anal phase, themes of autonomy versus shame and doubt are paramount. The oedipal phase brings questions of initiative versus guilt. The latency years, between the oedipal phase and adolescence, are concerned with issues of industry versus inferiority. The adolescent must consolidate an identity, or he faces "role diffusion," in which the lack of a firmly established identity endangers his ability to develop clear goals and ideals about his occupation and sexual identity.

The *epigenic principle* says that developmental tasks must be mastered sequentially.

In the third and fourth decades of life, Erikson believed the adult enters a stage of "intimacy versus isolation," in which she must develop the ability to form long-lived attachments such as friendships and marriage, as well as to find a set of life tasks to which she becomes devoted. Failure to establish intimacy threatens her with isolation—a life without long-standing relationships and without important central tasks.

The fifth and six decades bring the stage of "generativity versus stagnation," in which healthy adaptation leads the adult to nurture younger generations and to continue finding new creative goals. Finally, in the "integrity versus despair" stage of later years, the individual is confronted with his own mortality and the closing of tasks; the "life cycle" must be accepted as it draws to a close.

Lack of resolution at any stage leaves characteristic symptomatology. Erikson might view someone in her 40s who has yet to establish long-standing relationships and a career identity as still struggling with the developmental stage of "intimacy versus isolation." Most importantly, Erikson believed that change is possible at any age. It is never too late to grow, to master old tasks, and to resolve conflicts.

Erikson's theory is largely observable in the process of individuals living their lives. Unlike the previous psychodynamic models, it does not require the existence of an unobservable entity like the unconscious. If a patient in her early 20s is talking about conflicts in career choice and sexual relationships, and these are problems that someone her age typically encounters, then it is justified to say these issues constitute a stage which, on the whole, people have to navigate at that time in their lives. However, the model may tend to overgeneralize. Erikson's model is not the only way in which the problems of living can appear, and it tends to produce this illusion.

Carl Jung

Carl Jung's great contribution to dynamic psychology is twofold. First he developed the concept of *psychological types*, or personality styles. These are popularly famous as the *introvert versus extrovert*, although Jung's typology is more complex, having additional dimensions such as *thinking versus feeling* and *intuition versus sensation*. Jung also developed the concept of *archetypes*, universal prototypical human experiences that form a part of how human beings structure their understanding of the world (Jung, 1961).

Like Sigmund Freud, Jung believed that a psychological domain called the unconscious lay beneath the conscious mental activity of human beings. But in Jung's psychology, the unconscious has two layers: a *personal* layer and a *collective* layer. Jung observed that in most human cultures certain themes inevitably recur: birth and death, fear of night and strangers, eating, and sexual coupling, to name a few. These are "archetypal" human situations, forming the structure upon which an individual human life is built. The personal unconscious of each individual is thus constructed upon a collective unconscious, which is passed both genetically and in the nature of the human situation. The personal unconscious is predisposed to a certain style—introvert or extrovert, for example. The former tend to be introspective and withdrawn, the latter primarily concerned with affairs of the world.

Jung's psychology has had relatively minor influence on American psychiatry, partly as a result of politics. Jung was originally a disciple of Freud, and the two had a parting of ways because of their differing models of the psyche. American psychiatry followed Freud, and Jung's influence is restricted largely to Europe. But if Freud's model is weakened by its reliance on the unobservable unconscious, Jung's model is doubly so, since it hypothesizes two layers of the unconscious. How do we know what constitutes an archetype? There would seem to be an infinite number of possibilities. That certain themes return again and again in human cultures does not imply that human psychology must overlie them. Jung thought that clinical material supported his belief in the collective unconscious, but this is difficult to prove. However, Jung's psychology is less mechanistic than Freud's and paved the way for psychologies of object and the self previously examined.

> Jung's *psychological types* classify personalities through a series of opposites, including "introvert vs. extrovert."

> An *archetype* is a universal prototypical human experience that forms a part of how people structure their understanding of the world.

Existentialism

It has been an important criticism of Freud's drive theory that it tends to be mechanistic. It suggests that human beings' psychological states result from an impersonal "mental apparatus" that discharges drives in one particular way or another, shaped purely by the forces of experience upon the apparatus. Lost in this perspective are human beings' unique experiences. This loss was partly recaptured by object relations theory and self-psychology, but even these psychologies have a peculiar blind spot—they do not specifically address the experience of finite human beings in an infinite universe.

That experience, as the existential psychologists and philosophers realized, includes experiences of death and meaninglessness. Death haunts every moment of human existence. It is the force perpetually pulling at life, against which life cannot ultimately prevail. This finitude draws into question the meanings we take for granted which structure the experience of ourselves and our lives. In the immensity of space and time, what does it really mean to have particular experiences and values, since all are ultimately swept away?

Existential psychology holds that all anxiety is fundamentally anxiety about death. The prospect of death, especially our own, is something we work very hard to keep screened from consciousness. Freud's own theory may be one example of this denial. It is remarkable, as Ernst Becker pointed out in *The Denial of Death* (1973), that Freud's brilliant theories of anxiety managed to generally ignore fear of death, focusing instead on anxiety's origin in unconscious conflict. In fact, Freud supposed that rather than being afraid of death, human beings had a drive to die—the controversial third drive of the death instinct.

Existential psychology says that when we are anxious, we are fundamentally anxious about death. Anxiety is a signal of danger, and so in a basic sense serves to alert the organism to potentially fatal problems. Like all living organisms, human beings fear death. But of all creatures, human beings alone have the unique ability to understand the certainty of death. This knowledge haunts us continually as a subterranean fear lurking beneath every thought and act. Inescapably, that fear threatens to render our existence meaningless: If we must die, then does all we hold important die with us? When we experience this meaninglessness, as every human being must, we experience both the truth of our mortality and the evanescence of meaning. What meaning our lives have, existentialism holds, we give them. Thus, for psychological health, the individual must come to terms with his finitude and with his responsibility for the meaning of his life (Frankl, 1984).

Thus, existential psychotherapy focuses on the fear of death, experiences of meaninglessness, and changes in life as fundamental sources of psychopathology (Yalom, 1980). By coming to terms with these issues and entering into a new, creative experience despite our finitude, the hope of existential psychotherapy is that we can free our stymied lives. If, instead of repressing the awareness of our mortality we admit and examine our fears, then we can stop living for unconscious fantasies—such as immortality—that can never be realized. As Irvin Yalom said, "full awareness of death ripens our wisdom and enriches our life . . . though the *fact*, the physicality, of death destroys us, the *idea* of death may save us" (1989).

Key points

- The *four dynamic psychologies*—drive, ego, object, and self—can be used in concert.

- Erikson viewed development as occurring in a series of sequential stages, mastered in order, throughout the lifespan—this is the *epigenic principle*.

- Erikson's stages are trust versus mistrust, autonomy versus shame and doubt, initiative versus guilt, industry versus inferiority, identity versus role diffusion, intimacy versus isolation, generativity versus stagnation, and integrity versus despair.

- Jung developed the theories of *psychological types* and of the *collective unconscious*, a shared archetypal unconscious common to all human beings.

- *Existential psychology* focuses on fear of death, isolation, and loss of meaning as sources of psychopathology.

The learning psychologies, part I: cognitive psychology 17

Learning psychologies

The psychodynamic psychologies imply that unseen motives drive psychological states, that unconscious conflicts and dramas power our psychological lives. Of course, these unconscious patterns are learned in a very broad sense. But implicit in the psychodynamic psychologies is the idea that the fundamental forces beneath human psychology are the same for all of us. The particulars of each individual shape these forces so they appear as different psychological styles and issues, but essentially the same types of things motivate everyone.

In contrast, learning theories hold that the only thing we can really say about what drives human psychology is that people learn to do what they do. In this view, people's unconscious motives are forever hidden from examination. They can only be inferred, not directly observed, and so are largely unverifiable. Who can say whether people really have oedipal complexes, since it is impossible to verify the existence of the unconscious? On the other hand, learning is a process that is readily observable in human beings and in other animals. It can be studied directly. If a child persistently misbehaves at school, learning theory says that the child has learned this behavior through reinforcement, modeling, and other specific learning processes. He may or may not be motivated by an unconscious conflict, but that is impossible to know. What can be observed is that some circumstances of the environment reinforce particular behaviors, and some ways of thinking have demonstrable errors. The hope of the learning psychologies is that both of these problems can be directly corrected with the appropriate learning—in other words, that people can learn themselves out of their problems as well as into them.

Cognitive psychology

The central claim of cognitive psychology is that people perceive the world through a system of beliefs and assumptions. These beliefs and assumptions form a mental set that influences how each individual interprets the world. Events in the world are neutral. They simply occur, and they are meaningless until interpreted through a mental set. Thus, it is the beliefs and assumptions of the mental set that determine our emotional state. An event is either good or bad depending on how we understand it. In other words, *thinking precedes feeling* (Beck, Rush, Shaw, & Emory, 1979; Burns, 1992). We do not have emotional responses and then interpret them. Rather, we interpret the world, and our interpretations determine our resulting emotions. If, for example, you are walking down the hall and a coworker fails to return your greeting, your emotional response will be determined by how you interpret the event. If you think that Bob must be stressed and preoccupied to have missed your greeting, you will perhaps feel pity and concern for him. If, on the other hand, you are sure you must have done something to anger Bob and that he didn't greet you because he no longer likes you, then you may feel worthless and depressed. In either case, the interpretation determines the emotional state.

Cognitive theorists such as Albert Ellis and Aaron Beck discovered that psychopathology tends to result from a particular mental set. Depression and anxiety, for example, are often the results of a habitual tendency to see the world in ways that reinforce feelings of depression and anxiety.

Cognitive distortions

One of the early investigators in cognitive psychology was Albert Ellis, who found that individuals with depression and anxiety typically evidenced a number of what he called "irrational assumptions" about the world (Ellis, 1997). These irrational assumptions, he theorized, caused symptoms of depression and anxiety. One common irrational assumption Ellis found in his patients was the belief that "everyone must like me." While common enough, this clearly is an unrealizable aspiration. Not every human being on the face of the planet is going to like you, no matter what you do. Actions that some people appreciate will be revolting to others. Ellis found that another common irrational assumption was, "I need to do everything right." Since everyone makes mistakes, this assumption naturally leads to failure, and failure leads to feelings of depression and anxiety.

Irrational assumptions systematically distort our perceptions of the world. Cognitive psychologists call an irrational assumption about the nature of the world a *cognitive distortion*. Cognitive distortions occur when the world is interpreted through a belief that is demonstrably false or incoherent. When cognitive distortions become habitual, then psycho-pathology may result.

Case example

Ms. E presented with symptoms of depression and social phobia. Every time she was in a group of people, she became paralyzed with fear. Once, sitting with friends at a bar, she became over-whelmed with panic and fled. When questioned about this pat-tern, E was vague. "I just got nervous," she said, and shrugged. Clearly, just thinking about the episode made her uncomfortable. When the psychiatrist persisted, E admitted that she was afraid her friends would think she was, in her words, "crazy." The psy-chiatrist asked what E thought that would mean. E said she be-lieved her friends would think she was weak for becoming anx-ious, and that they would not want to be friends with someone who was so weird. In fact, she was afraid that she might never have friends again, which led to depressing fantasies of always being alone.

Cognitive distortions are demonstrably untrue beliefs and assumptions that increase depression and anxiety.

E's beliefs about her friends were, at first glance, unremark-able. Most people fear rejection at one time or another and some-times worry that their idiosyncracies will draw criticism. Yet, closely examined, E's thinking contained a number of demonstrable er-rors. What, for example, did she mean by "crazy"? What judg-ment was it *exactly* that she thought was being visited upon her? The psychiatrist asked her this very question.

E: I don't know. That I don't have any self-control.

P: So anyone who doesn't have any self-control is crazy?

E: I guess.

P: Do you have any self-control?

E: No.

P: Because you ran out of a room once?

E: Right.

P: But you're sitting here now.

E: Yes.

P: So, in fact, you do have some self-control.

E: Some, I suppose.

In other words, E's concept of "crazy" was an empty concept, de-void of meaning. When asked to define her terms, E picked what crazy seemed to her to represent—a lack of self-control. But she overgeneralized. She said that someone who is crazy has *no* self-control. This is actually an absurd statement, since everyone, even the most impaired, has *some* degree of self-control. E's self-control might not have been what she wanted when she ran out of the bar, but that is a different statement than saying she has no self-control at all. After all, she was not running into a wall as she ran from the bar—perhaps not the sort of success she would typically congratulate herself for achieving, but an activity of control nevertheless. Someone with multiple sclerosis might be thrilled to be able to walk reliably. E's belief that she has no self-control is at once untrue and damaging to her self-esteem.

This was E's problem. She didn't reward herself for what she was doing well, instead focusing only on her perceived failures, and she *overgeneralized*, using a meaningless but derogatory term to *label* herself. The result was that she felt depressed. Who wouldn't feel bad if she really was a crazy person who had no self-control? But this judgment was simply inaccurate when applied to E. In fact, it would be inaccurate when applied to anybody.

In addition, E had *assumed* that the reaction of others to her running out of the room would be scorn. What a crazy fool, she imagined her friends saying, and then concluded that they would not want to be her friends anymore. But did E really know what her friends were thinking? She hadn't asked them, and there were other possibilities. Perhaps some of them were worried about her, thinking she was ill. Maybe others had had panic attacks themselves and knew exactly how she was feeling. Still others might have thought they had done something to make E run away and became worried that she wouldn't want to be friends with them. Of course, it is possible that some people were thinking she was crazy. But that isn't the only possible conclusion, or even the most likely. Yet E chose the most negative possible response and assumed it was true for everyone. She then made other unproven assumptions.

"If they think I'm crazy, they won't want to be my friends," E thought. But this is not necessarily true. Maybe some of her crowd would glamorize her sensitive nature, admire her for having a quirk or for unabashedly doing what she felt like doing. Again, others might feel concern, and this might strengthen the bonds of friendship. Even if no one in that particular group wanted to be her friend anymore, did that mean she was destined never to have a satisfying relationship in her life? In her mind, E had gone from having a panic attack in a bar to a doomed life of utter isolation, a judgment that was decidedly premature. In other words, she *catastrophized*.

E's way of looking at the world was characterized by a style that systematically distorted reality and in so doing generated feelings of depression and anxiety. Cognitive psychologists call characteristic ways of interpreting events a *cognitive schema* or a *cognitive set*.

The main premise behind cognitive psychology is that thoughts determine feelings rather than vice versa. If I believe everyone has to like me if I am to be a happy and self-satisfied person, then I am destined to feel unhappy whenever I get a negative response from someone. The appropriate intervention in this situation therefore is to detect and correct these irrational assumptions or, as they later came to be called, *cognitive distortions.*

It may seem strange for cognitive theorists to assert that a particular perspective is "irrational" and "distorted." Yet this is precisely what cognitive distortions demonstrably are. E's overgeneralization of the term "crazy" makes it applicable to every human being. Since in some sense every single person on the face of the planet is "out of control"—whether running amok in the streets, not getting paperwork finished, or eventually dying—our lives are never completely in our control. Thus by E's standard, everyone is crazy, in which case her definition of crazy is so vague and broad that it is meaningless. Furthermore, if E was going to be consistent, she would have to agree that anyone who had a panic attack was crazy. But she did not believe this. Instead, she felt compassion for people who experienced them. Only she was to be singled out for contempt.

Cognitive schemata are characteristic ways of interpreting events.

Later cognitive theorists moved from simply describing particular assumptions (such as Ellis delineated) to outlining how cognitive distortions operate as an overall style of thinking. The following is derived from Beck, Rush, Shaw, and Emory (1979) and from Burns (1992), who theorized that cognitive distortions tend to follow a particular pattern. *Labeling* occurs when one attaches an oversimplified description to one's self—for example, by saying "I'm a failure," rather than simply saying that a particular desired outcome was not achieved. *Overgeneralization* occurs when one overemphasizes the importance of a particular characteristic to the exclusion of others. Saying you are a failure implies that you never have done and never will do anything whatsoever correctly. *All-or-nothing thinking* (splitting) consists of seeing oneself or the world as either perfect or worthless, rather than as having both good and bad qualities. Cognitive distortions tend toward the *minimization* of positive events, leaving only the negative ones. They also tend to *magnify* the importance of or *catastrophize* about unwanted outcomes. Finally, *unjustified assumptions* may be made about others' thoughts without adequate data.

To some extent, everyone engages in cognitive distortions. Labeling is a necessary element of language usage. Thinking in broad concepts may be very useful, allowing the condensation of large amounts of information into a single bit of data. The statement, "Pablo is a medical student," oversimplifies by ignoring the myriad facts about Pablo that could be listed; but it accomplishes a purpose by avoiding extraneous information. However, if the pattern of cognitive distortion is demonstrably untrue and tends to reinforce low self-image, depressed mood, anxiety, and so on, then the distortions need to be corrected so that they are factually true.

Cognitive versus psychodynamic psychology

It is natural to wonder why some individuals' distortions lead to depression and others do not. The style of cognitive distortion does seem in many cases to clearly antedate psychiatric problems. At other times, however, significant cognitive distortions do not appear until it is clear the individual is psychiatrically ill. In the former case, perhaps childhood experiences lend to the development of the style, which later leads to a tendency to have psychiatric illness. For example, in E's case, her father was a perfectionist who was highly critical of her. This may have accounted for how E learned her particular cognitive schema. It also may have predisposed her to have difficulties with depression.

But these questions, while interesting, are of secondary concern to the cognitive psychotherapist. In the cognitive model, it does not matter how you ended up with distorted cognitions, only that you have them now and that such a pattern of thinking must be corrected through insight and practice. Unlike the psychodynamic models, "insight" here does not mean a lifting of repression but, rather, simply the elucidation of one's cognitive style. Most people take their perspectives of the world for granted. For example, it never occurred to E to wonder exactly what she meant by the word "crazy," or if her friends were really thinking that about her—she simply assumed it was true and was unaware that an alternative possibility existed. In fact, E was unaware of these judgments at all. When she felt depressed, she did not realize she was actually passing judgment on herself and others. She just automatically felt depressed, lonely, and worthless, without apparent reason. Pressured to do so, however, she could eventually bring her underlying thought processes to light.

The character of cognitive distortions that lead to psychopathology is similar to that seen in the immature ego defenses. Remember that the immature ego defenses include splitting, distortion, and projection. In splitting, the world is habitually divided into polar opposites of good and bad; in distortion, the facts of the external world are mentally altered; and in projection, a person's internal states are ascribed to the outside world.

When using a distorted cognitive schema, individuals are thinking in the same way as seen in the immature ego defenses. Overgeneralizing, for example, is a distortion of reality. It is grossly inaccurate for someone to say, "I never do anything right." When a woman says, "I'm a bad mother," she splits the world into good and bad, with those in the "bad" camp having no redeeming qualities at all, whereas those who are "good" are not fallible in any way. Similarly, when assumptions are made about the thoughts of others without clear evidence, that is the result of projection. So if someone doesn't call as expected, and without further evidence you think, "I guess she doesn't like me after all," that is a projection of internal insecurities rather than an objective assessment of the situation. However, cognitive psychology makes no assumptions about why a cognitive style exists. It simply recognizes that it does, presumably through learning, and that cognitive sets can be relearned.

Cognitive psychotherapy

The essential premise of cognitive psychotherapy is that cognitive distortions should be explicitly corrected. Cognitive psychotherapy generally is time-limited. Like the brief psychodynamic psychotherapies, it attempts to correct specific problems within a relatively circumscribed timeframe. The process begins by educating the patient about the nature of cognitive distortions and showing him how they operate to cause psychiatric distress. In the early stages of cognitive therapy, the patient is encouraged to simply write down what thoughts he has whenever he experiences a disturbing emotion, such as depression or anxiety. The therapist then helps the patient to see what cognitive distortions were operating at the time, and how those distortions might have led to the emotions experienced. It does not matter that the patient may think his thoughts have no bearing on what emotions he experiences. It is the fundamental premise of cognitive psychology that all emotional states arise from data processed through a cognitive schema. The nature of that schema will determine the subsequent emotions. If the schema contains a large number of cognitive distortions, then the succeeding emotions may well be negative. For E, such a chart might look like the one presented in Table 17.1.

In later sessions, the patient is encouraged to develop the skill of spotting cognitive distortions and their impact on emotions. At first this proceeds slowly, through written homework assignments. The patient writes the emotion, followed by the associated thoughts, followed by an identification of the cognitive distortions involved. Finally, the correction of the cognitive distortions is charted.

With practice, cognitive distortions can be corrected automatically. Just as the initial cognitive schema is habitual, so that the individual usually has no idea it is in operation, a learned cognitive schema can become habitual. When that happens, emotional disturbances will be less frequent and, when they do occur, they will be quickly corrected, resulting in a return to equilibrium.

Indications.   Like psychodynamic issues, cognitive distortions may be present in any mental disorder. Because cognitive therapy uses a relatively limited repertoire of interventions compared to psychodynamic psychotherapy, it is more easily standardized between practitioners. Therefore, it is a comparatively straightforward process to expose large

Table 17.1. Cognitive Psychotherapy

Emotions	Associated thought	Cognitive distortion	Realistic correction
Anxiety and depression	I'm out of control.	Overgeneralization	I'm in control in some ways.
	My friends think I'm crazy.	Labeling, mind-reading	I really don't know what they think.
	No one will ever want to be my friend.	Magnification	Even if they don't like me, some people will.

Thoughts associated with each emotional state are listed. The cognitive disortions present in each thought are identified. Finally, the realistic correction of each cognitive distortion is catalogued. Adapted from Burns (1992, p. 63).

numbers of patients with the same psychiatric diagnosis to cognitive psychotherapy that is consistently practiced (usually using technique manuals). So, unlike psychodynamic psychotherapy, cognitive psychotherapy has been studied extensively in controlled trials and shown to be effective in particular clinical situations.

Cognitive psychotherapy clearly is indicated for major depression, panic disorder, and generalized anxiety disorder (Barlow & Craske, 1994; Sadock & Sadock, 2000). Evidence for the effectiveness of cognitive therapy for substance use disorders, bipolar disorder, and schizophrenia also is accruing. Cognitive therapy may be combined with behavioral therapy (see Chapter 18) and is indicated for obsessive-complusive disorder, eating disorders, and borderline personality disorder (Linehan, 1993; Sadock & Sadock, 2000).

Caveats. Cognitive psychology is not without its own set of difficulties. Often, distorted cognitive schemata are not something people simply discover they have and then discard. People cling to their worldviews. For example, Ms. E was ready to admit that her standards for being a "success" versus being a "failure" were arbitrary—she couldn't really justify why being friends with certain people constituted success and that losing those friends meant she was a failure who would never have friends again. Furthermore, once E came to realize this, she also found out she had a double standard. E did not believe, for example, that everyone who doesn't have the precise friends they desire is a failure—only she was.

When pressed, however, E showed a marked resistance to changing this view of the world. In attempting to debunk these cognitive distortions, the psychiatrist ran into a common problem. E really didn't want to give up the cognitive schema she used to understand the world! She wanted to have high standards for herself and, in spite of recognizing the cognitive distortions inherent in this view, she couldn't give up those standards.

Part of the trouble, it turned out, was that her male therapist inadvertently recreated a drama E had played out with her harshly critical father. Every time the therapist provided insight into E's cognitive schema, no matter how gently, E perceived it as criticism—even her thinking wasn't correct! Thus, her childhood experiences with her father were repeated in the treatment, the phenomenon described in psychodynamic psychologies as transference. Cognitive psychology deals with the problem of transference without using the language of psychodynamic psychology, simply by calling transference a learned cognitive distortion—the therapist really isn't judging, just pointing out facts. So if a patient assumes without justification that he is being judged, that is a cognitive distortion. Whereas the psychodynamic psychotherapist is interested in determining *why* the patient has ended up with a particular transference reaction, the cognitive therapist wants to identify the cognitive distortions inherent in the transference, and then correct them.

It often turns out, however, that patients want more than a simple correction of erroneous thinking. They want a relationship that comforts them and that does not repeat the problems of earlier relationships, despite their expectation that it will (an expectation that may be conscious or unconscious).

Key points

- *Cognitive psychology* holds that thinking determines subsequent feelings.

- Everyone perceives the world through a *cognitive schema*, a way of interpreting events.

- *Cognitive distortions* in a cognitive schema are demonstrably untrue beliefs and assumptions that increase depression and anxiety.

- Common cognitive distortions include *overgeneralization, labeling, mental filtering, making unwarranted assumptions, all-or-nothing thinking*, and *catastrophizing*.

- Cognitive therapy works to consciously and systematically replace cognitive distortions with realistic expectations and beliefs.

The learning psychologies, part II: behavioral psychology 18

Although it is a learning psychology, cognitive psychology bears a resemblance to psychodynamic psychologies in one important respect: Because cognitive psychology explores thoughts—often hidden thoughts—that emerge only under scrutiny, it is, in a sense, a "depth psychology." It assumes there are thoughts, reasons, and assumptions beneath external behaviors. Strict behavioral psychology, on the other hand, demands exclusive attention to the behavior of the subject. Behavior is objectively observable, in contrast to thoughts and feelings, which are available for inspection only by the report of the subject or by inference from her behavior. Behavioral psychology does not rely on the report of the subject and does not attempt to infer her internal mental state. Instead, behavioral psychology is interested in discovering what influences a particular behavior to increase or decrease in frequency. As an illustration, recall the case of Ms. S.

Behavioral psychology is interested in discovering what observable causes influence a particular behavior to increase or decrease in frequency.

Case example

Ms. S was moving with the help of her older brother. She was driving behind her brother's truck to her new house when, crossing a bridge, he had to swerve to avoid a pedestrian and rolled his truck on its side. Fortunately, he was unhurt. But the experience was unnerving to S. Seeing his truck swerve, she thought for a moment that he would topple over the side of the bridge, and she was convinced for an instant that he was going to die.

Months later, S was still fearful. Not long after the accident, she was driving on a highway overpass when she was suddenly overwhelmed with the sensation that she was going to lose control of the car and kill someone in the resulting accident. As this thought flooded her mind, she began to hyperventilate. She felt she could barely catch her breath, and this heightened her fear that she would lose control of the car—S was afraid she would pass

215

out. Her heart pounded, she broke into a sweat, she felt dizzy and had a bizarre sensation of being outside of her body. In a panic, she pulled her car over to the side of the road, got out, staggered to a pay phone, and called her mother to pick her up.

After this experience, S was terrified to drive over bridges. She refused to drive herself over highway overpasses, and could do so as a passenger only by closing her eyes and counting out loud until it was over. Even this tactic was not always successful. Often, the panic occurred anyway, and she made the driver turn around. This was becoming a significant problem, because her workplace was on the other side of the highway from her house, and she had to cross a bridge in order to work.

Unlike psychodynamic psychology, behavioral psychology does not attribute S's anxiety and avoidance to the repression of aggressive or sexual impulses. Instead, it explains her panic disorder as the result of a learning process that is experimentally observable in human beings and animals. S had *learned* to avoid bridges.

Classical conditioning

Classical conditioning is a learned response to the association of repeated stimuli.

The first investigations into the process of learning were done by Ivan Pavlov, a Russian scientist who in the early twentieth century discovered *classical conditioning*. In his now-famous experiment, Pavlov fed dogs regularly with meat, which naturally resulted in salivation during feeding. Feeding with meat in this case is the *unconditioned stimulus* that results in salivation, an *unconditioned response* (Sadock & Sadock, 2000). No learning is involved. Salivation is an automatic, intrinsic response of the dog to feeding.

Next, Pavlov introduced a *conditioned stimulus*. Whenever the dogs were fed, he rang a bell. This procedure was repeated a number of times. Finally, the bell was rung without the presence of meat. The result— salivation! The dogs had learned to pair the previously neutral sound of the bell ringing with the presence of meat. Thus, salivation had become a *conditioned response* to the *conditioned stimulus* of the bell ringing.

1. Unconditioned stimulus (meat)/unconditioned response (salivation), paired with

2. neutral or conditioned stimulus (bell), produces

3. conditioned response (salivation) to conditioned stimulus (bell).

When S saw her brother nearly crash his truck, she experienced a rush of pure terror. In this case, fear was the unconditioned response to the unconditioned stimulus of danger. No learning was required. It was an automatic response for S to become fearful with danger. Paired with this unconditioned response (fear) were a number of neutral stimuli. For example, the setting—driving over a bridge—is not normally a stimulus that provokes fear and anxiety. Paired with the unconditioned response of fear, however, the previously neutral setting becomes the conditioned stimulus that provokes the conditioned response—fear of bridges. Thus, S learned to become fearful of driving over bridges by classical conditioning. She learned to associate the neutral stimulus of driving over a bridge with terror, and so driving over a bridge produced terror.

Operant conditioning

A second learning process now comes into play. Because S had several terrifying episodes driving over bridges, she developed *anticipatory anxiety*. She feared the prospect of driving over bridges. However, unlike the classically conditioned response, this fear was under her control. She could reduce the unpleasant sensation produced by driving over bridges simply by avoiding bridges entirely. This procedure dramatically reduced her anticipatory anxiety, an outcome S found preferable. In other words, she was *rewarded* for the behavior of avoiding bridges by experiencing anxiety reduction. Avoiding bridges thus became a *reinforced behavior*. Thereafter, she regularly engaged in it, despite other adverse consequences, so long as those consequences were not severe enough to override the reinforced behavior.

> *Operant conditioning* occurs when a subject operates upon the environment to produce rewards and punishment that reinforce a behavior.

This process is called *operant conditioning* (Sadock & Sadock, 2000). S operated upon the environment to produce the rewards that led to reinforced behavior. Whereas classical conditioning is an entirely passive process, operant conditioning requires reciprocal interaction between the environment and the learner. In S's case, operant conditioning taught her to increase her bridge avoidance by rewarding her with decreased anticipatory anxiety. Unfortunately, this learned pattern resulted in a severe disability. Avoiding bridges can be an effective short-term strategy for anxiety reduction, but over the long term it has serious drawbacks.

Rewards and punishments

In behavioral psychology, anything that increases the frequency of a behavior is called a reward. A reward may be either positive or negative. A *positive reward*, or *positive reinforcement*, will increase the frequency of a behavior through the organism's desire to obtain more of the reward. A *negative reward*, or *negative reinforcement*, will increase the fre-

A *reward* or *reinforcement* is anything that increases the frequency of a behavior.

quency of a behavior through the organism's desire to avoid an outcome. When a rat is rewarded with cocaine by pushing a lever, the rat's lever pushing will increase because it wants to obtain more of the reward. In this case, cocaine is a positive reward. On the other hand, if a rat can avoid electrical shocks by pushing a lever, its lever pushing will be increased so as to avoid the shocks. In this case, reduced electrical shock is a negative reward. When S experienced reduced anxiety by avoiding bridges, the operant conditioning involved was negative reward. S increased the frequency of her avoidance so as to experience the removal of an unpleasant sensation.

Negative rewards and punishments often are confused, but they are not the same. Punishments are events that decrease the frequency of a behavior. Like rewards, punishments can be either positive or negative. A *positive punishment* will decrease the frequency of a behavior by causing the organism to seek more of a stimulus. If lever pushing decreases the availability of food, then the rat will decrease its rate of lever pushing so as to obtain more food. A *negative punishment* will decrease the frequency of a behavior by causing the organism to seek less of a stimulus. So, if pushing a lever induces an electrical shock in a rat, its frequency of lever pushing will decrease as the rat seeks to avoid electric shocks.

To summarize:

Rewards increase the frequency of a behavior.

- Positive rewards increase the frequency of a behavior by causing the organism to seek more of a stimulus.

- Negative rewards increase the frequency of a behavior by causing the organism to avoid a stimulus.

Punishments decrease the frequency of a behavior.

A *punishment* is anything that decreases the frequency of a behavior.

- Positive punishments decrease the frequency of a behavior by causing the organism to seek more of a stimulus.

- Negative punishments decrease the frequency of a behavior by causing the organism to seek less of a stimulus.

A behavior whose frequency increases or decreases as a result of conditioning is said to be *reinforced*. So, when S learned to avoid bridges with increasing frequency through the reward of lowered anxiety, that behavior was reinforced. The unlearning of a behavior (particularly if it is eliminated) through the removal of reinforcement is called *ex-tinction*.

Operant rewards and punishments may be either *continuous* or *intermittent*. Rewards and punishments that occur every time a behavior is enacted (or at regular intervals) are said to be continuous. If a reward or punishment appears at unpredictable intervals, on the other hand, it is called intermittent. It has been determined experimentally that intermittent reward and punishment leads to more rapid reinforcement and a prolonged extinction period.

A reinforced behavior is one whose frequency increases or decreases as a result of operant conditioning.

Behavioral therapy

Behavioral therapy proposes simply to replace one learned behavior with another. S can be taught, both intellectually and especially experientially, to engage in behaviors that are less detrimental to her well-being than bridge avoidance. There are two main ways to do this: One is by a gradual approach, and the second is by flooding.

Graded response

One possible way to change S's behavior is to have her approach the feared situation gradually. First, an alternative behavior to avoidance must be available. If S can escape anxiety by engaging in a behavior besides avoidance, over time that behavior will be reinforced. One likely substitution is to use conscious relaxation techniques, including deep breathing and reduction of muscular tension. By learning to relax rather than flee, and by having relaxation rewarded by reduced anxiety, fleeing eventually is unlearned (extinguished) and relaxation learned as the operant response to an anxiety-provoking stimulus (reinforcement). So, S will learn first to deliberately relax. Then, the conditioned stimulus (namely, bridges) can be paired with the new behavior for conditioning to occur. In other words, S must tolerate bridges until it is possible for her to relax in their presence. To do this, she must inhibit her tendency to engage in her previously learned behavior. This process is known as *response prevention*. Once this happens, new learning—or conditioning—will occur.

Extinction is the unlearning of a behavior.

But S is extraordinarily fearful of bridges, and her newly learned relaxation techniques (introduced by behavioral therapy) are fragile. If she goes straight to a bridge and tries to relax, her anxiety may overwhelm her relaxation skills, which will be very detrimental. If S avoids the bridge again, that response will be reinforced—the opposite of what was intended. Thus, *graded response techniques* rely on gradually entering the feared situation through a series of progressively intensifying steps. Since S becomes somewhat anxious just at the idea of driving over a bridge, initial graded exposures might simply have her imagine driving over a bridge while she consciously practices relaxation. Then she might get in a car and anticipate driving over a bridge; then drive toward a bridge, stopping short of crossing it; and at last actually drive over a bridge. As S achieves mastery of each successive step, the relaxation response becomes reinforced and the avoidance response becomes extinguished.

Graded responses involve desensitization through gradual exposure.

An alternative behavioral school would argue that graded response runs the risk of reinforcing avoidance, since none of the graded steps except the last actually forces S to change her behavior in the feared situation. Furthermore, the learning of relaxation, although valuable, usually is somewhat tenuous—it takes skill to systematically relax when you are very anxious. For that reason, some behavioral therapists argue that *flooding*, a second way to learn alternative behaviors, is the appropriate behavior modification technique to use.

Flooding

During flooding, the feared situation is entered head-on and endured until the fear dwindles. Contrary to what the individual fears—that his anxiety will be overwhelming and endless—peak anxiety is a transient experience. The body can maintain extreme arousal for limited periods, usually less than 10 to 15 minutes. Furthermore, the anxiety *is* bearable, no matter how bad it gets. According to this theory, all that would be required for S is that she plunge in and hold on until she feels better. The one thing she must *not* do is avoid the situation once she is in it. In fact, once behavioral therapy is brought up as an option, hesitation is tantamount to avoidance, which is then reinforced.

Flooding involves entering a feared situation directly and waiting for the anxiety to decrease.

Despite its harsh demeanor, exposure therapy is extremely effective. There often is prompt relief of symptoms after just a single flooding experience. This was the case for Mr. F—introduced at the start of Part 3—whose obsessions about contamination decreased after a single exposure session. But frequently patients such as F have another agenda. They want understanding more than advice. Behavioral therapists point out that this can simply be avoidance. In F's case, he was actually doing behavioral therapy to his benefit. However, behavioral therapy could not address the meaning of obsessive anxiety for F. How did his obsessions defend against other anxiety, and what would it mean to give up his obsessions? Also left unexamined in this case is how behavioral therapy itself might have meaning. What was it like for F to engage in behavioral therapy? Did he experience the psychiatrist as a harsh parental figure? Exposure therapy cannot address such issues except by pointing out the avoidance. Behavioral therapy in a broader sense can. In a case like F's, the behavioral therapist will point out how the behavioral response of wanting attention rather than advice from the therapist is a learned behavior and will seek to modify it. This can be a successful tactic.

Behavioral therapy is clearly indicated in treating anxiety disorders. It is the treatment of choice for specific phobias (such as the fear of flying or of heights), as well as for OCD. It also may be effective for mood disorders and substance use disorders. Behavioral therapy also is effective in couples' therapy for sexual disorders, particularly for arousal disorders and premature ejaculation.

Cognitive-behavioral therapy

Typically, it is difficult to convince individuals that exposure to what they fear is the proper treatment for the fear. After all, they already fear something terrible will happen to them. How can deliberately entering that situation be healthy? Even if they accept the intellectual foundation of behavioral psychology, many people approach treatment with great trepidation.

These problems are difficult to address through purely behavioral techniques. Often the patient's fears involve many cognitive distortions. It is not unusual for individuals with panic disorder to catastrophize, for example. When asked to imagine the worst possible outcome of a feared situation, reasoning such as the following often emerges: If I try to drive across a bridge, I will have a panic attack, which will cause me to lose control of my vehicle. I will then run across the road and hit another vehicle, sparing me but killing the other driver. The accident will be my fault, and I won't be able to live with the intolerable guilt of this. My entire life will be ruined.

These are cognitive distortions, displaying the tendency to make a number of unwarranted assumptions that turn the event into the worst of all possible situations and to assign blame to oneself for uncontrollable outcomes. Often cognitive strategies can be effective in ameliorating these concerns and allowing behavioral therapy to move forward. This requires flexibility on the part of the behavioral therapist. Conversely, the cognitive therapist usually hopes to see more than simply the correction of cognitive distortions; she also hopes to see a replacement of maladaptive behaviors.

Cognitive and behavioral psychotherapies often are executed together, in a synergistic psychotherapy known as *cognitive-behavioral therapy* (CBT). The CBT of panic disorder, for example, often proceeds first with education about the condition and the therapy, followed by the teaching of relaxation techniques and controlled breathing, which are practiced outside the therapy. In the meantime, the frequency and character of the patient's panic attacks are rigorously charted and cognitive distortions about the attacks are corrected. Finally, as panic occurs, the newly developed skills in relaxation and breathing are applied as response prevention to the development of panic, and the feared or avoided situations are entered into again.

Similarly, the CBT of OCD is conducted first with education about the condition and the therapy. Since individuals with OCD often have a tremendous amount of fear (based on cognitive distortions) about the consequences of not engaging in their rituals, these cognitive distortions are addressed so as to make later exposure therapy more tolerable. Relaxation techniques are taught. Ultimately, the patient must enter his feared situation (perhaps a public restroom, if cleanliness is an obsession) and engage in response prevention (denying handwashing after touching articles in the restroom). Often, the therapist accompanies the patient during exposure and engages in the same behaviors. This provides the opportunity for another type of learning to occur. Here the therapist *models* desired behavior for the patient.

Key points

- *Behavioral psychology* focuses solely on observable behavior.

- *Classical conditioning* begins with an unconditioned stimulus that causes an unconditioned response. When a new conditioned stimulus is introduced along with the unconditioned stimulus and response, it eventually will cause the original unconditioned response to occur with it, which is known as the conditioned response. Classical conditioning is a passive process.

- *Operant conditioning* requires the active operation of the organism upon the environment.

- *Rewards* increase the frequency of a behavior. *Punishments* decrease the frequency of a behavior.

- *Reinforcement* occurs when conditioning results in learning. *Extinction* occurs when the learned response is eliminated.

- *Modeling* is the learning of behavior through the observation of others.

- *Behavioral therapy* is particularly effective for the anxiety disorders and the sexual disorders.

- Behavioral therapy of the anxiety disorders focuses on *exposure* to feared situations and *response prevention*.

- Behavioral therapy may take either a graduated approach (*graded response*) or abrupt immersion (*flooding*).

Social IV
Models

Introduction to social models 19

Human beings live in a social environment, and that environment may either increase or decrease their stress levels. The *social model of mental illness* proposes that mental illness derives from pathological social interactions.

Case example

J was 14 years old and having trouble at school. He often was truant and had been in a number of fights. Despite above-average intelligence, his grades were poor, because he seldom completed assignments and never studied. He had several friendships characterized by shared counterculture interests. J seemed to enjoy antagonizing others. Once he had been suspended for pushing a teacher.

When such instances occurred, J's mother, Ms. T, seemed unsure of how to respond. She tended to believe J's explanations that the school principal and teachers were lying when they accused him of misdeeds. T had been a teenager herself when J was born, and J had never had a significant relationship with his father. When J was a young boy, his mother had become involved with a man who was a professional gambler and was verbally abusive to her. This man mostly ignored J. When T broke off the relationship after a number of years, she felt guilty that she had exposed J to this man's influence. She did not want her relationship with J—his only significant adult relationship—to be an adversarial one. Thus, she characterized their relationship as "friends." Although T was disappointed with J's behavior at school and at home—he did none of the few chores asked of him, for example—she never punished him. J had a large allowance that was never withheld, and T did not make good on threats to ground him when he misbehaved. T had few social relationships outside of J. She worked and was friendly with her coworkers, but she had not had a romantic relationship in several years.

> The *social model of mental illness* proposes that mental illness derives from pathological social interactions.

J's style with his mother was friendly at times, but often he affected a stand-offishness, an apparent cynical maturity. When asked what he would like out of life, he said he would like to move out of the home because he was old enough to be an adult. When T pointed out to him that he would have to get a job in order to make this possible, J became irritated and took the position that he knew things about the world that made it unnecessary for him to "buy into" her value system.

Descriptively, J exhibited symptoms of oppositional-defiant disorder. The etiology of this problem is multifaceted. Biological evidence shows that oppositional-defiant-disordered children may have abnormalities in noradrenergic and serotonergic neurotransmission. Psychologically, a good case might be made that oedipal issues were paramount for J. He had successfully displaced his biological father at a young age, and his mother's boyfriend in his early adolescence, when sexuality was beginning to appear as a crucial developmental issue. He was, it is said, an "oedipal victor." He had displaced the father figures from his life and become his mother's primary companion—she did not date and she treated J as an equal—not her child, but as a "friend." J thus had accomplished the forbidden, and he was haunted by unconscious fears of retaliation. He therefore used the ego defenses of projection and acting out, lashing out at authority figures in an attempt simultaneously to place blame on them and to provide a reason for punishment other than his oedipal transgression.

Whether this formulation is correct is a matter of speculation. J was not in a position to embark on the sort of one-on-one treatment that might resolve these issues in psychodynamic psychotherapy, a time-consuming and expensive process. J was getting in a lot of trouble, heading for expulsion and jail time. He needed help now.

According to the biopsychosocial model, J's problems could be understood from the perspective of his social setting, particularly within his family of origin. J's relationship with his mother was marked by poorly demarcated boundaries. There were obvious sexual undercurrents within their relationship that were being defended against; but, more importantly, there were basic flaws in certain broad areas: For example, what exactly was the nature of their relationship? Were they friends, or were they still parent and child? Who made the decisions? How were rules defined and enforced? How were differences communicated and resolved?

In the process of answering these questions, it became clear that J and T had poorly defined roles. J was treated at times as an adult, at others as a child; T, although the breadwinner and nominal adult, was rather adolescent at times, without clearly defined values and goals. As a result, decision-making in the family was unpredictable. Sometimes the two would make decisions as equal partners; at other times T would expect obedience, only to be stymied, leaving her uncertain how to proceed. There were no clear expectations as to how each was to behave. T always did her family duties, such as working. J largely escaped his duties, such as cleaning his room and setting the table for dinner. Yet, when rules and expectations were violated, there were no clear repercussions. T might feel sorry for J, or she might attempt to ground him. In either event, he got his allowance.

Treatment began by pointing out these difficulties. Despite his aspirations toward immediate adulthood, J clearly lacked the capability to navigate the complex world of modern American society independently. He was "pseudomature," aspiring to an independence with which he would be unable to cope. As such and by necessity, his life would be dictated by adults to a significant degree. Although reciprocity and empathy are important in parent–child relationships, it is necessary for adults to make decisions for their children. J clearly did not have the capacity to make his own long-term decisions—his actions, as is common for teenagers, were dictated by his whims of the moment. But poor short-term decisions often have adverse long-term effects. For example, getting kicked out of school means not having an education. No education in a technological, information-based society threatens permanent economic disenfranchisement. It is one thing to reject the technological, information-based society on philosophical grounds, with a clearly defined alternative; it is quite another to reactively reject it without a programmatic sense of why it is being rejected or what the alternatives are. J's aggressive behavior was not directed *toward* a particular goal, but was generally distributed without regard for what it accomplished. He simply had no idea what the long-range consequences of his actions were. Freedom is quite liberating for those who can set their own boundaries, but it can be devastating for those who cannot. J was certainly not able to set boundaries for himself.

So he needed adults to do it for him. Unfortunately, this was not occurring at home. T had not established clearly that she was the parent and in control of the family. Although it is important for children, particularly adolescents, to have some autonomy, ultimately someone with greater capacity for long-range planning and decision making must be clearly and unequivocally in charge of setting rules and limits and of enforcing them. Not only had T not defined the relationship roles in the family, she also had not set clearly defined rules. Her half-hearted attempts to require housecleaning and other chores failed because she did not really expect them to be done, and there were no consequences for J's defiance. For example, he received his allowance whether he did what T asked or not. Thus, T reinforced the misbehavior both by rewarding it and by not punishing it (a process described in the section on behavioral psychology).

In this case, however, the behavioral problem involved two people rather than just one. When (as we saw in Part 3) Mr. F felt a compulsion to wash his hands, he was the only one involved. But in J's case, although he was the one whose behavioral problem was being reinforced, it was not he who was doing the reinforcing, but his mother. So, solving this problem required a *two-person psychology*. It might be possible to get J to motivate himself with rewards and punishments, but this was unlikely when the status quo was being rewarded at home by his mother. Although ultimately it was J who had the problem—and J who would suffer the consequences of his own behavior in the long run—it would be impractical to simply say that J alone had the problem and had to change. Very likely, J would not do this without the social structures around him changing, too. This may seem to absolve J of any responsibility for his actions. But this is a value judgment that does not necessarily follow from the raw observation that J was, to a significant degree, influenced by the behavior of others around him. Placing the blame entirely on J would be like examining only one dimension of the biopsychosocial model—it might be correct, but it would miss part of the picture and thus lose opportunities for successful resolution of the problems.

Nor does the social perspective on J's difficulties end with his immediate family. When J's nuclear family was unable to meet the challenges of successfully regulating his behavior, what other social structures were available to help? J lived in a diffuse community in a large city. He and his mother, like many city-dwellers, did not know even their close neighbors. Extended family support was absent. T's mother lived in the same city, but she was across town and, in any event, was debilitated by alcoholism. The only consistent community presence in J's life was his school. Since the school staff could not be available 24 hours a day, J could successfully split school off as an isolated object whose efforts to control him were rendered futile. If J were suspended from school, it would simply mean a holiday, as there were no communitywide repercussions for being suspended. Indeed, J's friends might view it as a badge of honor. J would then become a rebel, a highly prized role in his peer group, and his behavior would be reinforced by that reward.

Biopsychosocial treatment must take into account the social circumstances of the individual patient. As we saw earlier, the continuum of natural systems takes into account the pairs, groups, communities, and populations in which individuals participate and which ultimately affect their mental states. Even the biosphere at large may play a role in the development of psychopathology. Natural disasters may result in PTSD. Crops may fail, precipitating a change in the economy. The comprehensive biopsychosocial treatment of the patient makes use of all these factors.

Key points

- *Social models* of mental illness propose that mental illness results from pathological patterns of stress and social interactions.

- *Pathological social interactions* may occur at the level of pairs, groups, communities, or the biosphere at large.

The individual in society 20

Attachment

There is abundant evidence that human beings are inextricably inter-twined with one another from the earliest moments of infancy. From birth, the human infant appears hard-wired to seek human interaction. Even in their first weeks of life , infants who are barely aware of their environments seek out human faces and prefer them to other objects in the environment. Almost immediately, mother and infant set up a pattern of empathic attunement with each other. Infants generally evidence three distinct cries, representing hunger, anger, and pain, which mothers are able to distinguish. Mothers generally hold their babies at the distance optimal for a child's visual acuity, and they typically reflect the infant's mood with reciprocal facial gestures. The child thus becomes increasingly aware of other human beings as distinct objects in the environment.

Attachment is the reciprocal bonding between mother and child.

John Bowlby (1969) called this bonding between mother and infant *attachment.* And, naturally enough, he called the objects of such attachment *attachment objects*. The infant and mother have an innate drive to become attached to one another, Bowlby said—to become reciprocally important. This drive is transferable across objects. Infants become attached to other caregivers if the mother is not available, without apparent detriment.

Without some kind of human attachment, however, infants wither and may die. René Spitz demonstrated the dramatic effects of inadequate attachment in his study of orphaned infants cared for in large hospital wards (Sadock & Sadock, 2000). Despite adequate material conditions, such as food and changing, these infants did poorly, often showing "failure to thrive" and even death. Spitz also discovered that a subset of infants survived the hospital experience relatively intact. The babies in this group, it turned out, were able to garner some attention from the nursing staff, who played with them, touched them, and made reciprocal facial gestures. Spitz concluded that such attachment behavior was crucial for infant survival.

The consequences of social separation are by no means limited to childhood. There is ample evidence that even in adulthood, isolation from social interaction has deleterious effects, including increased mortality, particularly from cardiovascular disease, suicide, and accidents. Those who live alone following a heart attack are twice as likely to die as those living with others. Of those who live alone and have no close confidants, 50% die within 5 years of a heart attack, compared with 18% of individuals who are married or have other close social ties (Case et al., 1992). Suicide rates have been documented to increase when social connectedness decreases (Kreitman, 1988). Breast cancer survival also is improved by social support groups (Spiegel, Bloom, Kramer, & Gottheil, 1989). Overall, isolated individuals are twice as likely to die during a given study interval as those with social support. Social isolation is stressful to humans.

Stress

It comes as no surprise that stress has adverse effects on organisms. Stress forces the body to work harder to maintain its integrity in the face of a world that is constantly threatening to destroy it. Ideally, equilibrium can be maintained, but this is not always the case. The immune system may fight invading microorganisms quietly, beyond conscious awareness, for months or even years. Then suddenly, the invaders gain a foothold and illness appears. This stress then becomes palpable, and all resources are directed toward meeting it.

Stress is accompanied by physiological changes that are deleterious in the long run. Hormones such as cortisol increase to meet the demands of stress. Unfortunately, chronically high levels of cortisol lead to problems such as decreased immune function, hippocampal atrophy, learning impairments, and stunted growth. Stress also is associated with the development of many of the major mental illnesses, even some that are clearly biological in origin. It is common, for example, for schizophrenia to make its appearance during a time of stress, such as leaving home for the first time. The evidence is that stress itself does not cause schizophrenia, but stress can *precipitate* the appearance of the illness. Although the disease process may have been unnoticeable in a familiar environment with predictable social support, separation from that support may strain an already burdened psychological equilibrium—so, delusions worsen, auditory hallucinations become persecutory, and general functioning deteriorates.

So what is stressful to human beings? Threats are stressful. Illness, injury, and natural disasters are all threats that tax the human organism to respond in order to avoid death or serious debility. However, potentially harmful events are not the only things that prove stressful. Someone who is about to be married would seem to be doing something that is beneficial. Marriage is more than gratifying. As we have already discussed, it actually decreases mortality from coronary artery disease and suicide, lessens the risk of depression and alcoholism, and often improves finances through the combining of resources. So, why do people find marriage stressful?

Most living organisms dislike change because it requires the use of additional resources, and human beings are no different. In 1972, Rahe constructed a table of life's major stressful events (or *stressors*) and assigned a relative numerical value to each stressor. Rahe found that a cumulative score of over 300 in one year predicted psychiatric and medical problems. The full list is available in the appendices. Examples from the list:

Death of spouse	100
Divorce	73
Marital separation	65
Jail	63
Marriage	60
Fired from work	47
Retirement	45
Pregnancy	40
New mortgage	30
Personal achievement	28
Christmas	12

Notice that many of the stressors on the list are interpersonal. Death of loved ones, marriage, a change in relationships—even seemingly neutral stressors such as a change in occupation—have marked social ramifications. Often the stress of a new job consists not so much in the change of work itself but in the change of social settings. Job-changers face new superiors and supervisees, new social networks, new first impressions, a host of new names and schedules, and perhaps changes in sleep cycles and interference with outside activities such as time with family and friends.

That human stress is often social stress should come as no surprise, given the evidence that human infants depend on social interactions from the moment of birth, not just for the provision of material requirements but to sustain their emotional equilibrium. Social stress is profoundly unsettling to people, particularly when it threatens them with isolation. This threat may be actualized, such as in the death of a loved one or divorce, or it may be covert. Losing one's job means more than just facing loss of income. It also means a loss of social status and predictable social networks, and perhaps even a loss of friends gained through the workplace. Moving places the individual in an unfamiliar environment, but more than that it disrupts her social ties. It should hardly be surprising that as change in social interactions brings real or threatened loss, people are faced with psychological stress that may become overwhelming.

A study by Rozanski, Bairey, Krantz, Friedman, Resser, and Morell (1988) looked at the effects of mental stress on patients with coronary artery disease. They found that 59% of the patients showed signs of poor circulation through the coronary arteries in response to mental stress. What mental stress had the greatest effect on heart circulation? Public speaking turned out to be the event that consistently produced the greatest stress in the subjects. The stress of public speaking is obviously entirely social, arising from a fear of the scrutiny of others. Human beings are social, and social stresses are among the most extreme. It probably is no accident that social phobia—the fear of others' scrutiny—is perhaps the most common anxiety disorder.

Any thorough psychiatric assessment, therefore, must take into account the patient's current stressors—which often will be social, interpersonal stressors—and attempt to reduce the impact of these. The biological and psychological models we have discussed so far can have a significant effect on the impact a given social stressor has on an individual. A negative interaction with a spouse may be much less damaging, for example, when a person is not in the throes of a major depression. Whereas prior to treatment an argument led to inevitable hopelessness and suicidal thoughts, it might be taken in stride after antidepressant medication or psychotherapy. Biological and psychological interventions with a single individual also may alter the nature of her social stressors, and changes in the social structure may affect her biology and psychology.

Often, however, social stressors must be addressed as problems in their own right. Physical abuse, for example, must be stopped. Social interaction may be encouraged if the patient has faced recent losses. Marital or family therapy may be indicated if there are significant interpersonal stressors within the family. A referral to a career counselor may help if job loss or transition has been a recent stressor. The best biological or psychological therapy may be ineffective if it is countered by social stress and, conversely, the need for biological or psychological therapies may evaporate if stressors are reduced.

Interpersonal psychology

In the 1980s it became apparent to a group of researchers that individuals with depression typically had a common recurrent psychosocial theme: Most of them had recently experienced some sort of interpersonal distress (Klerman, Weissman, Rounsaville, & Chevron, 1984). The researchers hypothesized that relationship distress plays a key role in the pathogenesis of depression, and they proposed a psychotherapy designed to alleviate precisely these problems, with a resulting decrease in depressive symptoms. The psychotherapy is called *interpersonal psychotherapy*.

Interpersonal psychotherapy is indicated when a depressed patient is experiencing distress in at least one of four interpersonal domains (Klerman et al., 1984).

- Grief and loss
- Role transitions
- Interpersonal disputes
- Interpersonal deficits

Interpersonal psychotherapy targets grief and loss, role transitions, interpersonal disputes, and deficits in treating depression.

Klerman et al. found that when these themes were targeted specifically in a time-limited psychotherapy, depression could be significantly reduced compared to placebo therapy. Interpersonal psychotherapy is time-limited since it is designed to focus specifically on these few predetermined themes, rather than attempting wholesale reconstruction of the personality, as might be the aim in psycho-analytically-oriented psychotherapy. Since depression often is associated with interpersonal stress, it is hoped that rapid alleviation of the interpersonal stress will lead to resolution of the depression. The therapy sessions are not allowed to wander far from interpersonal topics. Psychodynamic issues generally are avoided, and interpretation of transference is discouraged. Cognitive distortions and behavioral problems may be dealt with, but only insofar as they relate to the four key themes.

Case example

Ms. L was evaluated for complaints of depression. Over the preceding several months she had begun to develop depressed mood, anhedonia, sleep and appetite disturbances, and feelings of hopelessness. L was able to connect the development of these symptoms to several recent events in her life. She lived and worked with her boyfriend, who owned his own business. The two had been fighting, and L had started to look for another job. She approached this with some trepidation, as she had not been employed outside her boyfriend's business for several years. Complicating matters, her father had been diagnosed with cancer and had an uncertain prognosis. L had always had a difficult relationship with her father. She found him distant and critical, and the two had never been able to maintain consistent communication. After a time, one of them always broke off contact for a while.

The psychiatrist was able to identify three areas of focus for interpersonal psychotherapy. L was experiencing feelings of grief and loss after her father's recent diagnosis of cancer. She also was having interpersonal disputes with both her father and her boyfriend. Finally, she was transitioning out of the somewhat sheltered employment of her boyfriend's business and into the general workforce. L found great relief in talking about these issues with her therapist, and her depression improved dramatically as she came to have a feeling of deepening mastery over the changes in her life.

Religion

Religious beliefs are an important part of identity and social life for much of the world's population. There are literally thousands of religious beliefs; in fact, most people have religious or spiritual beliefs, whether those beliefs represent organized religion or are entirely personal (including atheism and agnosticism). Generally, religion is a social phenomenon. Most people adhere to the dominant religious beliefs of the culture they inhabit. Religious beliefs often are substantially influenced by the local social forces around an individual, including his community and his family.

Because religious beliefs are so varied, psychiatrists of necessity often treat patients of many differing religious convictions. This will be true even of individuals who ostensibly share the same faith. The differences between a Unitarian and a Southern Baptist, for example, may be enormous, even though both denominations are varieties of Christianity. Unless the psychiatrist specifically seeks out only those patients with very similar religious backgrounds, most of those who come for treatment will have different religious beliefs.

The biopsychosocial model views religion as one dimension of the human being. This approach to religion is pragmatic, as it is to all models of the mind. The role of the psychiatrist in religious questions is the same as it is in any other area of inquiry—to help the patient clarify her thinking so that she can make autonomous decisions. Just as the psychiatrist would seldom offer direct advice about whether a patient should divorce, even if the psychiatrist has a core conviction about what would be best for that patient, so religious questions are ultimately up to patients to decide for themselves. The psychiatrist can be of great assistance in helping explore the questions, including what beliefs are actually held (people may not admit to themselves what they really believe), how those beliefs serve and how they undermine, and what are the alternatives.

As in any area of life, religious beliefs often reflect underlying psychological themes. Psychodynamic and cognitive-behavioral issues often power perceptions of religious questions just as they affect other beliefs.

Case example

Mr. R's psychology was dominated by splitting, in which he divided the world into opposites of good and bad. Not surprisingly, his religious beliefs mirrored this splitting: He avowed a well-studied and highly personal brand of evangelical Christianity. Since R tended to split the world into polar opposites, the same split happened in his religious views about people and events. R idealized those who agreed with him precisely. But, as this could never happen consistently, he usually ended up demonizing even those who agreed with him on most issues. Since most of his friends and family members were Christians as well, disagreements tended to center around minor differences in biblical interpretation. Yet these differences were sufficient to distress R, and he dealt with this distress by splitting.

As therapy progressed and R was gradually able to relinquish this style of thinking, his religious perspective changed as well. He became more tolerant of other beliefs and found that this enhanced rather than diminished his own Christianity, since he was able to find biblical passages that supported this change. At no time in therapy was the literal correctness or incorrectness of his beliefs at issue, nor did the psychiatrist suggest any particular religious viewpoint. Instead, the therapy explored how R's beliefs worked for him and how they failed him, and why he had them. With greater insight and less need to split the world into opposites to find it tolerable, R found himself able to choose his beliefs, rather than being reflexively driven by them.

Thus, the psychiatrist usually focuses on how particular religious beliefs held by the patient help and hinder, and how they may be related to the appearance and resolution of symptoms. Like any dimension of the biopsychosocial model, the psychiatrist does not assume that she has the right answer. Any theory of mental illness is just that—a theory—and so is open to testing. If a particular approach to symptoms has explanatory power and resolves the symptoms, then it is supported. An approach that fails to do this is questioned, no matter how convincing it appears to be. Disregard of this principle can be disastrous.

Case example

Mr. M began seeing a therapist because he was experiencing severe depression. The therapist espoused a charismatic Christian healing plan and engaged M in prayer as the dominant modality of treatment. M participated and was at first hopeful that the technique would heal him. But as his depression deepened, M became plagued by doubt. If God had not healed him, he decided either that God did not exist or that God did not care about him because he was worthless. Both prospects seemed intolerable, and M became psychotic, with the delusional belief that he was the devil. M finally made a suicide attempt and was hospitalized. Antidepressant and antipsychotic medication and a therapy that focused on bolstering his ego defenses led to significant improvement. As his depression lifted, M was able to reenter his religious community, which had been impossible for him when he felt he had been rejected by God.

Violence

Physical and sexual abuse

Two social stressors not found on the Rahe list are physical and sexual abuses. There has been a recent explosion in awareness of the problem physical and sexual abuses pose for society. The prevalence of such abuse went largely unrecognized until the last few decades. Most current estimates indicate that 11% of men and 10.3% or women will be physically or sexually abused in their lifetimes (Sadock & Sadock, 2000). Three million children suffered documented abuse in 1992, and 2 million cases of spousal abuse were reported.

Although ongoing abuse can precipitate disorders such as major depression and anxiety, abuse during childhood can lead to additional adult disorders. A large majority of individuals who have borderline personality disorder have histories of repetitive childhood physical or sexual abuse. And current estimates indicate that 85% to 97% of individuals who have dissociative identity disorder were repeatedly sexually abused during childhood (Sadock & Sadock, 2000). So common is a clear history of sexual abuse in those with dissociative identity disorder that such abuse is currently thought to be causative—numerous distinct personalities emerge as a defense against overwhelming trauma. Ongoing abuse is one area where the physician unambiguously must attempt to intervene, with (at a minimum) advice tailored to end the abuse. More drastic action, including the involvement of legal authorities, also may be required.

The prediction of violence is inherently difficult. It is impossible to accurately predict the violent actions of others. Nevertheless, some risk factors for the commission of violence clearly stand out. The number one risk factor is a history of violent acts. Major mental disturbances such as psychosis, mania, substance use, depression, and antisocial personality disorder also are risk factors for violence, probably because they are disinhibiting.

Suicide

Every year approximately 30,000 completed suicides are officially reported in the United States (however the actual number may approach 100,000), along with perhaps 300,000 suicide attempts (National Center for Health Statistics, 1994). Suicide is the eighth leading cause of death in the United States, and the second leading cause in teenagers. Ninety-five percent of suicides involve the presence of a major mental illness. Over 50% of those who commit suicide suffer from depression, either bipolar or unipolar (Asgard, 1990). As many as 15% of those with unipolar major depression will ultimately die by suicide, with a similar figure for bipolar disorder. Additionally, 10% of individuals with schizophrenia (5% of all suicides) and 10% of those with borderline personality disorder will die by suicide (Miles, 1977). One-third of those who commit suicide have a substance use disorder. Medical illness also contributes substantially to suicide. Individuals with HIV may have a 30-fold greater risk of suicide than those without the virus (Sadock & Sadock, 2000).

Early studies of suicide were primarily sociological. Emile Durkheim (1951) discovered that propensity for suicide was influenced heavily by social integration. Durkheim found that those with greater privilege and autonomy, specifically wealthy Protestant males, were actually more likely to commit suicide. He concluded that the greater liberty afforded by these advantages in the Europe of his time came with an increased risk for suicide. In contrast, those from poorer classes, while having less freedom, were apparently protected from suicide (but suffered higher rates of homicide). Suicide is thus heavily influenced by social factors.

Static risk factors for suicide—those not subject to modification—are gender, age, race, history of attempts, and recent hospital discharge.

Risk factors. Risk factors for suicide can be divided into *static* and *dynamic* categories. Static risk factors are those not subject to modification, whereas dynamic risk factors can be changed.

Static risk factors. Male gender is a static risk factor for suicide. Women attempt suicide three times as often as men, but men use more lethal means and so succeed three times as often. Age also is a static risk factor. Studies show a bimodal distribution, with teenagers and those over 45 at greater risk for suicide. Caucasians are at highest risk for suicide, followed by Blacks and then by Hispanics. A history of previous suicide attempts increases the risk of suicide, as does recent hospital discharge.

These risk factors are significant. Unfortunately, none can be changed. Dynamic risk factors also play a crucial role in the pathogenesis of suicide, and they can be modified.

Dynamic risk factors. Mental illness is present in 95% of those who complete suicide. Depression, both unipolar and bipolar, is present in

52% of suicides. That makes depression the number one risk factor for suicide. Substance use disorders are second—being present in 32% of suicides—with alcohol accounting for the overwhelming majority. Psychosis is less common (5% of suicides), but when present is a significant risk factor. Recent studies have indicated that anxiety may be a key predictor for suicide, particularly panic disorder. Individuals with personality disorders also are at greater risk for suicide. Up to 10% of those with borderline personality disorder may ultimately complete suicide. Ongoing medical illness may lead to pain, humiliation, and demoralization, and so increases the risk of suicide. Social isolation (being single or divorced) and bereavement increase the risk of suicide, as do recent financial losses and homelessness. Imminent intent, available means, and hopelessness complete the list of dynamic risk factors.

Dynamic risk factors for suicide— those that can be changed— include depression, substance abuse, anxiety, psychosis, illness, social isolation, and hopelessness.

The assessment of the suicidal individual begins with an appropriate history. Every psychiatric evaluation should include inquiries into suicidal ideation. The therapist should ask about a patient's thoughts about death, thoughts that life is not worth living, thoughts of suicide, intent, plan, available means, hopelessness, and other risk factors.

Prediction of suicide and treatment.   The prediction of suicide, as for violence in general, is difficult. The presence of many risk factors indicates merely that—risk. It does not imply that an individual *will* make a suicide attempt. On the other hand, the absence of risk factors does not completely rule out the possibility of suicide. It also is possible for patients to lie. For this reason, if serious concern is present and the data are unclear, it is wise to attempt to contact others who may know the patient—whether family, friends, or other health-care providers. Even with complete and accurate information, however, predicting dangerousness is extremely difficult. Most data show that psychiatric professionals are somewhat better than chance at predicting violence within a short time-frame, perhaps 48 hours. Beyond that, prediction is no better than chance. Compounding problems, any net cast wide enough to include most high-risk individuals will result in a large number of false positives—that is, individuals with risk factors who are not actually going to make a suicide attempt. Hospitalizing everyone at high risk for suicide would lead to an unmanageable number of needless hospitalizations. Prospective attempts to accurately predict suicide have failed to do so and found unacceptably high false-positive rates in the instruments used.

Ultimately, it is little more likely that a mental health professional could accurately predict a suicide attempt than that an oncologist could predict the day a patient will die from cancer. The oncologist can certainly identify those at high, medium, and low risk, but precise prediction is a virtual impossibility.

The purpose of evaluating for suicidal ideation is thus less to prevent immediate harm, although that is certainly desirable, and more to identify and reduce dynamic risk factors. Successful detoxification; reducing depression, anxiety, and psychosis; assembling social support; eliminating available means; and giving hope can greatly reduce the likelihood of suicide. Given the positive response of the major mental disorders to treatment, the reduction of dynamic risk factors is likely to be a more successful strategy than sequestering large populations of at-risk individuals. However, as we will see in Chapter 22, involuntarily commitment sometimes is a necessary tool in the prevention of violence to the self and to others.

Key points

- *Stress* profoundly affects psychological functioning.

- *Social stressors* are among the gravest faced by human beings.

- *Change* of any kind, for better or worse, can be stressful.

- The *interpersonal theory* of depression says that depressed individuals usually are experiencing social stress in at least one of four domains: grief and loss, role transitions, interpersonal disputes, and interpersonal deficits.

- *Violence* can be a key contributor to psychopathology.

- *Suicide* is a leading cause of mortality, and risk for suicide can be divided into static and dynamic factors.

- *Static risk factors* include gender, age, race, history of attempts, and recent hospital discharge.

- *Dynamic risk factors* include depression, substance use, anxiety, psychosis, medical illness, social isolation, intent, means, and hopelessness.

Group psychology 21

Social relationships can affect individuals as much as their biology and psychology. As sociologists have long observed, society is a structure that, although composed of individuals, exists apart from any given individual within it. An individual may contribute to the structure of a pair, a group, or a society, but he does not have sole responsibility for the composition of that grouping. The workings of the larger entity of society affect the individual profoundly. Precisely how they will do so, of course, involves personal biology and psychology. But the world presents the individual with circumstances, and those circumstances are to a certain extent "outside" the individual. Individuals may have an impact on the world, but the world also has an impact on individuals. Society is encountered as a force that can help or harm individual mental functioning.

The pattern of a social network may become pathological in a number of ways. As noted above, although any social system is the combined work of the individuals that compose it, the system itself can be viewed as an individual entity. Just as the body can be conceptualized as a single entity even though it is made up of millions of individual cells, each with independent but interrelated functionings, so the social system can be viewed as a single entity composed of independent but interrelated human beings. That social entity, like the human body, can become dysfunctional in various ways. For example, the interactions of the individuals involved in the system may have a tendency to reinforce rather than reduce undesirable behaviors. The social system may cast one individual in a certain role necessary to the stability of the system, even if that stability is pathological and that individual is harmed by the role. The structure of alliances and antagonisms within the social system may lead to individual symptoms of psychopathology. In any of these events, it is in a sense the social system as a whole that has become distressed and dysfunctional, even though it may be a single person who becomes "ill." Correcting the system may be necessary to help the individual.

Cybernetics

Feedback occurs when a system can provide itself with information about its functioning. Feedback loops abound in the human body. During neurotransmission, for example, some neurotransmitters go on to affect other cells, while the remainder return to the parent neuron and hit a receptor called an autoreceptor. The effect of the neurotransmitter on the autoreceptor is to reduce the firing rate of the parent neuron (see Chapter 3). The neuron thus regulates its own firing. When enough neurotransmitters have been released, the autoreceptor is stimulated, reducing the rate at which the neuron continues to release neurotransmitters.

This phenomenon is known as a *negative feedback loop*. Negative feedback loops occur when feedback in a system decelerates a process through reciprocal inhibition. The purpose of the negative feedback loop in neurons is to avoid excessive release of neurotransmitters. Without an autoreceptor to tell the presynaptic neuron, in effect, "mission accomplished, return to resting state," the neuron would continue firing until depleted of neurotransmitters, which would be an extremely undesirable situation if the neuron was one that regulated a critical function such as breathing.

We might also imagine an opposite circumstance in which agonism of the autoreceptor increases firing of the neuron. In that event, every time the neuron released neurotransmitters, it would stimulate itself to release more, which stimulates more firing, and so the process accelerates. This "vicious cycle" is known in cybernetics as a *positive feedback loop*. Positive feedback loops occur when feedback in a system accelerates a process through reciprocal reinforcement.

The natural world is full of feedback loops. Most hormones in the body are regulated by negative feedback loops. The release of thyroid hormone from the thyroid gland is stimulated by the pituitary hormone thyroid stimulating hormone (TSH). Thyroid hormone has the effect of decreasing the pituitary gland's release of TSH (see Chapter 4). The result is that secretion of thyroid hormone acts as an inhibitor to the release of more TSH—a negative feedback loop.

Feedback loops also can be seen at the ecological level. The availability of large amounts of food may lead to increased reproduction in a particular species. Gradually, however, the increasing number of organisms begins to deplete the food sources, so the number of organisms is reduced through starvation. More food, more organisms; more organisms, less food; less food, fewer organisms; fewer organisms, more food. This is an example of mixed negative and positive feedback loops. Here organisms and food each act to increase or decrease the prevalence of the other so as to maintain a stable system.

Cybernetics is the study of feedback loops. Cybernetic interactions abound in the natural world and, like many natural systems, human relationships also may be regulated by feedback loops. The actions of one person may have a tendency to increase or decrease the actions of another. The actions of the second individual may likewise influence the first. If individuals affect each other so that the actions of one increase the actions of the other, and thus ultimately increase their own actions, a positive feedback loop is established.

Case example

Cybernetics is the study of feedback loops.

Ms. J had become depressed and found it difficult to enjoy anything. Her energy was low and interaction with others was painful. In her depressed state, she preferred to sleep. Her husband, B, found this upsetting. He was worried about J and had always reacted to adverse circumstances by taking charge. At first he tried to encourage J, but when this had no effect, he began to feel frustrated and ineffectual. These feelings were particularly difficult for B, since his mother had experienced major depression when B was a young child. When his mother became withdrawn, the young B had naturally assumed, in the self-centered way of children, that her depression and withdrawal were his fault. Since he was a talented child, B was able to figure out ways to make his mother smile, or to briefly win her approval, but for many months his successes were only temporary, and her depression continued.

Having faced the apparent withdrawal of his mother's love at a sensitive phase in his development, B came to have the nagging feeling that he had to perform in order to be loved. If others were not giving him the response he needed, he felt this was his fault. B developed an inner conviction that if he just tried hard enough, others would come through with the love he needed and, if they didn't, it was his fault for not finding the right way.

When his wife became depressed, B experienced this as a threat. Unconsciously he believed that her depression was his fault, and that J no longer loved him. He therefore set out to prove that this was not the case, by attempting to force her to demonstrate that she did in fact love him. But J did not have the resources to provide B with what he needed. As a result, B felt threatened and, as often happens when people feel threatened, he became angry and defensive. This had the effect of making J feel worthless and so worsened her depression and withdrawal. The more J withdrew, the more hurt and resentful B became, and thus a vicious cycle was born in which the behavior of each partner further aggravated the other, escalating the conflict.

We can see cybernetics at work in J and B's interactions. J's depression stimulated B to anger. B hoped that his anger would have the effect of decreasing J's withdrawal. In other words, he hoped his anger would be an inhibitor of her depressed mood and withdrawn behavior. This would establish a negative feedback loop in which J's depressed behavior would have the effect, through B, of decreasing itself. Unfortunately, all B's anger did was stimulate J's feelings of failure and hopelessness, leading to more withdrawal. This, of course, made B more irritable, which made J more depressed—creating a positive feedback loop.

Once established, positive feedback loops are difficult to break. Since the actions of each partner are driving the loop forward, it tends to accelerate, stimulating more undesirable behavior in an increasing spiral. The solution is to break the positive feedback loop.

Change could come through work with each partner individually. J or B might make changes in their own mental states that result in secondary changes in the pattern of their relationship. Perhaps B's individual psychotherapy would allow him to tolerate his wife's emotional absence, which could in turn lead to her feeling a sense of support through her suffering, thus lessening her sense of hopelessness and failure, which then would decrease the stress her depression had on him. Or J might begin antidepressant therapy, which would decrease her depression, thus allowing her to be less withdrawn and so ending the feelings of threat her husband experienced. The first would be an example of a psychological intervention impacting the social sphere, whereas the latter is a biological intervention that likewise has repercussions in the social realm.

Alternatively, the couple might enter therapy together, with the aim of changing their interactions and, through this, changing both the marriage as an entity and the symptoms of the individuals composing the marriage. Often, behavioral therapy can change the nature of feedback loops. The therapist points out the interaction, then develops strategies with the couple to alter the cybernetic cycles.

Systems theory

In the late nineteenth century it became fashionable in the newly emerging field of sociology to view societies as autonomous structures in their own right, with qualities and behaviors that exist independently of any particular individual. Although a society is made up of individual human beings, the sum of their interactions creates a structure known as a society. Such societal entities are organic. They are not fixed and static, but are constantly in flux. Like any organism, societies require certain things to maintain their stability and perpetuate themselves.

Any affiliation of people forms a social system. Since human beings have an innate drive for affiliation, social systems are ubiquitous in human life. Like any organic system, these social systems will attempt to become stable entities. Obviously, this does not happen out of conscious intent, since social systems are not thinking entities. Neither is the body. Both systems are *self-organizing*. Natural systems have a tendency to organize themselves into stable, self-perpetuating entities, whether at the level of the cell, the individual human body, or as pairs of organisms or ecosystems. Since human beings want to be with one another, this drive to attachment powers social systems to be highly self-organizing.

One way that natural systems are perpetuated is by differentiating individual components to play certain roles and fulfill specific functions. The body is not composed of trillions of identical cells. Rather, each cell has a specific role to play in maintaining the stability of the body as a whole. Heart cells pump blood cells, which carry oxygen to brain cells, which send signals to muscle cells, which obtain food for processing by gastrointestinal cells, and so on.

In the 1950s, sociologist Talcott Parsons attempted to describe the ways in which families and other social systems maintain themselves by differentiating specific roles for their individual members according to requirements necessary for the stability of the group structure (Parsons, 1964). Since women bear and nurse children and are less well-adapted for hunting and defense, the argument went, the role of woman as caregiver is necessary for the stability of the social system, while the man as hunter-gatherer is similarly stabilizing.

The accuracy of this particular interpretation of social roles is less important than the principle. Systems theory proposes that social systems differentiate specific roles for their individual members so as to remain stable. Any set of roles is conceivably stabilizing, particularly since the affiliative tendency of human beings makes them likely to continue in their social setting regardless of how dysfunctional it is. What becomes important for psychiatry is when an individual's role begins to cause problems in some way.

Systems theory proposes that social systems differentiate specific roles for their individual members so as to remain stable.

Case example

Mr. N came in for treatment because he was feeling anxious in his high school classes. He maintained a driven, perfectionistic lifestyle, working hard for top grades with a plan to go to an Ivy League college, competing on the lacrosse team, and keeping his room immaculate. Although popular, N required that his social activities be productive and that they be scheduled. He had difficulty just sitting around because he kept in his mind an endless list of duties he had to complete, even duties his friends found relatively trivial, such as making his bed. As someone dedicated to controlling his world, N despised having his grades depend on others. He studied for hours, digesting every conceivable nuance of the material, but always there lurked the nagging possibility that the professor would single out some fact that he had overlooked, or that—even worse—a question would be worded unclearly and his grade would suffer despite his preparation. He began to experience panic attacks during classes and tests.

Biologically, N might be viewed as having an anxiety disorder and possibly an obsessive-compulsive personality disorder. Correspondingly, he had some response to antianxiety medications. These reduced his panic, but his overall character style was unchanged. New data emerged in the course of treatment. N was the oldest of two boys. His younger brother P was in adolescent rebellion. Whereas N fulfilled his parents' wishes for achievement and orderliness, his brother kept a sloppy room, had mediocre grades, and showed little ambition. N was closer with his mother than his brother was. His father, who was a sought-after stockbroker, had a rather cool relationship with both boys, which N attributed to ongoing depression and a general character style that was uncomfortable with intimacy. N's father would emerge from his distant coolness, however, to express pride in N's achievements and dismay at P's relative failures.

Psychologically, N might be seen as having an overdeveloped superego—driving perfectionism and guilt—through identification with his father. This might have two sources. First, his father did not express approval except in response to achievement. Since N wanted his father's approval, he achieved, particularly in light of the alternative that his younger brother experienced. Also, N's close relationship with his mother was unconsciously threatening because of its oedipal overtones, and so he defended against these feelings by identifying with his father, a normal developmental process but one that had become overdeveloped in N. Thus, when N felt that achievement might not be realized, he became panicky, first because it threatened his relationship with his father, and second because unacceptable oedipal impulses threatened to break through the defense of perfectionism. Finally, N had a tendency to catastrophize about the consequences of failure.

Although these biological and psychological perspectives on N's problem may be true, they leave out important information. How did the family system contribute to N's anxiety and to trouble with other family members? N and his brother had assumed two opposite roles in the family—N as the son who lives in harmony with his parents and fulfills their hopes and expectations, P as the disappointment. How did this happen? Systems theory suggests that it was no accident and was not solely a result of the individual psychologies of each family member. The roles are lived because they lend to family stability.

N's family had low levels of expressed emotion, particularly affection. Concern tended to be evidenced by showing disapproval when expectations were not met, as when N's brother did not clean his room. P received attention—albeit negative attention—from his parents. Why didn't P just try to meet the parents expectations the way N did and get attention that way? N made it plain through his behavior that, without his role, chaos might have ensued. He panicked at the idea of not being the best child, the one who fulfilled expectations. If he were challenged in this role, conflict would be the result. P also idolized N, and felt he would never be able to match up to N in competition for his parents' approval. N made it apparent that he could not tolerate the parents' disapproval—he was glad to have his brother receive negative attention. In the system that gradually evolved, both children could receive attention without entering into conflict with one another, and in the process spare their parents the painful decision of who should get the positive attention. The net result was that the family was stabilized by the roles the brothers occupied. In a family with little tolerance for disorder, it is organizing to have one child be good and the other bad, and that they be predictable in these roles.

The price for this stabilized family was individual psychiatric symptoms. N was chronically anxious, thanks to the requirement that he fulfill his parents' expectations in order to remain in the role of the good child. Thus, he fought relentlessly for control, a battle he always lost, because no matter how regimented N was, some things were necessarily out of his control. When something threatened his role—if, for example, a professor were to ask unpredictable questions or graded in a way N had not anticipated, so that he failed a test—N was unbearably anxious. His anxiety was not just the biological discharge of neurons or the breaking through of unacceptable incestuous impulses. It was his accurate perception, albeit unconscious, of a threat to the family system.

Conversely, the lack of clearly defined roles also can cause problems. In Chapter 19 we saw the example of J, who was having difficulties in school and at home with his single mother. J's mother, T, had been divorced when J was a young child and was now single, without any ongoing romantic relationships. Her parenting style was marked by attempts to be J's friend rather than his parent. Although this produced a closeness and rapport between the two, problems emerged. When J misbehaved, there were no clear consequences for his misbehavior and, conversely, desired behaviors were not rewarded. Rather than earning his allowance, for example, J was simply given it regardless of his actions during the previous week.

J and T had failed to differentiate clear and consistent roles of parent and child. T was not clearly the parent, who would take appropriate action when he misbehaved, and J was allowed a freedom he was unequipped to handle. The result was chaos. The institution of appropriate roles restored some family functioning. J was ready to be rewarded and, despite his protestations that he was an adult, he did not really mind assuming the role of an unemancipated teenager—life in the adult working world was not really his goal yet.

For J and T, systems therapy might work with the two to establish more suitable and clearly delineated roles by encouraging T to increase the consistency of her parenting and diffusing J's need to rebel.

Family therapy for N and his family might proceed by trying to disrupt established roles. N had revealed in individual therapy that he actually had quite a bit of anger and disappointment in his relationship with his father, but it went unspoken. A family therapist might attempt to jostle the family so that this conflict could emerge, and N could abandon his role as the good child. Once out of the established roles, the family might achieve greater emotional and communicative flexibility. If in the safety of therapy, with the therapist as a stabilizing influence, conflicts could be brought to light, the family would learn that conflict does not mean catastrophe. And, if conflict is not catastrophic, then it can be tolerated without anxiety. Instead of feeling anxious at the possibility of failing his parents' expectations, N could be himself, free to fail without being cast into the opposite role his brother currently occupied.

Bowenian and structural theories

When roles become blurred, as in the case of J and T, we say that the family lacks consistent *boundaries*. Every interpersonal relationship is characterized by limits on the intimacy and closeness of individuals. No two individuals can be entirely enmeshed so as to have the identical experience. There always exists some space, both physical and mental, between people. This space between individuals is maintained by boundaries. There are certain things we cannot do in our relationships with one another and certain limits on how much influence others can have on our thoughts and decisions. Also, no one can completely understand the experiences of another. Thus, there is always a boundary between individuals.

Boundaries are limits placed on the intimacy and closeness of relationships.

An optimal mix of intimacy and separateness leads to the development of a flexible and adaptive sense of self and one's relationships. The toddler needs to have not only the autonomy to explore the world but also the security of knowing that mother is keeping a watchful eye and is readily available. Older children who are beginning to experience more directed sexual urges (such as occur during the oedipal period) need the security that the fantasized sexual relationship with the other-sex parent will not actually happen. Mother and father need to have a relationship distinctly separate from the child without excluding intimacy.

In J's case, the lack of boundaries between him and his mother had led to a destructive excess of freedom. J was young and immature, not capable of making all the decisions in his life. In other words, there was a boundary between his world and the world of adults. But this boundary needed to be made explicit. J needed to be told from a consistent external source what was and was not acceptable, and what constituted good versus bad decisions. If J was given this guidance, he would gradually learn to control his impulses, to make long-term plans and choices consistent with those plans. Such guidance would be a boundary on his behavior.

It might seem that placing boundaries on J represents an unfair usurpation of his freedom. But, in fact, J's freedom was illusory. He was unable to regulate his behavior according to well-developed plans and goals. He was reactive rather than proactive. True freedom would come when he could make deliberate plans that were in his best long-term interest, a capacity Freud identified as synonymous with a mature ego. Since J's ego was as yet immature, he required regulation from an outside source—namely, the important adults in his life—and this necessitated boundaries established by adults. T needed to set consistent limits on what was and was not acceptable. As J matured and his decision making improved, he would take on increasing responsibility, until eventually he was ready to be self-sufficient, setting his own boundaries for himself.

Bowen

When boundaries are insufficient, psychopathology may result. This was the thesis of Murray Bowen, the founder of the *family systems theory* of family psychology. According to Bowen, family psychopathology is a result of inadequate differentiation of the self from others in the family, which leads family members to an enmeshment wherein they lack the freedom to act as autonomous individuals (Bowen, 1978). In any group structure, in addition to boundaries there will be alliances and conflicts. Bowen observed that the structures of groups often occur as *triangles*. Triangles appear as the exclusion of one group member in favor of a relationship between two others. The primary interaction between a duo leading to the exclusion of the third may be an alliance, but it may just as easily be a conflict. In N's family, for example, the structure of the family showed numerous triangles that were alternately dominant. N had an alliance with his parents that led to the exclusion of his brother. However, P compensated by escalating his conflict with the parents, thus excluding N. N and P were then required to alternately escalate their respective relationships with the parents in order to be the dominant rather than the excluded member of the triangle. This process led to pathological oppositional behavior in P and to intolerable anxiety and perfectionism for N.

According to Bowen, pathological family systems may be helped by disrupting triangular alliances and by strengthening boundaries between family members so that they have greater autonomy.

Structural therapy

Structural therapy, as developed by Salvador Minuchin, focuses on how the family structure that is formed by boundaries between individuals and generational hierarchies within the family may lead to psychopathology (Minuchin, 1974). Boundaries between family members may be too weak, as we saw in the case of J and T, or they may be too rigid. As the case example below demonstrates, overly rigid boundaries may be just as problematic as weak boundaries.

Family systems theory posits that family psychopathology results from inadequate differentiation of self from others in the family and from patterns of alliance and exclusion.

Case example

Mr. R came to a psychiatrist for consultation because he had been depressed for some time. R was a very controlled person who needed to structure his life completely in order to feel comfortable. When his wife was injured in an automobile accident, damage to her brain resulted in a tendency toward irritability. R found himself unable to tolerate her outbursts of anger. He became angry in return, which was most troubling, since in his family of origin anger was simply not expressed. He recalled an ever-present veneer of civility between him and his parents throughout his life, and he had never seen his parents fight.

The result of these excessively rigid boundaries during R's childhood was that he was unable to tolerate negative emotions in himself or anyone else. The covert message of his family's cool reserve was that anger and other strong emotions are dangerous, and that terrible things will happen if they are expressed. Consequently, R was careful to make sure anger was not a part of his life. When his capacity to keep anger out of his awareness broke down, he became depressed.

How much structure is enough? Theories of family therapy all suggest a compromise between autonomy and intimacy, between freedom and boundaries. Healthy family systems allow their individual members to freely express their emotions, but regulate this expression sufficiently that the experience of emotionality is not overwhelming. There are no absolute guidelines that define a healthy family system, in part because each family is different. What works well for one family might be intolerable for another. The question is whether a given family system operates in such a way as to be generally satisfactory *to its members*. This standard not only will vary between families but also will be different depending on the surrounding culture. Western culture places greater emphasis on independence and autonomy, whereas Eastern societies view the individual less as an autonomous unit and more as an element of society. Thus, what constitutes pathological enmeshment in an American family might be perfectly normal and adaptive for a Japanese family. Conversely, a family that is functioning well in the United States might been seen as pathologically autonomous in Japan.

Just as there is no objective standard for boundaries, there is no single objective standard for what constitutes a pathological family structure in general. All family structures are successful to some extent, and all have difficulties. The question becomes whether or not the structure is largely successful and tolerable, or whether it leads to significant problems and symptoms of psychopathology in its members.

Structural and Bowenian therapy attempts to point out and alter pathological structures within the family. How this is accomplished varies widely from therapy to therapy. In the case of N and his family, a family therapist might attempt to shift the triangles by promoting improved relationships between N's brother P and his parents, thus altering the alliance between N and his parents.

Culture-specific syndromes

Many of the psychiatric disorders are found in virtually all cultures. Bipolar disorder, for example, is found in all societies in approximately the same prevalence as in the United States. With minor differences, all societies have approximately the same rate of major depression and, as in the United States, the ratio of female cases to male is roughly 2:1. Anxiety disorders such as OCD, panic disorder, and posttraumatic stress disorder are found everywhere in the world.

Although many of the major mental disorders are found in all cultures, some psychiatric disorders are found only in certain cultures. In other words, they are *culture-specific*. Examples from the United States and Western Europe are anorexia nervosa and bulimia nervosa. Eating disorders are rare in nonaffluent societies, although they may be more common than previously thought. One reason for the occurrence of anorexia nervosa and bulimia nervosa is thought to be the combination of Western affluence with a cultural norm that values thinness over other virtues. Western women, who have a much higher prevalence of eating disorders than men, are deluged with scientifically designed media images that inspire them to believe they are failures if they do not realize a highly idealized body image of excruciating thinness (Field, Camargo, Taylor, Berkey, & Grahm, 1999). The availability of limitless supplies of food in Western societies makes control of weight a symbol of control in general. Because Western societies congregate in cities of highly mobile individuals with little sense of community, Westerners are forced to judge one another largely based on appearances, as people come and go rapidly and are not known in depth. This emphasis on image is fostered by a media that attempts to sell products—and so generate money—by promoting enticing appearances. Westerners, particularly women, are often left with the sense that if they are not sufficiently attractive they have no place in society, and indeed their fears in this regard are not unfounded.

It is clear that whatever biological and psychological mechanisms may underlie the development of eating disorders, they are uncommon without the appropriate cultural context. Cultural context has historically been a local phenomenon. One hundred years ago, culture varied significantly from locale to locale because travel and communication was difficult and slow. In today's world of rapid transit and instant communication, cultural values take place on a much wider scale. As individuals come to reside less and less in stable small communities, they turn to the media of mass society for information regarding others. It is not unusual for Americans to know television characters better than their neighbors, and Californians watch largely the same television shows as New Yorkers. Thus, culture-specific syndromes in mass media societies tend to be disorders common to the mass media culture at large.

A number of culture-specific syndromes also have been reported in smaller societies around the world (American Psychiatric Association, 1994). In Southeast Asia, *amok* is a homicidal rampage which frequently ends in suicide. *Koro* is an intense fear that the penis is retracting into the body, threatening death (in Asia). In Trinidad, *tabanka* is a male depression with a high incidence of suicide following abandonment by the wife.

To say that illness is influenced by culture is, of course, to abandon a certain objectivity about illness. Clinicians often would like to believe that the illnesses they treat are objective problems that could afflict anyone at any time. That those illnesses may be manifestations of a particular culture at a particular time seems to diminish the scientific luster of clinical medicine.

This is a difficulty only if one believes that there are problems that exist independent of culture. Broken bones are not a culture-free problem, they are simply less influenced by culture than are disorders of the human brain and mental state. Anorexia nervosa may be a problem of late twentieth-century Western culture, but it is very real and very fatal—up to 18% of anorexic individuals die from complications of the disease (Sadock & Sadock, 2000).

What human beings think, perceive, and feel and how they behave are highly influenced by the social world provided by other human beings. It is only natural that psychiatric problems will be highly influenced by social phenomena as well. Coronary artery disease and colon cancer have different prevalences in different societies. Hypertension does not even exist in some South American tribal cultures. Does this mean that those cultures simply have a different biology? Possibly, but it does not follow that biology is not influenced by culture. The high-fat diet of some cultures may well have some influence on their rates of hypertension and coronary artery disease. The consumption of smoked food in Japan may increase the rate of gastrointestinal cancers. Because human beings are social, there are no problems of human beings that are not, to some extent, social. The biopsychosocial model captures this critical fact.

Key points

- *Cybernetics* is the study of feedback loops in systems.

- *Positive feedback loops* accelerate interactions in a system through reciprocal reinforcement.

- *Negative feedback loops* decelerate interactions in a system through reciprocal inhibition.

- *Systems theory* proposes that family and group members play roles, such as victim, rebel, authority, and caretaker.

- These *roles* stabilize the system but may have pathological consequences.

- *Bowenian theory* focuses on autonomy within families and triangular structures of alliance and exclusion.

- *Structural theory* proposes that the structure of boundaries and alliances in groups may result in psychopathology.

- *Structural therapy* addresses relationship boundaries and generational issues within the family structure.

- Most major psychiatric syndromes occur cross-culturally.

- A few syndromes are *culture-specific*, occurring specifically in particular cultures.

Ethical and legal considerations 22

Ethics

Ethical codes have been a formal part of medical practice for most of recorded history. Hippocrates famously opined that *the care of the patient for the good of the patient* was the requirement of ethical medical practice (Porter, 1997). Later ethical codes have focused on the duty of the state to care for its members or to respect their autonomy. Ethical codes are ubiquitous in medical practice because the care of a patient by a physician is inherently a social phenomenon and, like any social interaction, must be regulated by ethical considerations.

All human activity is interwoven with value. Science and medicine are no different. The saving of life and the amelioration of pain and suffering are sought because they are sources of human concern. What values guide us toward these goals are never fixed; instead, they evolve constantly. There is not always agreement about what constitutes an ethical stance toward patient care. As recently as the nineteenth century, it was considered not only acceptable but a matter of necessary treatment for "lunatics" to be physically abused with cold water, shocks, and extended physical restraint (Porter, 1997). The history of ethical philosophy leaves little hope that all ethical dilemmas will disappear by the virtues of a single ethics. Yet that need not be cause for despair. If there is not an ethical formula that is beyond dispute, this simply means the human condition is complex and replete with competing interests. Ethics can be worked out, and have been. The application of the biopsychosocial model takes place within a well-established ethical canon that dates back to the ancient Greeks. Some medical schools still swear their new graduates to the Hippocratic Oath. Even where this practice is outdated, some of its principles remain as pillars of the professional ethics of medicine.

The ethical physician, including the psychiatrist, approaches the patient within the following principles.

Beneficence

Beneficence is the principle that a physician's duty is to minister to the patient in the patient's best interests.

As Hippocrates said, it is the responsibility of the physician to minister to the patient *in the patient's interests*. It is only for the good of the patient that treatment is entered into.

Nonmaleficence

A corollary to the principle of beneficence, the principle of non-maleficence implies that there should never be any interest in harm on the part of the physician toward the patient. Even in those situations where harm must be undertaken, such as in surgically incising the abdomen, it not for the sake of harm but for healing that the wound is created, perhaps to remove an inflamed appendix that might otherwise prove lethal. This is the principle behind the famous commandment "Primum non nocere," or "First do no harm." The enjoinder is not against all harm, if some harm must occur in the name of beneficence, but rather that the primary purpose of harm is forbidden.

Nonmaleficence is the principle that says a physician should never hold any interest in harming the patient.

Autonomy

The trend in the Western world since the Enlightenment of the seventeenth and eighteenth centuries has been toward increasing individual liberty and respect for the uniqueness of the individual and her autonomy. Liberty has become a dominant Western value, following the chain of libertarian philosophy descending from John Locke, Adam Smith, and John Stuart Mill.

The principle of autonomy holds that individuals are the best judges of their own best interests, and as such should enter relationships and engage in activities voluntarily, without coercion. A patient seeks treatment with the physician voluntarily. In general, with few exceptions, the patient is free to refuse treatment even if others think the treatment is in his best interest.

Implicit in the concept of voluntary treatment is *informed consent*. The patient voluntarily consents only when she is fully apprised of her medical condition and understands the risks and benefits of various options available.

Autonomy is the principle that says that individuals are the best judges of their own best interests.

Sadly, it has not always been the practice of psychiatry to foster patient autonomy; in fact, the contrary was true until the latter half of the twentieth century. Earlier approaches to the psychiatric patient— and to the medical patient in general—favored the contrary doctrine of *paternalism*, holding that the physician, by virtue of superior knowledge and reason, could make better decisions on the patient's behalf than the patient could. This was particularly true for psychiatric disorders, wherein the very organ and faculties required for decision making may be impaired—that is, the brain and the reasoning process.

The scope of involuntary treatment has been greatly curtailed, and it is the aim of all treatment today to be between consenting individuals. This is almost always possible. Yet even as staunch an advocate of individual liberty as John Stuart Mill found himself forced, in his treatise *On Liberty* (1859/1983), to temper his championing of liberty in cases where an individual is so incapacitated that his "rational faculty" is impaired. Modern medical ethics have tended to expand the emphasis on liberty and autonomy to a great degree; however, there remain instances of involuntary treatment, and this is an area of vigorous debate.

Paternalism is the principle that physicians, by virtue of superior knowledge and reason, can make better decisions on the patient's behalf than the patient could.

Legal considerations

Involuntary treatment

Because Western societies place a high premium on individual freedom, they tolerate a high degree of idiosyncrasy before imposing on this freedom. This stems from a belief in the sovereignty of individual autonomy unless one's actions interfere with others. When this happens, every society reserves the right to restrict an individual's liberty. Such restriction is necessary to the functioning of an orderly society.

In the United States, the criteria for involuntary psychiatric treatment—although specifically regulated at the state level—are restricted to imminent danger to self or others or grave disability (usually interpreted as the inability to organize subsistence tasks, such as maintaining basic safety and finding food and shelter). This standard was mandated in the Supreme Court case of *O'Connor v. Donaldson* (1975). In that case, O'Connor had been committed to a mental hospital merely because he had schizophrenia. O'Connor sued, and the Court found that mentally ill individuals may be involuntarily committed only if they are imminently dangerous to themselves or others, or if they are incapable of surviving outside the hospital. A psychiatric diagnosis alone is not sufficient grounds for involuntary treatment. State law has subsequently followed this decision, and these are the general requirements for involuntary commitment, although the details vary from state to state.

Following decisions such as *Wyatt v. Stickney* (1971, 1979), involuntary commitment must be for the purpose of treatment, and not simply for domiciling. Since the purpose of involuntary commitment is treatment, psychiatrists and other mental health providers are necessarily involved in involuntary proceedings. However, the imposition of involuntary treatment is not the business of psychiatrists, but of the courts. Psychiatrists often advocate for involuntary treatment, but the final decision lies in the hands of a judge. Involuntary status is specifically regulated on a state-by-state basis, but in general it does not restrict rights to visitation or communication, the right to vote, and so on.

Jail or treatment?   The commission of acts that are dangerous to others is behavior that every society penalizes. The decision of whether the criminal justice system or the mental health system should deal with those who commit acts dangerous to others is an area of ongoing controversy. Generally speaking, since the M'Naghten case in England in 1843, American and European societies have made provision for the effects of mental illness on culpability (Sadock & Sadock, 2000).

The M'Naghten case is named after the defendant, Daniel M'Naghten, who, in the thrall of paranoid delusions, murdered Edward Drummond. The M'Naghten decision produced the *M'Naghten rules*, by which the English courts attempted to codify grounds for an insanity defense. The essence of the rule is that:

> the party accused was laboring under such a defect of reason, from a disease of the mind, as not to know the nature and quality of the act he was doing, or if he did know it, he did not know he was doing what was wrong. (Sadock & Sadock, 2000, p. 3286)

The M'Naghten rule remains the centerpiece of the insanity defense in American and British law and forms the basis of the current American Law Institute's test of criminality, the model penal code of 1962. However, the American Law Institute's test includes the addendum that criminal conduct in itself does not constitute a mental illness (Sadock & Sadock, 2000).

Thus, under U.S. law, the test of criminality is, in essence, a test of *competency*. Competence is the state in which one is responsible for one's actions and choices.

Competency.   In general, the criteria for competency are that one

1. understand one's condition, including the consequences of one's acts and choices,
2. have an opinion about choices related to one's condition, and
3. be able to express that opinion.

If one has no understanding of one's condition, then one is not competent to make decisions. Given one's condition, one must actually have an opinion about it (not everyone does). Finally, one must be able to express that opinion. A person with a stroke in the dominant hemisphere language center may well understand his condition and have an opinion about the course of future events, but if he cannot communicate that opinion, then someone else must make his decisions. Ideally, family and friends become the decision makers in such circumstances, but this is by no means always the case and, in any event, even family cannot guarantee that the decisions made will be congruent with what the patient would want.

Competency has nothing to do with the perceived rationality of opinions expressed. Plaintiffs have consistently been allowed by the courts to refuse lifesaving treatments, so long as the risks and benefits of refusing or accepting are understood. Competent capacity is required in a number of domains, including managing one's estate, standing trial, and making medical decisions, and incapacity in one area does not imply incapacity in all. Competency in each area in question must be assessed individually, although it often happens that incapacity generalizes to include all areas.

Competency is the state in which one is responsible for one's actions and choices.

Thus, the key feature of criminality—*criminal responsibility*—is competency. If in the course of a criminal act, one understands the nature of the act and its morality, then one is competent to make decisions around that act and therefore is culpable for the outcome of those decisions. In such cases, the criminal justice system handles one's dangerousness to society. Alternatively, if one is not competent, then the criminal justice system does not act. Instead, medical treatment to attempt to alleviate the incompetency or chronic care by proxy ensues. An individual with Alzheimer's disease might require treatment for a urinary tract infection and placement in a nursing home. In the case of mental illnesses such as schizophrenia, this might mean hospitalization and treatment with antipsychotic medication.

Incompetency by virtue of mental illness usually is handled by different state statutes than incompetency by "medical" illnesses, and typically in a stricter manner. This legal distinction is a remnant of bygone days in which it was held to be meaningful to speak of mental illness as distinct from central nervous system dysfunctions. Today the evidence of a neuropathological basis for mental disorders is overwhelming. Despite this anachronistic division, the end result is substantially the same, whether one is incompetent because of a medical or a mental illness. If one is incompetent by virtue of the effects of a mental illness, then involuntary treatment is indicated, just as if one were demented from Alzheimer's disease.

Mental illness per se does not immunize one against the consequences of one's actions, provided one actually understands such consequences. Contrary to popular opinion, very few insanity pleas are actually filed, and even fewer are successful. Juries tend to be quite dubious of claims that one is not responsible for one's actions. Most mentally ill individuals are competent to manage their own affairs.

Duty to protect. Despite the impossibility of accurately predicting violence toward others and suicide, the courts have clearly established a legal duty to do so for any providers caring for the mentally ill, including primary care and other nonpsychiatric physicians. This duty arises from the two *Tarasoff v. California Board of Regents* cases (1973, 1976a, 1976b, 1976c). Tarasoff was murdered by her boyfriend, who had made credible threats to his psychiatrist that he was going to murder Ms. Tarasoff.

Although the psychiatrist alerted the authorities, he did not contact Ms. Tarasoff directly to warn her of the danger. The court found that mental health providers have a duty to warn third parties of credible threats of violence from their patients. *Tarasoff II* expanded this to a general duty to protect both society and patients themselves from their acts. The former "duty to warn" now falls under the penumbra of acts that a mental health provider may be required to undertake in order to fulfill a broader "duty to protect." Warning a potential victim is not necessarily sufficient, and involuntary hospitalization or other protective steps may be required. On the other hand, if a patient is involuntarily hospitalized and the danger resolves, warning the former target may not be necessary.

While the courts unfortunately have established a requirement that psychiatrists do something that cannot be done—predict the future—this does help to focus those caring for the mentally ill on the presence of risk factors for dangerousness to self and others, and encourages steps to mitigate those risk factors. Although psychiatrists cannot predict the future, they can make destructive outcomes less likely through appropriate biopsychosocial treatment.

Key points

- The principles of ethical treatment of patients include *beneficence*, *nonmaleficence*, and *autonomy*.

- *Involuntary psychiatric treatment* is based on the principle of *paternalism* and is indicated in cases of dangerousness to self or others or of grave disability.

- *Incompetency* occurs when an individual does not understand her condition and the consequences of various possible courses of action.

- Mental health providers have a *legal duty to protect* society from the violent acts of patients and to protect patients from their own violent acts.

Biopsychosocial Psychiatry V

The process of 23 diagnosis

The diagnostic cascade

The cases presented in this book, although real clinical examples, have been selected for their illustrative quality. Each exemplifies a particular psychiatric diagnosis. But how do psychiatrists sort through so many symptoms systematically, so as to correctly classify them and find their cause?

The medical approach to assessment is through the process of *differential diagnosis*, the purpose of which is to generate a list of possible causes for the presenting problem and then systematically search for the presence or absence of each possible illness until a result is reached. For example, if a person comes into the emergency room with severe abdominal pain, possible causes include appendicitis, gallstones, ulcers, a ruptured organ, organ infarction, and so on. Based on the patient's history, a physical examination, and laboratory tests, physicians can sort through these possibilities systematically and make a correct diagnosis. The purpose of this approach is to avoid missing any possible causes— it is all too easy to reach an incorrect diagnosis based on one's first impressions.

Psychiatric practice is no different in this regard. For example, hallucinations may be the result of problems as diverse as Alzheimer's disease, head injury, seizure, schizophrenia, mania, major depression, and drug intoxication. Learning to generate differential diagnostic schemes is one of the primary learning tasks in medical school and residency training. Sorting through a differential diagnosis is the heart of medical assessment.

The practice of differential diagnosis in psychiatry can be organized by a priority list based on possible severity of illness. In descending order, from more important to less:

- Delirium
- Psychiatric disorders due to a general medical condition
- Dementia

Differential diagnosis is the process of generating a list of possible causes for a presenting problem, then systematically searching for the presence or absence of each.

- Substance use disorder
- Mania
- Primary psychotic disorders
- Major depression
- Anxiety disorders

These disorders usually are considered the major mental illnesses, since they cause much morbidity and mortality, are highly prevalent, and have a clear body of data establishing their causes. The remaining *DSM-IV* diagnoses are considered next, and include personality disorders, dissociative disorders, eating disorders, somatization disorders, sleep disorders, sexual disorders, childhood disorders, malingering/factitious disorders, adjustment disorders, and impulse control disorders.

Obviously, this list can be modified based on the clinical symptoms. An eating disorder may be one of the first considerations in an adolescent girl who weighs 20% less than her ideal body weight and who believes she is overweight. But the list must be considered in its entirety. Brain tumors, for example, can cause profound weight loss, as can paranoid fears that one's food is poisoned.

Case example

Let us take the example of mutism, which is the complete or nearly complete lack of verbal output. A worried family brings in their 25-year-old son, who has not spoken to anyone for the last two days. Without going into more details, a general differential diagnosis for the problem of mutism might look like this:

- ***Delirium***, leading to an altered level of consciousness, could produce mutism.

- Mutism may be caused by ***general medical problems***, such as vocal cord (laryngeal) dysfunction (either through direct damage to the larynx, as might be seen in simple inflammation of the larynx), trauma, a vocal cord tumor, or damage to the nervous system control of the vocal cords. The latter might include problems such as strokes, amyotrophic lateral sclerosis, multiple sclerosis, infections, and tumors.

  Additionally, the ***nervous system*** may be damaged in such a way as to impair language production rather than directly affecting vocalization.

  Injury to the ***dominant cerebral hemisphere***, possibly by mechanisms just listed, may cause aphasia—the inability to understand, organize, and produce language. (There are many subtypes of aphasia, such as Broca's aphasia, in which language comprehension is intact but language production impaired, and Wernicke's aphasia, which has the opposite presentation.)

Damage to prefrontal cortex may produce a syndrome called *akinetic mutism*, in which there is a virtual absence of movement and lack of initiation.

Seizures, particularly complex partial seizures, also can result in mutism.

- ***Dementia*** must be considered, with various causes such as AIDS dementia complex or spongiform encephalopathy in a young person.

- ***Intoxication or withdrawal states*** certainly could be responsible for mutism. Intoxication with opiates such as heroin or withdrawal from chronic cocaine use may cause the symptom of mutism. In addition, intoxication or withdrawal from prescription medications and herbal preparations must be considered, as well as poisoning from heavy metals and other toxins.

- ***Mania*** is seldom a cause of mutism.

- ***Primary psychotic disorders*** can cause mutism. Mutism may be the result of catatonia, for example, which can be related to primary psychotic and mood disorders or can be the effect of certain medications (such as antipsychotic medications). Alternatively, the patient might be preoccupied with internally generated stimuli (hallucinations) and so not respond to the environment around him. Severe paranoia might make a person too afraid to speak. The negative symptoms of schizophrenia, such as anhedonia (the inability to experience pleasure) and abulia (lack of spontaneity), also might be responsible for mutism.

- ***Major depression*** can present with symptoms of catatonia or profound withdrawal, resulting in mutism.

- ***Anxiety disorders*** such as posttraumatic stress disorder occasionally can result in mutism. Severe OCD with a compulsion to remain mute is a possible etiology.

- ***Dissociative disorders***, such as a spontaneous trance state, would be in the differential diagnosis for mutism.

Having sorted through this differential diagnosis, we are left with the possibility that the patient has conscious intent to produce mutism. Perhaps he has taken a vow of silence or is simply very angry and does not wish to speak to anybody. Or he may have another reason to want to be taken to the hospital (such as insurance fraud), and mutism is a way to accomplish this.

The process of differential diagnosis may be quite long. Fortunately, the process shown here is somewhat theoretical, for the purposes of illustration. In practice, the patient's history, a physical examination, and laboratory data will aid in quickly eliminating many of the possibilities. Some are mutually exclusive. For example, someone who is mute because of a coma cannot, by definition, be malingering.

Despite the benefits of systematically considering the various diagnostic possibilities for each case, the process is not foolproof. Patients' stories can be misleading and symptoms can be confusing and not readily categorizable. The state of the art in medical practice is only the best that is currently available. There still are many problems modern medicine does not understand, and some it has not even identified. This is expected as a part of scientific investigation. Some of our cherished theories eventually will be discarded, and new ideas as yet unknown will arrive. Still, differential diagnosis is the best process by which to critically assess problematic symptoms.

Key points

- Psychiatric symptoms should be evaluated using a *differential diagnosis* to systematically sort through the possible causes.

- A *diagnostic cascade* aids in prioritizing possible diagnoses.

The biopsychosocial 24
interview

The biopsychosocial framework

A complete biopsychosocial assessment includes the following items:

- Identifying data, including the patient's name, age, sex, ethnicity, marital status, sexual orientation, and employment and living situations

- The chief complaint, in the patient's own words

- A history of the present illness, including symptoms relevant to the chief complaint looking toward *DSM-IV* classification and differential diagnosis, duration, precipitants and mitigants, and a review of systems to rule in or out the major mental illnesses (delirium, psychiatric disorder due to a general medical condition, substance use disorders, dementia, bipolar disorder, primary psychotic disorders, major depression, and anxiety disorders)

- Allergies

- Medications

- Past medical history, including information on alcohol and drug use, nicotine, and caffeine

- Past psychiatric history, including previous treatment episodes, medication history, hospitalizations, suicide attempts or violence, and psychotherapy

- Family history for structure and medical and/or psychiatric illnesses

- Social history, including developmental history, psychodynamic factors, physical or sexual abuse, education, military service, employment history, legal history, sexual or marital situation, religious beliefs, support system, and stressors

- A physical examination, if any, typically limited to a neurological examination, but may include any general physical examination as required

- A mental status examination, including general appearance, behavior, interaction, speech, mood (subjective emotional state), affect (external expression of mood), thought process (organization), thought content (suicidal or homicidal, hallucinations, and delusions), formal cognitive testing (level of consciousness, orientation, recent and remote memory, attention, language, praxis, naming, and abstraction), judgment, and insight

- Laboratory data

- *DSM-IV* diagnoses:

  Axis I: Psychiatric Diagnoses except Personality Disorders

  Axis II: Personality Disorders/Mental Retardation

  Axis III: Medical Disorders

  Axis IV: Current Stressors, none to catastrophic

  Axis V: Current and Remote Functioning, 1–100 scale

- Biopsychosocial formulation

  Biological contributors to *DSM* diagnosis, genetic contributions, medical and substance use contributors

  Psychological/psychodynamic formulation (drive, ego, object, self) and cognitive-behavioral formulation

  Social structure deficits and stressors

- **Plan** addressing biological, psychological, and social factors

  (Five axis diagnostic categories used with permission from the **Diagnostic and Statistical Manual of Mental Disorders**, Fourth Edition. Copyright 1994, American Psychiatric Association.)

A biopsychosocial interview

What follows is an interview derived from actual psychiatric practice, with annotations describing the psychiatrist's thinking as the interview progresses. The reader will note that although the psychiatrist attempts to fill out most of the information required in the preceding outline, she does not follow a strictly programmatic interview, but instead gathers the information as it becomes available. The interview begins with open-ended questions that the patient can answer as she wishes. Later, more specific questioning is undertaken. The transcribed text cannot reflect the nuances of intonation or the extensive nonverbal communication that always occurs between physician and patient. It represents a real interview operating within constraints such as scheduling, and so may not show an ideal interview in every regard.

> Ms. N appears for the appointment early and fills out the preliminary paperwork. The psychiatrist introduces herself in the waiting room, and leads Ms. N to her office, where Ms. N is offered a seat wherever she chooses. Already, the psychiatrist has noted that Ms. N is neatly dressed and timid almost to the point of obsequiousness.

Psychiatrist (P): Well, what brings you to see me today?

Ms. N (N): I guess it's this depression.

The psychiatrist nods without commenting.

N: I've been feeling really bad. Over the last couple of months.

P: In what way are you feeling bad?

N: Just really down. (***Although timid and quiet, she begins to talk readily.***) I don't feel very good about myself. I really don't feel like doing anything. I'm kind of . . . beating myself up all the time.

P: What are you beating yourself up about?

N: I just don't feel like I do anything right anymore. I cry a lot. (***N looks very gloomy.***)

P: (***nods***) You've been feeling pretty sad. (***Reflecting.***)

N: Yeah.

P: And this started a few months ago?

N nods, looking at the floor.

P: Do you connect this with anything?

N: Well, when I was little, my mother went through a phase where she was very depressed. It was just after my little brother was born.

The psychiatrist is surprised to hear this distant developmental history, since she herself had been thinking about recent precipitating events, but notes the family history of depression and pursues the developmental information.

N: I remember her just lying in bed for days at a time. My dad was at work a lot. My grandmother came over to look after us, but she had to look after my brother. My older sister and I just kind of kept to ourselves. I remember spending a lot of time alone.

P: What did you think about that?

N: (*looking terribly sad*) I felt awful.

When she does not elaborate, the psychiatrist again reflects.

P: You felt awful.

N: Like I do now. I just felt like no one . . . (*She trails off.*)

P: Like no one what?

N: Like I was alone.

P: You felt abandoned. (*A trial clarification.*)

N: I did. I've been depressed a lot over the years. This definitely isn't the first time. (*N responds well to the clarification.*)

P: When were you depressed before?

N: The last time was about 5 years ago.

P: Hmm. So you were doing fine since then?

N: (*nods*) Yeah. Then I just started to feel myself sinking. I tried to ignore it, but . . . it just kept getting worse. The last few months . . .

P: Do you have any ideas about why this is happening now?

A long pause ensues, in which N clearly is thinking about a difficult topic. The psychiatrist does not interrupt this process.

N: Well. I've been . . . involved with this man at work. I mean, it's entirely . . . nothing's happened. It's just that he pays a lot of attention to me. This is embarrassing.

She pauses and the psychiatrist sits quietly.

N: I don't know why I want him to like me. I mean, I don't want to have an affair. I'm happily married.

The psychiatrist considers that this may either be a reaction formation as a ego defense against the anxiety-provoking idea of having an affair, since N is clearly intrigued by the man at work, or an object relationship in which she really does not want to have an affair but needs attention to fulfill an object need.

P: What do you suppose he wants out this relationship?

N: That's just it. I don't think he wants one either. He's married. He must be happy.

P: How do you know that?

N: I just . . . well, he seems very . . . I just assumed he did.

The psychiatrist notes the transference to the man at work which assumes he is happily married without factual basis. She also notes the cognitive distortion of mind-reading, assuming what another thinks without basis.

P: Why did you assume that?

N: He just seems so well-adjusted. Confident.

P: Hmm. And yet he's paying attention to you.

N: Right.

P: And yet you're sure he's happily married.

N: Well. I just . . . (***long pause***) I guess I'm sure I couldn't measure up.

The psychiatrist notes the possible rivalrous connotation as well as the self-deprecation.

P: Measure up in what way?

N: Well, I don't feel very good about myself at all.

P: How?

N: I just don't think . . . I'm not good-looking enough, for starters.

P: Not good-looking enough for what?

N: To . . . I don't know. Be the sort of person I would like to be.

P: And what sort of person is that?

N: You know. Confident.

P: You'd like to feel good about yourself.

N: Right.

P: So how good-looking would you have to be to feel good about yourself?

N: I . . . better than this.

P: So it's hard to really say.

N: I just feel like I'm ugly.

P: I . . . I'm not sure how you'll know when you're good-looking enough to feel good about yourself.

She is trying to get N to examine the cognitive distortions of labeling (I'm ugly), arbitrary standards, and dichotomous thinking.

N: I don't know.

P: I don't either. I think that's because you really haven't set a particular standard. You just think you're ugly.

N: Well . . . what you see on magazines.

P: I see. So anyone who doesn't look like a magazine can't feel good about themselves?

N: Of course they can.

P: Except you.

N: I guess.

P: Sort of a double standard. It's okay for them to feel good about themselves if they don't look a certain way, but not you.

N: Yeah. I just feel that way about myself.

Although the preceding interaction may have had therapeutic value, this is not a therapy session, but an evaluation. The psychiatrist moves back to gathering data rather than continuing to pursue the distortions.

P: Mmm-hmm. So what's been happening with this person at work?

N: Well, we spend a lot of time together. We work on some of the same projects. So we talk a lot during the day. He seems to pay a lot of attention to me. And the other day, he brought me a flower. He was real casual about it, but it was very pretty, and I thought . . . . He asks me to lunch sometimes.

P: How do you feel about this attention?

N: I feel like he must . . . but I end up feeling like he couldn't possibly like me.

P: Even though he pays attention to you?

N: Mmm-hmm.

The psychiatrist notes that N turns the obvious interpretation of her coworker's behavior on its head, and again wonders if this is an ego-defensive behavior.

P: How would your husband feel about this?

N: Oh. I'm sure he wouldn't mind. He's very sweet. I mean, I have everything I could ever want in a husband. He's kind, and he's a good provider.

P: Hmm. Okay. What about your romantic relationship?

N: That's good too. (*She does not elaborate.*)

P: But, for some reason, you're drawn to this man at work.

N: I want him to like me, but I feel like he won't.

Since the theme has returned and the hour is passing, the psychiatrist decides to move on. She has noted the ego defenses (reaction formation and isolation-of-affect) and the possible oedipal themes of forbidden affection. Cognitive distortions are prominent.

P: So all this has left you feeling pretty depressed?

N: Yes.

The psychiatrist pursues symptoms of depression. N's psychomotor retardation has already been noted.

P: Has it been hard to enjoy things? Do you not get much pleasure out of life anymore?

N: I don't feel like doing anything.

The psychiatrist notes anhedonia.

P: What did you used to like to do?

N: Read a lot. Hiking. I just don't feel like it anymore.

P: Have you been tired?

N: Very.

P: How well do you sleep?

N: It's been a problem.

P: How so?

N: I go to sleep okay. But I wake up a lot. Then I can't get back to sleep.

The psychiatrist notes decreased sleep with early a.m. awakening.

P: How about your appetite?

N: That's been fine.

N looks rueful about her weight, which is not exceptional.

P: You don't feel too good about that?

N: I'm too heavy.

Here the psychiatrist could again pursue the cognitive distortion of arbitrary standard setting and labeling, but since the presence and character of cognitive distortions has already been established, as well as some of their psychodynamic bases, she chooses to gather more data needed for the complete evaluation. In so doing, she moves from open-ended to more directed questioning.

P: Can you concentrate on things?

N: That's been terrible. Maybe that's part of why I don't read much. I look at a page, and it just doesn't sink in.

P: Let me ask you this: Have you had any thoughts that perhaps life isn't worth living anymore?

She is beginning the assessment of suicidal ideation.

N: Yeah, I have. I know that's terrible.

The psychiatrist notes the self-criticism.

N: But sometimes I just feel like it's not worth it. Not that I'd ever do anything about it. I mean I'd never . . . . (***trails off***)

P: Have you actually had any thoughts of ending your life?

N: No, I'd never do that. The kids . . . and I have a strong faith. I really think that's wrong.

P: But it sounds like you haven't been very optimistic.

N: No. That I haven't been.

P: Okay. Now you told me that this isn't the first time you've been depressed. Could you tell me what sort of treatment you have had for this over the years?

The diagnosis of depression established, she moves on to past psychiatric history.

N: Well, my family doctor put me Zoloft (sertraline).

P: How much of that are you taking?

N: I don't know. It's a little blue one . . . .

P: Fifty milligrams?

N: I guess.

P: How long have you been on that?

N: About 2 months.

P: Has it helped?

N: Not really.

P: Any problems with it? Any side effects?

N: No. It's fine.

P: Okay. (***She stops to take a current medical history.***) Are you taking any other medications right now?

N: Just birth control.

P: You're not being treated for any medical problems?

N: No, I'm fine.

P: Any serious medical problems in the past?

N: No, not really.

P: How about any operations?

N: I had my appendix out.

P: Any head injuries, serious trauma?

N: No.

P: How about any allergies to any medications?

N: Just penicillin.

The psychiatrist moves back to N's psychiatric history.

P: All right. You're taking the Zoloft now. Have you been on any other antidepressant medications over the years?

N: I took amitriptyline.

P: When was that?

N: That was 5 years ago.

P: Did it help?

N: I think so. I don't really remember.

P: Who prescribed that for you?

N: A psychiatrist. (***She names a physician in a nearby town.***)

P: I see. So you were in psychiatric treatment then?

N: Right.

P: Did he put you on anything else?

N: (***looking sheepish***) I . . . I'm not sure. I really don't remember.

P: Let me name a few and see if you remember. (***The psychiatrist names a few medications, but none of them seem familiar to N.***)

N: Sorry. I just don't really remember.

P: That's okay. Any other times you've been in psychiatric treatment?

N: Well, I was hospitalized once before.

P: Oh. When was this?

N: I was about 25.

P: What happened?

N: (*sighs*) I was engaged. My fiancé left me. I was pretty . . . I was devastated.

P: How did you end up in the hospital?

N: I checked myself in. I couldn't stop crying.

P: How was that experience?

N: Not great. They discharged me pretty fast.

The psychiatrist has noted the recurrent theme of loss precipitating episodes of depression. The association N has already made with her childhood experience of her mother's depression is crucial. However, she opts to finish the history taking before using the rest of the hour to explore that theme.

P: Okay, well, let me ask you just a few more questions about some specific things.

N: Okay.

P: First, have you had any severe anxiety? For example, any panic attacks?

N: I don't think so.

P: That's where you suddenly feel so scared you feel like you might die right there on the spot. Heart pounding, shaking, sweating . . . ?

N: No.

P: Okay. How about any recurring thoughts that you just can't get out of your head, no matter how hard you try?

She is looking for OCD.

N: I don't think so.

P: Sometimes, you know, people get so concerned about germs or contamination that they feel compelled to wash their hands over and over . . . .

N: Oh, I see. No. I haven't.

P: All right. How about any unusual symptoms? Things you've had a difficult time accounting for?

N: Not really.

The psychiatrist is looking for any history of psychosis.

P: For example, have you ever heard any funny things? Voice say your name, you turn around and there's nothing there?

N shakes her head.

P: How about seeing anything odd? Shadows out of the corner of your eye? Things like that?

N: No.

P: Okay. (***Now she is looking for episodes of mania.***) Now, sometimes when people have depression, it's actually part of a cycle, where they go from being depressed to feeling okay, to feeling so good it seems very odd. You know, so much energy they don't know what to do with it all, talking really fast, maybe they only need 4 or 5 hours of sleep and they feel great . . . anything like that?

N: (***almost laughs***) I've never felt like that. I wish I would.

P: All right. Let me ask you about alcohol.

N: Well, I have a glass of wine with dinner sometimes. Maybe a few times a month.

P: Any time when you felt like alcohol was a problem for you in any sort of way?

N: Not . . . no, not really. I drank more in college. It never was a problem though.

P: You've never missed work or had any school problems because of drinking?

N: No, nothing like that.

P: No relationship problems because of alcohol?

N: Oh, no.

P: What about other drugs? Marijuana, cocaine . . . ?

N: Hmm. I did use marijuana a few times in college. I didn't really like it though.

P: Tobacco? Do you smoke?

N: I quit. Ten years ago.

P: Good for you.

N: Actually, it was easier than I thought. I just said one day, that's it. And I never touched another one.

P: Okay. Any time in your life when you felt in great danger?

N shakes her head.

P: Were you ever assaulted? Or raped?

N: No.

P: Was there any time in your life when you were physically or sexually abused?

N: (***thinks for a second, and takes a breath***) No.

The interview is not complete. In the remaining time, the psychiatrist works on some of the psychological issues raised in the interview, performs some brief cognitive tests that reveal no significant abnormalities (because N complained of poor concentration), and then moves on to coordinating a treatment plan based on her assessment. The assessment is as follows:

Diagnostically, N appears to be suffering from recurrent major depression, of moderate severity. No other Axis I disorder is present, and there is no clear evidence of a personality disorder. The differential diagnosis includes depression due to a general medical condition, substance-induced depressive disorder, and bipolar disorder. The information gathered is reassuring that none of these is present. No significant comorbidity (such as an anxiety disorder) is present.

Biologically, N's depression appears to have a genetic predisposition passed on by her mother. N has tried a somatic therapy (the antidepressant sertraline) with limited success, but at a subtherapeutic dose. She seems to be tolerating the medication. Medically, she takes birth control pills, which occasionally are associated with the appearance of depressed mood. However, N has taken estrogen/progesterone supplements for years and has been euthymic for long periods of time while taking the supplements.

Psychologically, N's ego functioning is largely neurotic. There is little evidence of immature ego defenses (although she tends to view herself in all-or-nothing terms), and no psychotic ego defenses are present. Instead, she relies primarily on reaction formation (assuming her coworker is not attracted to her when he obviously is and denying that she could have any interest in an affair with him), isolation-of-affect (she talks about her mood more than she shows it), and repression. In *drive psychological terms*, she has evidence of an oedipal complex (she has feelings of guilt, for example), but this seems to be somewhat immature (her superego is quite punitive). She defends herself vigorously against sexual impulses. Her formative experience of her mother's abandonment (through depression) occurred during the genital phase and seems to have left some self-psychological deficits, in which she wishes to be admired (but thinks she cannot be) and tends to idealize others (such as her coworker and the psychiatrist). N's object relations are evident in the session. She has a transference, evident in her timid behavior, to the psychiatrist that is at once idealizing of the doctor and self-denigrating.

Cognitively, N's psychology is marked by prominent cognitive distortions that perpetuate her depression. She thinks, for example, that she must measure up to certain arbitrary standards, or she will be a failure. *Behaviorally*, she has withdrawn from many of the activities that formerly gave her pleasure, and acts in a manner consistent with her low sense of self-worth.

Socially, N has reasonable social support in her nuclear family, although there are questions of subterranean conflicts that she is currently unwilling to discuss. It is not yet clear how her interactions with her husband may be contributing to her symptoms. N seems to have formed a positive feedback loop with her coworker, in which their mutual interest escalates with each interaction. N's finances are sound, and there have been few major changes in her life. Although she has depression and despondency, her risk for violence is low.

Accordingly, the psychiatrist formulated the following plan: *Biologically*, the antidepressant sertraline was increased to 100mg/day. N was sent for a complete blood count and thyroid studies to rule out the common conditions of anemia and hypothyroidism. *Psychologically*, N was enrolled in cognitive-behavioral therapy, although the psychiatrist suspected that psychodynamic therapy might eventually be necessary. *Socially*, N was encouraged to bring her husband in to an appointment so the doctor could observe their interactions.

This is the practice of psychiatry: Patient and physician meet together in a forum where a maximum of interpersonal understanding may grow, engage in a process of critical inquiry, apply various models of understanding with an ethic of caring, and reach solutions.

References

Adler, G. (1981). The borderline-narcissistic personality disorder continuum. *American Journal of Psychiatry, 138,* 46–50.

Aghajianian, G. K. (1994). Serotonin and the action of LSD in the brain. *Psychiatric Annals, 24,* 137–141.

Akbarian, S., Vinuela, A., Kim, J. J., Potkin, S. G., Bunney, W. E., Jr., & Jones, E. G. (1993). Distorted distribution of nicotinamide-adenine dinucleotide phosphate-diaphorase neurons in temporal lobe of schizophrenics implies anomalous cortical development. *Archives of General Psychiatry, 50,* 178–187.

American Psychiatric Association. (1994). *Diagnostic and Statistical Manual of Mental Disorders* (4th ed.). Washington, DC: American Psychiatric Association.

Andreasen, N. C. (1999). A unitary model of schizophrenia: Bleuler's "fragmented phrene" as schzencephaly. *Archives of General Psychiatry, 56,* 781–787.

Anton, R. F., & Burch, E. A. (1990). Amoxapine versus amitriptyline combined with perphenazine in the treatment of psychotic major depression. *American Journal of Psychiatry, 147,* 1203–1208.

Arnold, S. E., Hyman, B. T., van Hoesen, G. W., & Damasio, A. R. (1991). Some cytoarchitectural abnormalities of the entorhinal cortex in schizophrenia. *Archives of General Psychiatry, 48,* 625–628.

Asgard, U. (1990). A psychiatric study of suicide among urban Swedish women. *Acta Psychiatrica Scandinavia, 82,* 115–124.

Baker, D. G., West, S. A., Nicholson, W. E., Ekhator N. N., Kasckon, J. W., & Hill, K. K. (1999). Serial CSF corticotropin-releasing hormone levels and adrenocortical activity in combat veterans with posttraumatic stress disorder. *American Journal of Psychiatry, 156,* 585–588.

Baker, H. S., & Baker, M. N. (1987). Heinz Kohut's self-psychology: An overview. *American Journal of Psychiatry, 144,* 1–9.

Barlow, D. H., & Craske, M. G. (1994). *Mastery of your anxiety and panic.* New York: Graywind Publications.

Bateson, G. (1979). *Mind and nature.* New York: Dutton.

Baxter, L. R. (1999). Functional imaging of brain systems mediating obsessive-compulsive disorder. In D. S. Charney, E. J. Nestler, & B. S. Bunney (Eds.), *The neurobiology of mental illness* (pp. 534–547). New York: Oxford University Press.

Baxter, L. R., Schwarz, J. M., Bergman, K. S., Szuba, M. P., Guze, B. H., Mazziota, J. C., Alazraki, A., Selin, C. E., Fering, H.-K., Munford, P., & Phelps, M. E. (1992). Caudate glucose metabolic rate changes with both drug and behavior therapy for obsessive-compulsive disorder. *Archives of General Psychiatry, 49,* 681–689.

Beck, A. T., Brown, G., Berchick, R. J., Stewart, B. L., & Steer, R. A. (1990). Relationship between hopelessness and ultimate suicide: A replication with psychiatric outpatients. *American Journal of Psychiatry, 147,* 190–195.

Beck, A. T., Jallon, S. D., Young, J. E., Bedrosian, R. C., Budenz, D., et al. (1985). Treatment of depression with cognitive therapy and amitriptyline. *Archives of General Psychiatry, 42,* 142–148.

Beck, A. T., Rush, A. J., Shaw, B. F., & Emory, G. (1979). *The cognitive therapy of depression.* New York: Guilford Press.

Becker, E. (1973). *The denial of death.* New York: Free Press.

Bellack, L., & Sheehy, M. (1976). The broad role of ego functions assessment. *American Journal of Psychiatry, 133,* 1259–1264.

Bellodi, L., Derna G., Caldorola D., Arancio C., Bertani A., & DiBella, D. (1998). CO2–induced panic attacks: A twin study. *American Journal of Psychiatry, 155,* 1184–1188.

Berman, K. F., & Weinberger, D. R. (1999). Neuroimaging studies of schizophrenia. In D. S. Charney, E. J. Nestler, & B. S. Bunney (Eds.), *The neurobiology of mental illness* (pp. 246–257). New York: Oxford University Press.

Biederman, J., Herzog, D. B., Rivinus, T. M., Harper, G. P., Ferber, R. A., Rosenbaum, J. F., et al. (1985). Amitriptyline in the treatment of anorexia nervosa: A double-blind, placebo-controlled study. *Journal of Clinical Psychopharmacology, 5,* 10–16.

Blehar, M. C., & Rosenthal, N. E. (1989). Seasonal affective disorders and phototherapy: Report of the National Institute of Mental Health-Sponsored Workshop. *Archives of General Psychiatry, 46,* 469–474.

Bogerts, B., Ashtari, M., Degreef, G., Alvir, J. M. J., Bilder, R. M., & Lieber-man, J. A. (1990). Reduced temporal limbic structure volumes on magnetic resonance images in first-episode schizophrenia. *Psychiatry Research, 35,* 1–13.

Boscolo, L., Cecchin, G., Hoffman, L., & Penn, P. (1987). *Milan systematic family therapy: Conversations in theory and practice.* New York: Basic Books.

Bowen, M. (1978). *Family theory in clinical practice.* New York: Jason Aronson.

Bowlby, J. (1969). *Attachment and loss (Vol. 1): Attachment.* London: Hogarth Press.

Braff, D. L. (1999). Psychophysiological and information-processing approaches to schizophrenia. In D. S. Charney, E. J. Nestler, & B. S. Bunney (Eds.), *The neurobiology of mental illness* (pp. 258–271). New York: Oxford University Press.

Bright, D. A. (1994). Postpartum mental disorders. *American Family Physician, 50,* 595–598.

Brenner, C. (1955). *An elementary textbook of psychoanalysis.* New York: Doubleday.

Brown G., Goodwin, F., Ballenger, J., et al. (1979). Aggression in humans correlates with cerebrospinal fluid metabolites. *Psychological Research, 1,* 131–139.

Burke, K. C., Burke, J. D., Rae, D. S., & Regler, D. A. (1991). Comparing age at onset of major depression and other psychiatric disorders by birth cohorts in five U.S. community populations. *Archives of General Psychiatry, 48,* 789–795.

Burns, D. D. (1992). *Feeling good: The new mood therapy.* New York: Avon Books.

Byne, W., Kemether, E., Jones, L., Haroutunian, V., & Davis, K. (1999). The neurochemistry of schizophrenia. In D. S. Charney, E. J. Nestler, & B. S. Bunney

(Eds.), *The neurobiology of mental illness* (pp. 236–245). New York: Oxford University Press.

Caper, R. (1988). *Melanie Klein's place in psychoanalysis.* New York: Jason Aronson.

Carboni, E., Imperato, A., Perezzani, L., & Di Chiara, G. (1989). Amphetamine, cocaine, phencyclidine, and nomifensine increase extracellular dopamine concentration preferentially in the nucleus accumbens of freely moving rats. *Neuroscience, 28,* 653–661.

Case, R. B., Moss, A. J., Case, N., McDermott, M., & Eberly, S. (1992). Living alone after myocardial infarction: Impact on prognosis. *Journal of the American Medical Association, 267,* 515–519.

Chan, C. H., Janicak, P. G., Davis, J. M., Altman, E., Andriukaitis, S., & Hedeker, D. (1987). Response of psychotic and nonpsychotic depressed patients to tricyclic antidepressants. *Journal of Clinical Psychiatry, 48,* 197–200.

Charney, D. S., Heninger, G. R., & Breier, A. (1984). Noradrenergic function in panic anxiety: Effects of yohimbine in healthy subjects and patients with agoraphobia and panic disorder. *Archives of General Psychiatry, 41,* 751–763.

Charney, D. S., Nestler, E. J., & Bunney, B. S. (Eds.). (1999). *The neurobiology of mental illness.* New York: Oxford University Press.

Cheng, A. T. A. (1995). Mental illness and suicide: A case-control study in Taiwan. *Archives of General Psychiatry, 52,* 594–603.

Cloninger, C. R. (1986). A unified biosocial theory of personality and its role in the development of anxiety states. *Psychiatric Developments, 3,* 167–226.

Cloninger, C. R. (1987). A systematic method for clinical description and classification of personality variants: A proposal. *Archives of General Psychiatry, 44,* 573–588.

Coffey, C. E., Weiner, R. D., Djang, W. T., Figiel, G. S., Soady, S. A. R., & Patterson, C. J. (1991). Brain anatomic effects of electroconvulsive therapy: A prospective magnetic resonance imaging study. *Archives of General Psychiatry, 48,* 1013–1021.

Coffey, C. E., Wikinson, W. E., Weiner, R. D., Parashos, I. A., Djang, W. T., & Webb, M. C. (1993). Quantitative cerebral anatomy in depression: A controlled magnetic resonance imaging study. *Archives of General Psychiatry, 50,* 7–16.

Cohen, L. J., Hollander, E., & Stein, D. J. (1997). The neuropsychiatry of OCD. In E. Hollander & D. J. Stein (Eds.), *Obsessive-compulsive disorders: Diagnosis, etiology, treatment* (pp. 75–88). New York: Marcel Dekker.

Cohen, L. J., Simeon, D., Hollander, E., & Stein, D. J. (1997) Obsessive-compulsive spectrum disorders. In E. Hollander & D. J. Stein (Eds.), *Obsessive-compulsive disorders: Diagnosis, etiology, treatment* (pp. 47–73). New York: Marcel Dekker.

Cooper, J. R. (1989). Methadone treatment and the acquired immunodeficiency syndrome. *Journal of the American Medical Association, 262,* 1664–1668.

Corder, E. H., Suanders, A. M., Strittinatter, W. J., Schmechel, D. E., Gaskell, P. C., Small G. W., et al. (1993). Gene dosage of apolipoprotein E type 4 allele and the risk for Alzheimer's disease in late onset families. *Science, 261,* 921–923.

Creese, I., Burt, D., & Snyder, S. (1984). Dopamine receptor binding predicts clinical and pharmacological potencies of antischizophrenic drugs. *American Journal of Psychiatry, 141,* 633–638.

Crits-Christoph, P., Luborsky, L., Dahl, L., Popp, C., Mellon, J., & Mark, D. (1988). Clinicians can agree in assessing relationship patterns in psychotherapy: The core conflictual relationship theme method. *Archives of General Psychiatry, 45,* 1001–1004.

Crow, T. J. (1980). Molecular pathology of schizophrenia: More than one disease process? *British Medical Journal, 280,* 66–68.

Crowe, R. R., Noyes, R., Pauls, D. L., & Slyman, D. (1983). A family study of panic disorder. *Archives of General Psychiatry, 40,* 1065–1069.

Cruts, M., Hendricks, L., & Van Broeckhoven, C. (1996). The presenilin genes: A new family involved in Alzheimer's disease pathology. *Human Molecular Genetics, 5,* 1449–1455.

Damasio, A. R. (1994). *Descartes' error: Emotion, reason, and the human brain.* New York: Putnam.

Damasio, A. R., Tranel, D., & Damsio, H. (1990). Individuals with psychopathic behavior caused by frontal damage fail to respond autonomically to social stimuli. *Behavioural Brain Research, 41,* 81–94.

Damasio, H., Grabowski, T., Frank, R., Galaburda, A. M., & Damasio, A. R. (1994). The return of Phineas Gage: Clues about the brain from a skull of a famous patient. *Science, 264,* 1102–1105.

Dilts, S. L., Jr. (1998). On the Szaszian argument. *Journal of Psychiatry and Law, 26,* 311–325.

Dodman, N. H., Moon-Fanelli, A., Mertens, P. A., Pfluger, S., & Stein, D. J. (1997). Veterinary models of OCD. In E. Hollander & D. J. Stein (Eds.), *Obsessive-compulsive disorders: Diagnosis, etiology, treatment* (pp. 99–143). New York: Marcel Dekker.

Dubovsky, S. L. (1994). Beyond the serotonin reuptake inhibitors: Rationales for the development of new serotonergic agents. *Journal of Clinical Psychiatry, 55,* 34–43.

Dubovsky, S. L. (1997). *Mind-body deceptions: The psychosomatics of everyday life.* New York: Norton.

Durkheim, E. (1951). *Suicide: A study in sociology.* New York: Free Press.

Eastman, C. I., Young, M. A., Fogg, L. F., Liu, L., & Meaden, P. M. (1998). Bright light treatment of winter depression: A placebo-controlled trial. *Archives of General Psychiatry, 55,* 883–889.

Ellis, A. (1997). *The practice of rational emotive therapy.* New York: Springer.

Emde, R. N. (1983). The prerepresentational self and its affective core. *The Study of the Child, 38,* 165–192.

Engel, G. L. (1980) The clinical application of the biopsychosocial model. *American Journal of Psychiatry, 137,* 535–544.

Erikson, E. (1980). *Identity and the life cycle.* New York: Norton.

Evans, E. A., Funkenstein, H. H., Albert, M. S., Scherr, P. A., Cook, N. R., Chown, M. J., Hebert, L. E., Hennekens, C. H., & Taylor, J. O. (1989). Prevalence of Alzheimer's disease in a community population of older persons. Higher than previously reported. *Journal of the American Medical Association, 262,* 2551–2556.

Farone, S. V., & Biederman, J. (1999) The neurobiology of attention deficit hyperactivity disorder. In D. S. Charney, E. J. Nestler, & B. S. Bunney (Eds.), *The neurobiology of mental illness* (pp. 788–801). New York: Oxford University Press.

Fein D., Joy, S., Green, L. A., & Waterhouse, L. (1996). Autism and pervasive developmental disorders. In B. S. Fogel, R. B. Schiffer, & S. M. Rao (Eds.), *Neuropsychiatry* (pp. 571–614). Baltimore: Williams & Wilkins.

Field, A. E., Camargo, C. A., Jr., Taylor, B. C., Berkey, C. S., & Grahm, G. A. (1999). Relation of peer and media influences to the development of purging behaviors among preadolescent and adolescent girls. *Archives of Pediatric and Adolescent Medicine, 153,* 1184–1189.

Fluoxetine Bulimia Nervosa Collaborative Study Group. (1992). Fluoxetine in the treatment of bulimia nervosa: A multicenter, placebo-controlled, double-blind trial. *Archives of General Psychiatry, 49,* 139–147.

Foucault, M.(1988). *Madness and civilization: A history of insanity in the age of reason.* New York: Vintage Books.

Fraiberg, S. (1969). Libidinal object constancy and mental representation. *Psychoanalytic Study of the Child, 24,* 9–31.

Francis, J., Martin, D., & Kapoor, W. N. (1990). A prospective study of delirium in hospitalized elderly. *Journal of the American Medical Association, 263,* 1097–1101.

Frankl, V. E. (1984). *Man's search for meaning: An introduction to logotherapy* (3rd ed.). New York: Simon & Schuster.

Frasure-Smith, N., Lesperance, F., & Talajic, M. (1993). Depression following myocardial infarction: Impact on 6–month survival. *Journal of the American Medical Association, 270,* 1819–1825.

Freeman, T. W., Clotheir, J. L., Pazzaguia, P., Leser, M. D., & Swann, A. L. (1992). A double-blind comparison of valproate and lithium in the treatment of acute mania. *American Journal of Psychiatry, 149,* 108–111.

Freud, A. (1936/1946). *The ego and the mechanisms of defense* (C. Baines, Trans.). New York: International Universities Press.

Freud, A. (1968). Acting out. *International Journal of Psychoanalysis, 49,* 165–170.

Freud, S. (1900/1964a). The interpretation of dreams. In J. Strachey (Ed. & Trans.), *The standard edition of the complete psychological works of Sigmund Freud* (Vols. 4–5, pp.1–627). London: Hogarth Press.

Freud, S. (1905/1964b). Three essays on the theory of sexuality. In J. Strachey (Ed. & Trans.), *The standard edition of the complete psychological works of Sigmund Freud* (Vol. 7, pp. 123–245). London: Hogarth Press.

Freud, S. (1912/1964c). The dynamics of transference. In J. Strachey (Ed. & Trans.), *The standard edition of the complete psychological works of Sigmund Freud* (Vol. 12, pp. 97–108). London: Hogarth Press.

Freud, S. (1914/1958). Remembering, repeating and working-through (further recommendations on the technique of psycho-analysis II). In J. Strachey (Ed. & Trans.), *The standard edition of the complete psychological works of Sigmund Freud* (Vol. 12, pp. 145–156). London, Hogarth Press.

Freud, S. (1915/1964d). The unconscious. In J. Strachey (Ed. & Trans.), *The standard edition of the complete psychological works of Sigmund Freud* (Vol. 14, pp. 159–215). London: Hogarth Press.

Freud, S. (1917/1964e). Mourning and melancholia. In J. Strachey (Ed. & Trans.), *The standard edition of the complete psychological works of Sigmund Freud* (Vol. 14, pp. 237–260). London: Hogarth Press.

Freud, S. (1923/1989). The ego and the id. In P. Gay (Ed.), *The Freud reader* (pp. 628–658). New York: Norton.

Freud, S. (1937/1964f). Analysis terminable and interminable. In J. Strachey (Ed. & Trans.), *The standard edition of the complete psychological works of Sigmund Freud* (Vol. 23, pp. 209–253). London: Hogarth Press.

Fulford, W. (1991). The concept of disease. In S. Bloch & P. Chodoff (Eds.), *Psychiatric ethics* (2nd ed., pp. 77–99). New York: Oxford University Press.

Gabbard, G. O. (1994). *Psychodynamic psychotherapy in clinical practice.* New York: American Psychiatric Association.

Games, D., Adams, D., Alessandrini, R., Barbour, R., Berthelette, P., Blackwell, C., et al. (1995). Alzheimer-type neuropathology in transgenic mice overexpressing V717F b-amyloid precursor protein. *Nature, 373,* 523–527.

Gastpar, M., Gilsdorf, U., Abou-Saleh, M. T., & Ngo-Khac, T. (1992). Clinical correlates of response to CST: The dexamethasone suppression test in depression: A world health organization study. *Journal of Affective Disorders, 26,* 17–24.

Goeders, N. E., & Smith, J. E. (1983). Cortical dopaminergic involvement in cocaine reinforcement. *Science, 221,* 773–775.

Goeders, N. E., & Smith, J. E. (1993). Intracranial cocaine self-administration in the medial prefrontal cortex increases dopamine turnover in nucleus accumbens. *Journal of Pharmacology & Experimental Therapeutics, 265,* 592–600.

Goldstein, R. B., Black, D. W., Nasrallah, A., & Winokur, G. (1991). The prediction of suicide. *Archives of General Psychiatry, 48,* 418–422.

Goodwin, F. K., & Jamison, K. R. (1990). *Manic-depressive illness.* New York: Oxford University Press.

Gorman J. M., Kent, J. M., Sullivan, G. M., & Coplan, J. D. (2000). Neuroanatomical hypothesis of panic disorder. *American Journal of Psychiatry, 157,* 493–505.

Gorman J. M., Papp, L. A., Coplan, J. D., Martinez, J. M., Lennon, S., Goetz, R. R., Ross, D., & Klein, D. F. (1994). Anxiogenic effects of CO2 and hyperventilation in patients with panic disorder. *American Journal of Psychiatry, 151,* 547–553.

Greenberg, P. E., Stiglin, L. E., Finkelstein, S. N., & Berndt, E. R. (1993). The economic burden of depression in 1990. *Journal of Clinical Psychiatry, 54,* 405–418.

Greist, J., Chouinard, G., Duboff, E., Halaris, A., Kim, S. W., & Koran, L. (1995). Double-blind parallel comparison of three dosages of sertraline and placebo in outpatients with obsessive-compulsive disorder. *Archives of General Psychiatry, 52,* 289–295.

Griffin, R. E., Gross, G. A., & Teitelbaum, H. S. (1993). Delirium tremens: A review. *Journal of the American Osteopathic Association, 93,* 924, 929–932, 935.

Guze, S. B. (1989). Biological psychiatry: Is there any other kind? *Psychological Medicine, 19,* 315–323.

Guze, S. B. (Ed.). (1997). *Mosby's neurology psychiatry access series: Washington University adult psychiatry.* St. Louis: Mosby.

Guze, S. B., & Robins, E. (1970). Suicide and primary affective disorders. *British Journal of Psychiatry, 117,* 437–438.

Halmi, K. A., Eckert, E., LaDu, T. J., & Cohen J. (1986). Anorexia nervosa: Treatment efficacy of cyproheptadine and amitriptyline. *Archives of General Psychiatry, 43,* 177–181.

Henriksson, M. M., Aro, H. M., Marttunen, M. J., Heikkinen, M. E., Isometsa, E. T., Kuoppasalmi, K. I., et al. (1993). Mental disorders and comorbidity in suicide. *American Journal of Psychiatry, 150,* 935–940.

Herman, J. L., Perry, C., & Van der Kolk, B. A. (1989). Childhood trauma in borderline personality disorder. *American Journal of Psychiatry, 146,* 490–495.

Janicak, P. G., Davis, J. M., Preskorn, S. H., & Ayd, F. J., Jr. (1997). *Principles and practice of psychopharmacotherapy* (2nd ed.). Baltimore: Williams & Wilkins.

Jeste, D. V., & Lohr, J. B. (1989). Hippocampal pathologic findings in schizophrenia: A morphometric study. *Archives of General Psychiatry, 46,* 1019–1024.

Johnson, S. W., & North, R. A. (1992). Opioids excite dopamine neurons by hyperpolarization of local interneurons. *Journal of Neuroscience, 12,* 483–488.

Jung, C. G. (1961). *Memories, dreams, reflections.* New York: Random House.

Kagan, J. J., Reznick, S., & Snidman, N. (1988). Biological basis of childhood shyness. *Science, 240,* 167–171.

Kandel, E. R. (1999). Biology and the future of psychoanalysis: A new intellectual framework for psychiatry revisited. *American Journal of Psychiatry, 156,* 505–524.

Kandel, E. R., & Schwartz, J. H. (1981). *Principles of neural science.* New York: Elsevier.

Kane, J. M., Honigfeld, G., Singer, J., & Meltzer, H. (1988). The Clozaril Collaborative Study Group. Clozapine for the treatment-resistant schizophrenic: A double-blind comparison versus chlorpromazine/benztropine. *Archives of General Psychiatry, 45,* 789–805.

Kaplan, H. I., Sadock, B. J., & Grebb, J. A. (Eds.). (1994). *Kaplan and Sadock's synopsis of psychiatry: Behavioral sciences and clinical psychiatry* (7th ed.). Baltimore: Williams & Wilkins.

Kapur, S., Zipursky, R., Jones, C., Remington, G., & Houle, S. (2000). Relationship between dopamine D2 occupancy, clinical response, and side effects: A double-blind PET study of first-episode schizophrenia. *American Journal of Psychiatry, 157,* 514–520.

Karno, M., Golding, J. M., Sorenson, S. B., & Burnam, M. A. (1988). The epidemiology of obsessive-compulsive disorder in five U.S. communities. *Archives of General Psychiatry, 45,* 1094–1099.

Keck, P. E., McElroy, S. L., Tugrul, K. C., & Bennett, J. A. (1993). Valproate oral loading in the treatment of acute mania. *Journal of Clinical Psychiatry, 54,* 305–308.

Kernberg, O. (1980). *Internal world and external reality: Object relations theory applied.* New York: Jason Aronson.

Kessler, R. C., McGonagle, K. A., Zhao, S., Nelson, C. B., Hughes, M., & Eshelman, S. (1994). Lifetime and 12–month prevalence of DSM-III-R psychiatric disorders in the United States. *Archives of General Psychiatry, 51,* 8–19.

Klein, E., Zohar, J., Geraci, M. F., Murphy, D. L., & Uhde, T. W. (1991). Anxiogenic effects of m-CPP in patients with panic disorder: Comparison to caffeine's anxiogenic effects. *Biological Psychiatry, 30,* 973–984.

Klerman, G. L., Weissman, M. M., Rounsaville, B. J., & Chevron, E. S. (1984). *Interpersonal psychotherapy for depression.* New York: Basic Books.

Kohut, H. (1971). *The analysis of the self.* New York: International Universities Press.

Kohut, H. (1977). *The restoration of the self.* New York: International Universities Press.

Kovelman, J. A., & Scheibel, A. B. (1980). A neurohistological correlate of schizophrenia. *Biological Psychiatry, 19,* 1601–1621.

Kreitman, N. (1988). Suicide, age, and marital status. *Psychological Medicine, 18,* 121–128.

Kupfer, D. J., Ehlers, C. L., Frank, E., Grochocinski, V. J., & McEachran, A. B. (1991). EEG sleep profiles and recurrent depression. *Biological Psychiatry, 30,* 641.

Kupfer, D. J., Frank, E., Perel, J. M., Cornes, C., Mallinger, A. G., & Thase, M. E. (1992). Five-year outcome for maintenance therapies in recurrent depression. *Archives of General Psychiatry, 49,* 769–773.

Lieberman, R. P., & Bedell, J. R. (1989). Behavior therapy. In H. L. Kaplan & B. J. Sadock (Eds.), *Comprehensive textbook of psychiatry* (5th ed.). Baltimore: Williams & Wilkins.

Liebowitz, M. R., Gorman, J. M., Fyer, A. J., Levitt, M., Dillon, D., Levy, G., et al. (1985). Lactate provocation of panic attacks II: Biochemical and physiologic findings. *Archives of General Psychiatry, 42,* 709–719.

Linehan, M. (1993). *Cognitive-behavioral treatment of borderline personality disorder.* New York: Guilford Press.

Linnoila, M., Virkkunen, M., Scheinin, M., et al. (1983). Low cerebrospinal fluid 5–HIAA concentration differentiates impulsive from nonimpulsive violent behavior. *Life Sciences, 33,* 2609–2614.

Lipowski, Z. J. (1987). Delirium (acute confusional state). *Journal of the American Medical Association, 258,* 1789–1792.

Loewald, H. W. (1960). On the therapeutic action of psychoanalysis. *International Journal of Psychoanalysis, 41,* 16–33.

London, E. D., Grant, S. J., Morgan, M. J., & Zukin, S. R. (1996). Neurobiology of drug abuse. In B. S. Fogel, R. B. Schiffer, & S. M. Rao (Eds.), *Neuropsychiatry* (pp. 635–678). Baltimore: Williams & Wilkins.

Loosen, P. T., & Prange, A. J. (1982). Serum thyrotropin response to thryotropin-releasing hormone in psychiatric patients: A review. *American Journal of Psychiatry, 139,* 405–416.

Lydiard R. B., Lesser, I. M., Ballenger, J. C., Rubin, R. T., Laraia, M., Dupont, R., et al. (1992). A fixed-dose study of alprazolam 2 mg, alprazolam 6 mg, and placebo in panic disorder. *Journal of Clinical Psychopharmacology, 12,* 96–103.

Mahler, M. S., Pine, F., & Bergman, A. (1975). *The psychological birth of the human infant: Symbiosis and individuation.* New York: Basic Books.

Maj, M., Veltro, F., Pirozzi, R., Lobrace, S., & Magliano, L. (1992). Pattern of recurrence of illness after recovery from an episode of major depression: A prospective study. *American Journal of Psychiatry, 149,* 795–800.

Mandlewicz, J., Papadimitrious, G., & Wilmotte, J. (1993). Family study of panic disorder: Comparision with generalized anxiety disorder, major depression and normal subjects. *Psychiatric Genetics, 3,* 73–78.

Mayberg, H. S., Liotti, M., Brannan, S. K., McGinnis, S., Mahuria, R. K., & Jerabek, P. A. (1999). Reciprocal limbic-cortical function and negative mood: Converging PET findings in normal sadness. *American Journal of Psychiatry, 156,* 675–682.

Miles, C. P. (1977). Conditions predisposing to suicide: A review. *Journal of Nervous and Mental Disorders, 164,* 231–246.

Mill, J. S. (1859/1983). *On liberty.* New York: Viking.

Miller, A. (1979). The drama of the gifted child and psychoanalyst's narcissistic disturbances. *International Journal of Psychoanalysis, 60,* 47–58.

Minuchin, S. (1974). *Families and family therapy*. Cambridge, MA: Harvard University Press.

Motto, J. A., Heilbbron, D. C., & Juster, R. P. (1985). Development of a clinical instrument to estimate suicide risk. *American Journal of Psychiatry, 142,* 680–686.

MTA Cooperative Group. (2000). A 14–month randomized clinical trial of treatment strategies for attention-deficit/hyperactivity disorder. *Archives of General Psychiatry, 56,* 1073–1086.

National Center for Health Statistics. (1994). *Advance report of final mortality statistics: Monthly vital statistics report.* Hyattsville, MD: U.S. Public Health Service.

Nemeroff, C. B., Widerlov, E., Bissette, G., Walleus, H., Karlson, I., Eklund, K., Likts, C. D., Loosen, P.T., & Vale, W. (1984). Elevated concentration of CSF corticotropin-releasing factor-like immunoreactivity in depressed patients. *Science, 226,* 1342–1344.

Nolte, J. (1988). *The human brain: An introduction to its functional anatomy* (2nd ed.). St. Louis: Mosby.

Nordstrom, A. L., Farde, L., Wiesel, F. A., Forslund, K., Pauli, S., Halldin, C., & Uppfeldt, G. (1993). Central D2 receptor occupancy in relation to antipsychotic drug effects: A double-blind PET study of schizophrenic patients. *Biological Psychiatry 33,* 227–235.

O'Connor v. Donaldson, 422 U.S. 563 (1975), remanded *Donaldson v. O'Connor,* 519 F2d 59 (5th Cir 1975).

Olds, J., & Milner, P. (1954). Positive reinforcement produced by electrical stimulation of septal area and other regions of the rat brain. *Journal of Comparative Physiology and Psychology, 47,* 419–427.

Parsons, T. (1964). *The social system.* New York: Free Press.

Penfield, W., & Jasper, H. (1954). *Epilepsy and the functional anatomy of the human brain.* Boston: Little, Brown.

Pine, F. (1988). The four psychologies of psychoanalysis and their place in clinical work. *Journal of the American Psychoanalytic Association, 36,* 571–596.

Pohl, R. B., Wolkow, R. M., & Clary, C. M. (1988). Sertraline in the treatment of panic disorder: A double-blind multicenter trial. *American Journal of Psychiatry, 155,* 1189–1195.

Pokorny, A. D. (1983). Prediction of suicide in psychiatric patients: Report of a prospective study. *Archives of General Psychiatry, 40,* 249–257.

Pontieri, F. E., Tanda, G., Orzi, F., & DiChiara, G. (1996). Effects of nicotine on the nucleus accumbens and similarity to those of addictive drugs. *Nature, 382,* 255–257.

Pope, H. G., Jr., Keck, P. E., Jr., McElroy, S. L., & Hudson, J. J. (1989). A placebo-controlled study of trazodone in bulimia nervosa. *Journal of Clinical Psychopharmacology, 9,* 254–259.

Porter, R. (1997). *The greatest benefit to mankind: A medical history of humanity.* New York: Norton.

Post, R. M. (1990). Sensitization and kindling perspectives for the course of affective illness: Toward a new treatment with the anticonvulsant carbamazepine. *Pharmacopsychiatry, 23,* 3–17.

Post, R. M., Rubinow, D. R., & Ballenger, J. C. (1986). Conditioning and sensitization in the longitudinal course of affective illness. *British Journal of Psychiatry, 149,* 191–201.

Rabins, P. V., & Folstein, M. F. (1982). Delirium and dementia: Diagnostic criteria and fatality rates. *British Journal of Psychiatry, 140,* 149–153.

Rahe, R. H. (1972). Subjects' recent life changes and their near-future illness susceptibility. *Advances in Psychosomatic Medicine, 8,* 2–19.

Raine, A., Lencz, T., Birhrle, S., LaCasse, L., & Colletti, P. (2000). Reduced prefrontal gray matter and reduced autonomic activity in antisocial personality disorder. *Archives of General Psychiatry, 57,* 119–127.

Regier, D. A., Boyd, J. H., Burke, J. D., Jr., Rae, D. S., Myers, J. K., Kramer, M., Robins, L. N., George, L. K., Kamo, M., & Locke, B. Z. (1988). One-month prevalence of mental disorders in the United States. *Archives of General Psychiatry, 45,* 977–986.

Ritvo, E. R., Freeman B. J., Scheibel, A. B., Duong, T., Robinson, H., Guthrie, D., & Ritvo, A. (1986). Lower Purkinje cell counts in the cerebella of four autistic subjects: Initial findings of the UCLA–NSAC autopsy research report. *American Journal of Psychiatry, 143,* 862–866.

Ritz, M. C., Lamb, R. J., Goldberg, S. R., & Kuhar, M. J. (1987). Cocaine receptors on dopmaine transporters are related to self-administration of cocaine. *Science, 237,* 1219–1223.

Robinson, D., Wu., H., Munne, R. A., Ashtari, M., Alvir, J. M. J., Lerner, G. (1995). Reduced caudate nucleus volume in obsessive-compulsive disorder. *Archives of General Psychiatry, 52,* 393–398.

Rogers, S. L., Farlow, M. R., Doody, R. S., Mohs, R., Friedhoff, L. T., & Donepezil Study Group. (1998). A 24–week, double-blind, placebo-controlled trial of donepezil in patients with Alzheimer's disease. *Neurology, 50,* 136–145.

Rozanski, A., Bairey, C. N., Krantz, D. S., Friedman, J., Resser, K. J., & Morell, M. (1988). Mental stress and the induction of silent myocardial ischemia in patients with coronary artery disease. *New England Journal of Medicine, 318,* 1005–1012.

Rubia, K., Overmeyer, S., Taylor, E., Brammer, M., Williams, S. C. R., & Simmons, A. (1999). Hypofrontality in attention deficit hyperactivity disorder during higher-order motor control: A study with functional MRI. *American Journal of Psychiatry, 156,* 891–896.

Sadock, B. J., & Sadock, V. A. (Eds.). (2000). *Kaplan and Sadock's textbook of psychiatry* (7th ed.). Baltimore: Williams & Wilkins.

Salokangas, R. K. R., Vilkman, H., Ilonen, T., Taiminen, T., Bergman, J., Haaparanta, M., Solin, O., Alanen, A., Syvalahti, E., & Hietala, J. (2000). High levels of dopamine activity in the basal ganglia of cigarette smokers. *American Journal of Psychiatry, 157,* 632–634.

Sano, M., Ernest, C., Thomas, R. G., Klauber, M. R., Shafer, K., Grundman, K., Woodbury, P., Growndon, J., Cotman, C. W., Pfeiffer, E., Schneider, L. S., & Thal, L. J. (1997). A controlled trial of selegiline, alpha-tocopherol, or both as treatments for Alzheimer's disease. The Alzheimer's Disease Cooperative Study. *New England Journal of Medicine, 24,* 1216–1222.

Schleifer, S. J., Keller, S. E., Bond, R. N., Cohen, J., & Stein, M. (1989). Major depressive disorder and immunity: Role of age, sex, severity and hospitalization. *Archives of General Psychiatry, 46,* 81–87.

Schleifer, S. J., Keller, S. E., Camerino, M., Thornton, J. C., & Stein, M. (1983). Suppression of lymphocyte stimulations following bereavement. *Journal of the American Medical Association, 250,* 374–377.

Sees, K. L., Delucchi, K. L., Masson, C., Rosen, A., Clark, H. W., Robillard, H., Banys, P., & Hall, S. M. (2000). Methadone maintenance vs. 180–day psychosocially enriched detoxification for treatment of opioid dependence: A randomized controlled trial. *Journal of the American Medical Association, 283,* 1303–1310.

Shelton, R. L., Winn, S., Ekhatore, N., & Loosen, P. T. (1993). The effects of antidepressants on the thyroid axis in depression. *Biological Psychiatry, 33,* 120–126.

Sherrington, R., Rogaev, E. I., Liang, Y., Rogaeva, E. A., Levesque, G., & Ikeda, M. (1995). Cloning of a gene bearing missense mutations in early-onset familial Alzheimer's disease. *Nature, 375,* 754–760.

Siever, L. J., Keefe, R., Bernstein, D. P., Coccaro, E. F., Klar, H. M., Zemishlany, Z., et al. (1990). Eye tracking impairment in clinically identified patients with schizotypal personality disorder. *American Journal of Psychiatry, 140,* 740–745.

Sifneos, P. E. (1972). *Short-term psychotherapy and emotional crisis.* Cambridge, MA: Harvard University Press.

Sirois, F. (1988). Delirium: 100 cases. *Canadian Journal of Psychiatry, 33,* 375–378.

Skre, I., Onstad, S., Torgerson, S., & Kringlen, E. (1993). A twin study of DSM-III-R anxiety disorders. *Acta Psychiatrica Scandinavia, 88,* 85–92.

Spiegel, D., Bloom, J. R., Kraemer, H. C., & Gottheil, E. (1989). Effect of psychosocial treatment on survival of patients with metastatic breast cancer. *Lancet, ii,* 888–891.

Steele, B. F. (1990). Some sequelae of the sexual maltreatment of children. In H. B. Levine (Ed.), *Adult analysis and childhood sexual abuse* (pp. 21–34). Hillsdale, NJ: Analytic Press.

Stern, D. (1985). *The interpersonal world of the infant.* New York: Basic Books.

Svrakic, D. M., Whitehead, C., Przybeck, T. R., & Cloninger, C. R. (1993). Differential diagnosis of personality disorders by the seven-factor model of temperament and character. *Archives of General Psychiatry, 50,* 991–999.

Szasz, T. S. (1987). *Insanity: The idea and its consequences.* New York: John Wiley.

Tarasoff v. Regents of the University of California, 33 Cal app 3d 275, 108 Cal Rptr 878 (1973).

Tarasoff v. Regents of the University of California, 17 Cal 3d 425, 131 Cal Rptr 14, 551 P2d 334 (1976a).

Tarasoff v. Regents of the University of California, 17 Cal 3d 439, 131 Cal Rptr 25, 551 P2d 345 (1976b).

Tarasoff v. Regents of the University of California, 13 Cal 3d 177, 118 Cal Rptr 19, 529 P2d 553, reargued, 17 Cal 3d425, 131 Cal Rptr 14, 551 P2d 334 (1976c).

Targum, S. D., & Marshall, L. E. (1989). Fenfluramine provocation of anxiety in patients with panic disorder. *Psychiatry Research, 28,* 295–306.

Tohen, M., Sanger, T. M., McElroy, S. C., Tollefson, G. D., Roy, C. K. N., & Daniel, D. G. (1999). Olanzapine versus placebo in the treatment of acute mania. *American Journal of Psychiatry, 156,* 702–709.

Tsuang, M. T., & Farone, S. V. (1995). The case for heterogeneity in the etiology of schizophrenia. *Schizophrenia Research, 17,* 161–175.

Vaccarino, F. J., Bloom, F. E., & Koob, G. F. (1985). Blockade of nucleus accumbens opiate receptors attenuates intravenous heroin reward in the rat. *Psychopharmacology, 86,* 37–42.

Vaillant, G. E. (1971). Theoretical hierarchy of adaptive ego mechanisms: A 30–year follow-up of 30 men selected for psychological health. *Archives of General Psychiatry, 24,* 107–118.

Vaillant, G. E. (1977). *Adaptation to life.* Boston: Little, Brown.

Volpicelli, J. R., Alterman, A. I., Hayashida, M., & O'Brian, C. P. (1992). Naltrexone in the treatment of alcohol dependence. *Archives of General Psychiatry, 49,* 876–880.

Wahlbeck, K., Cheine, M., Essali, A., & Adams, C. (1999). Evidence of clozapine's effectiveness in schizophrenia: A systematic review and meta-analysis of randomized trials. *American Journal of Psychiatry, 156,* 990–999.

Walsh, B. T., Gladis, M., Roose, S. P., Stewart, J. W., Stetner, F., & Glassman, A. H. (1988). Phenelzine vs. placebo in 50 patients with bulimia. *Archives of General Psychiatry, 45,* 471–475.

Weddington, W. W. (1982). The mortality in delirium: An underrecognized problem. *Psychosomatics, 23,* 1232–1235.

Weinberger, D. R., Berman, K. F., & Zec, R. F. (1986). Physiologic dysfunction of dorsolateral prefrontal cortex in schizophrenia, 1. Regional cerebral blood flow evidence. *Archives of General Psychiatry, 43,* 114–124.

Weissman, M. M., Wickramaratne, P., Adams, P. B., Lish, J. D., Horwath, E., Charney, D., Woods, S. W., Leeman, E., & Frosh, E. (1993). The relationship between panic disorder and major depression: A new family study. *Archives of General Psychiatry, 50,* 767–780.

Wells, K. B., Stewart, A., Hays, R. D., Burnam, M. A., Rogers, W., & Daniels, M. (1989). The functioning and well-being of depressed patients: Results from the Medical Outcomes Study. *Journal of the American Medical Association, 262,* 914–919.

Williams, R. B., Barefoot, J. C., Califf R. M, Haney, T. L., Saunders, W. B., & Pryor, D. B. (1992). Prognostic importance of social and economic resources among medically treated patients with angiographically documented coronary artery disease. *Journal of the American Medical Association, 267,* 520–524.

Winnicott, D. W. (1953). Transitional objects and transitional phenomena: A study of the first not-me possession. *International Journal of Psychoanalysis, 34,* 89–97.

Wise, R. A., Spindler, J. deWit, H., & Gerberg, G. J. (1978). Neuroleptic-induced "anhedonia" in rats: Pimozide blocks reward quality of food. *Science, 201,* 262–264.

Wisniewski, K. E., Dalton, A. J., McLachlan, D. R. C., Wen, G. Y., Wisniewski, H. M., et al. (1985). Alzheimer's disease in Down's syndrome: Clinicopathologic studies. *Neurology, 35,* 957–961.

Wolraich, M., Wilson, D., & White, W. (1995). The effect of sugar on behavior or cognition in children. *Journal of the American Medical Association, 34,* 1577–1583.

Woods, S. W., Charney, D. S., Silver, J. M., Krystal, J. H., & Heninger, G. R. (1991). Behavioral, biochemical and cardiovascular responses to the benzodiazepine receptor antagonist flumazenil in panic disorder. *Psychiatry Research, 36,* 115–124.

Wyatt v. Stickney, 325 F Supp 781 (MD Ala 1971), aff'd in part and remanded in part, and remanded sub nom *Wyatt v. Aderholt,* 503, F2d 1305 (5th Cir 1979).

Yalom, I. D. (1980). *Textbook of existential psychotherapy.* New York: Basic Books.

Yalom, I. D. (1989). *Love's executioner and other tales of psychotherapy*. New York: Basic Books.

Yokel, R. A., & Wise, R. A. (1975). Increased lever-pressing for amphetamine after pimozide in rats: Implications for a dopamine theory of reward. *Science, 187,* 547–549.

Young, E. A., Haskett, R. F., Murphy-Weinberg, V., Watson, S. J., & Akil, H. (1991). Loss of glucocorticoid fast feedback in depression. *Archives of General Psychiatry, 48,* 693–699.

Glossary

Acting out: the discharge of rage and frustration through purposeless action.

Advice and praise: techniques at the supportive end of the supportive–expressive continuum designed to encourage a patient in his or her progress.

Affirmation: a technique that simply registers the patient's situation.

Agnosia: the inability to recognize objects.

Altruism: the ability to place the interests of another above one's own.

Anaclytic depression: a condition that results from social or interpersonal deprivation.

Anorexia nervosa: an eating disorder characterized by caloric restriction, disturbed body image, and low body weight.

Anticipation: the ability to visualize a future event or state, and thus deal with it in advance.

Anxiety disorders: conditions characterized by fear responses in settings where they are maladaptive.

Aphasia: dysfunction in the production or comprehension of language.

Apraxia: the inability to plan and execute a motor task, despite normal strength.

Archetype: a universal prototypical human experience that forms a part of how people structure their understanding of the world.

Asberger's syndrome: a condition characterized by impaired social interaction skills and idiosyncratic, nonhuman interests.

Attachment: a state typified by the reciprocal bonding between mother and child.

Atypical major depression: a condition characterized by mood reactivity to positive and negative events.

Autism: a condition characterized by impaired communication, inhibited social interactions, and impoverishment of behaviors and interests.

Autonomy: the principle that says individuals are the best judges of their own best interests.

Autoreceptors: receptors that are stimulated by their own neurotransmitters.

Axons: extensions from a cell that terminate at a receiving cell.

Behavioral psychology: a field of study interested in discovering what causes a particular behavior.

Beneficence: the principle that says a physician's duty is to minister to the patient in the patient's best interests.

Biogenic amines: neurotransmitters that become dysregulated in depressive states.

Biological model: a theory which states that mental illness is caused by the dysfunction of tissues and cells.

Biopsychosocial model: a theory which holds that mental illness is caused by physical, psychological, and social causes.

Body dysmorphism: the preoccupation that a body part is defective.

Boundaries: the limits families place on the intimacy and closeness of their members.

Bulimia nervosa: an eating disorder characterized by episodes of binge eating followed by compensatory behavior such as purging, severe exercise, and dieting.

Clarification: summarizing information so it is clearer to the patient.

Classical conditioning: a learned response to a repeated stimulus.

Cognitive distortions: demonstrably untrue beliefs and assumptions that increase depression and anxiety.

Cognitive schemata: characteristic ways of interpreting events.

Cognitive-behavioral psychologies: schools of thought that focus on how conceptual assumptions and patterns of behavior shape psychopathology.

Competency: the state in which one is responsible for one's actions and choices.

Confrontation: pointing out what the patient may not want to face.

Conversion disorder: the unconscious production of a physical symptom to solve an unconscious conflict.

Core conflictual relationship theme: used in brief therapy to get quickly to problem issues.

Cross-tolerance: a tolerance for one substance that results from a tolerance for another.

Cybernetics: the study of feedback loops.

Delirium: the onset of alterations in level of consciousness, attention, and other cognitive deficits.

Delusions: fixed beliefs that are untrue and not culturally accepted.

Dementia: a disturbance in memory, typically with accompanying cognitive deficits.

Dendrites: cell projections that receive input from other neurons.

Denial: the refusal to acknowledge external realities that are anxiety-provoking.

Depersonalization: the sense that one is unsure of who one is.

Depression: a mood disorder characterized by sadness, a decline in interests and energy, and changes in sleep patterns, appetite, and concentration.

Depressive position: a state characterized by the realization that one's actions can affect others.

Differential diagnosis: the process of generating a list of possible causes for a presenting problem, then systematically searching for the presence or absence of each.

Displacement: the transfer of impulses from an unacceptable object to an acceptable object.

Dissociation: a condition in which the usual sense of self as a single state of consciousness is lost.

Dissociative amnesia: the loss of recall for personal information.

Dissociative fugue: a state in which a person may travel and assume a new identity while forgetting his or her formal identity.

Dissociative identity disorder: the formation of more than one personality in a single individual.

Distortion: the altered perception of external reality to make it congruent with internal states.

Dynamic risk factors: those suicide risk factors that can be modified, including depression, substance abuse, anxiety, psychosis, illness, social isolation, and hopelessness.

Dysthemia: a condition characterized by the same symptoms seen in major depression, but of lesser severity and shorter duration.

The ego: the part of the self that is concerned with achieving gratification of the id's drives.

Ego defenses: means by which the ego protects itself from anxiety.

Ego-dystonic fears: those fears which the sufferer cannot recognize as senseless.

Ego-systonic fears: those fears the sufferer recognizes as senseless.

Empathic validating: expressing understanding and empathy for a patient's internal state.

Encouragement to elaborate: asking the patient to say more about a particular topic.

Epigenic principle: a theory which holds that adults as well as children face development tasks that must be mastered sequentially.

Exhibitionism: the need to expose one's genitals to strangers for sexual arousal.

Explicit learning: knowledge that is semantic and can be expressed linguistically.

Explicit memory: the conscious awareness of information.

Extinction: the unlearning of a behavior.

Factitious disorder: intentional feigning of symptoms for sympathy.

Family systems theory: a model which posits that family psychopathology results from inadequate differentiation of self from others in the family.

Fetishism: the need for stimulation using nonliving items.

Flooding: a treatment technique that involves entering a feared situation head-on and waiting for the anxiety to decrease.

Free association: the process of allowing a patient to say anything that comes to mind, without censoring the material.

Generalized anxiety disorder: a condition characterized by chronic and uncontrollable worry.

Graded response: a treatment technique that involves desensitizing a person to something her or she fears by gradual exposure.

Hallucinations: sensory perceptions that are internally generated.

Healing relationship: the relationship between therapist and patient that allows the patient to learn new ways of relating to others.

Heteroreceptors: receptors that are agonized by neurotransmitters other than those released by the presynaptic neuron.

Humor: the capacity to step back from one's situation and laugh at it.

Hypochondriasis: the preoccupation that one has a particular illness.

Hypomania: a condition characterized by the same symptoms as mania, but in milder form.

The id: the part of the self that comprises two libidinal drives: aggression and sexuality.

Idealizing transference: a state in which individuals see those who evoke the sense of parents in an idealized way.

Impaired reality testing: a state that includes delusional thinking and hallucinatory perceptions.

Implicit learning: knowledge gained through doing, like riding a bike or playing the piano.

Implicit memory: the part of the mind responsible for learning implicit skills such as riding a bike.

Insight: the act of consciously recognizing one's previously unconscious processes.

Insomnia: the prolonged abnormal inability to obtain adequate sleep.

Intellectualization: the attempt to develop rational, rather than an emotional, understanding of a problem.

Intermittent explosive disorder: a condition characterized by impulsive aggression toward others.

Interpersonal psychotherapy: a therapy that targets grief and loss, role transitions, and interpersonal disputes and deficits in treating depression.

Interpretation: the act of pointing out ego defenses as they occur.

Isolation-of-affect: the attempt to keep overwhelming emotions at a comfortable distance.

Kleptomania: the repetitive stealing of unnecessary items.

Latent content: the associations, nonverbal cues, and unspoken connections of a conversation.

Malingering: the feigning of illness symptoms to meet some secondary objective.

Mania: a condition characterized by euphoria, energy, illusions of grandiosity, and lack of focus.

Manifest content: the overt meaning of the words a patient speaks.

Melancholic depression: a condition that is characterized by pervasive anhedonia.

Mental disorders: disturbances in one's thoughts, feelings, behaviors, perceptions, or cognitions.

Mental retardation: intelligence in the lower first percentile appearing before adulthood.

Mental state: one's thoughts, feelings, perceptions, cognitions, and behaviors.

Mind-reading: the assumption, without justification, of being judged.

Mirror transference: a condition in which individuals seek a state of complete empathic attunement, duplicating that between mother and child.

Mood: the subjective experience of emotion.

Narcissistic disturbance: a state characterized by oscillations between feelings of inferiority and grandiose self-importance.

Narcolepsy: a condition characterized by daytime attacks of refreshing sleep that occur even in dangerous settings.

Negative feedback loop: a state that occurs when neurotransmitters return to the parent neuron and hit an autoreceptor, thus reducing the firing rate of the parent neuron.

Neurons: primary operating cells in central nervous system activity.

Neurotransmitters: chemical messengers between cells.

Nonmaleficence: the principle that says a physician should never hold any interest in harming the patient.

Object relations: repetitions of old relationship patterns in current relationships.

Obsessive-compulsive disorder: a condition characterized by senseless fears that compel compensatory behavior.

Oedipal stage: the phase of childhood that is characterized by a child's rivalry with the same-sex parent for the attention of the opposite-sex parent.

Operant conditioning: operating upon the environment to produce rewards that reinforce a behavior.

Panic attacks: sudden rushes of intense fear in nondangerous situations.

Panic disorder: the fear of recurring panic attacks.

Paranoid–schizoid position: a state characterized by splitting, in which the ego cannot see the same object as a source of both bliss and pain.

Passive-aggression: a mechanism whereby aggressive impulses are expressed without the intolerable anxiety of consciously expressing them.

Paternalism: the idea that physicians, by virtue of their superior knowledge and reason, can make better decisions on their patients' behalf than the patients could.

Pathological gambling: repetitive gambling, despite serious adverse outcomes.

Pedophilia: sexual attraction to children.

Personality: a person's usual style of understanding the self and engaging the world.

Personality disorders: patterns of engaging the world that are predominantly inflexible and maladaptive in many contexts.

Positive feedback loop: a state that occurs when the return of a neurotransmitter to the parent neuron causes an autoreceptor to increase firing of the neuron.

Posttraumatic stress disorder: a persistent, extreme fear response resulting from a life-threatening event.

Primary insomnia: a condition that is characterized by excessive daytime somnolence with periods of unrefreshing sleep and shortened sleep latency.

Primary mental illnesses: those illnesses which result from particular biologies.

Projection: the attribution of internal events to the outside world.

Pseudodementia: a condition characterized by dementia symptoms that are caused by other psychiatric disorders.

Psychological model: a theory which states that mental disorders are the results of previous mental states.

Psychological types: Carl Jung's system of classifying people through a series of opposites, including "introvert versus extrovert."

Psychodynamic psychologies: fields of study that examine how pathological mental states arise from unconscious wishes, fantasies, and beliefs.

Psychosis: the experience of impaired reality testing.

Psychotic major depression: a condition characterized by symptoms of psychosis.

Punishment: anything that decreases the frequency of a behavior.

Pyromania: repetitive fire setting.

Reaction formation: the transformation of an urge into its opposite.

Reality testing: the ability to distinguish between stimuli generated from within and those coming from outside.

Receptors: tiny organs on the surface of cells that receive messages from other cells.

Reinforced behaviors: those for which frequencies increase or decrease as a result of conditioning.

Reliability: the degree to which diagnosticians agree that a diagnosis is present.

Repression: the submerging of anxiety-provoking conflict from one's conscious awareness into the unconscious.

Reuptake inhibition: the process of inhibiting the membrane pumps that transport biogenic amines.

Reward: anything that increases the frequency of a behavior.

Secondary mental illnesses: those illnesses that result from general medical conditions.

Self-objects: items we use to define our sense of self.

Short-term anxiety-provoking psychotherapy: a therapy technique in which the patient moves rapidly from assessment to interpretation of unconscious material.

Social model: a theory which states that mental disorders are caused by dysfunctional interpersonal interactions.

Social model of mental illness: the theory that mental illness derives from pathological social interactions.

Social phobia: a specific fear of social situations.

Somatization: the presentation of one's psychological distress as physical distress.

Somatization disorder: a condition that is characterized by multiple simultaneous physical symptoms that lack a definitive general medical etiology.

Somatoform pain disorder: a condition characterized by disproportionate distress and disability in response to a given disorder.

Specific phobias: fears of individual situations or objects.

Splitting: reduces the world to polar opposites, in which good and bad are incompatible qualities that cannot exist simultaneously.

Static risk factors: those suicide risk factors not subject to modification, including one's gender, age, race, history of attempts, and recent hospital discharge.

Structural model: Freud's theory which holds that people are possessed by aggressive and libidinal drives which they regulate to achieve greater pleasure, to avoid danger, and to appease a sense of right and wrong.

Sublimation: the attempt to divert drive energy into socially useful goals.

Substance abuse: the use of a substance in ways that cause repeated detrimental consequences.

Substance dependence: loss of control over use of a substance.

The superego: the part of the self that acts as the moral conscience, which regulates the ego and the id.

Suppression: the conscious choice to put information out of mind temporarily.

Systems theory: a model positing that social systems differentiate specific roles for their individual members so as to remain stable.

Temperament: a person's inborn characteristic inclination of emotional response.

Tolerance: the capacity to consume at least 50% more of a substance than was previously possible.

Transference: the redirection of feelings and desires unconsciously retained from childhood toward a new object.

Transitional objects: items children invest with emotional attachment.

Trichotillomania: repetitive hair pulling.

Two-person psychology: a treatment plan that involves both the person whose behavior is troubling and the person who contributes to or enables that behavior.

Undoing: the attempt to neutralize dangerous thoughts and feelings by reversing them.

Validity: the degree to which a diagnosis represents what it is intended to represent.

Withdrawal: the appearance of a physiological syndrome upon removal of the substance.

Index

About the author

Stephen L. Dilts, Jr., received a B.A. in English and a medical doctorate from the University of Colorado, where he was also chief resident in the department of psychiatry and received the Golden Apple award for best instructor to the graduating medical school class of 1997. He is board certified by the American Board of Psychiatry and Neurology.

Currently, Dr. Dilts is medical director of psychiatric consultation-liason services at WellSpann Health in York, Pennsylvania.